BASEBALL
AND THE PURSUIT OF
INNOCENCE

Richard Skolnik

Baseball

and the Pursuit of Innocence

A Fresh Look
at the
Old Ball Game

TEXAS A&M UNIVERSITY PRESS
College Station

Library of Congress Cataloging-in-Publication Data

Skolnik, Richard, 1940–
    The pursuit of innocence : a fresh look at the old ball game /
Richard Skolnik. — 1st ed.
        p.   cm.
    Includes bibliographical references (p.   ).
    ISBN 0-89096-559-5 (alk. paper)
    1. Baseball — Social aspects — United States.   2. Baseball — United
States — Philosophy.   I. Title.
GV863.A1S635   1994
796.357′0973 — dc20   93-30794
                                                        CIP

Contents

Contents

Acknowledgments

WRITING THIS BOOK on baseball was for me, a long-time sports fan, a labor of love. Still it was labor, eased considerably by the encouragement and assistance I received from many different people who deserve recognition. Special mention goes first to Noel Parsons of the Texas A&M University Press and Dr. Richard Costa, reviewer for the Press, who saw possibilities in my original manuscript and encouraged me to pursue the project to its completion.

I wish also to thank my lifelong friend, Bill Scher, for his support and for his eagerness to see the book appear after his appetite was whetted by reading a few early chapters. An appreciative nod goes to Robert Mason, Ronnie Glassman, Lester Rothman, and Earl Williams, all fellow sports fans, who indulged me on those occasions when I tried out a few of my ideas on them. I am most grateful to Louis Masur of the City College of New York, a lifelong Yankee fan, who reviewed the manuscript and was willing to overlook my National League bias and obvious affinity for the Mets. Lawrence Levy, a former collegiate pitcher who still can throw heat (when he's not writing columns and editorials for *Newsday*) was good enough to read the work and provided helpful comments throughout.

A special thanks goes to my wife, Louise, and my children, Seth, Sari, Deborah and Rebecca, who all allowed me to commandeer the basement television for hours at a time to pursue my baseball "research." Finally, Dorothy Hanley, my typist, once again worked her incomparable magic translating my indecipherable scrawl into clear, errorless copy.

And yes, I gratefully remember the superb baseball writers, reporters, and commentators—Tom Boswell, Roger Angell, Tim McCarver, Ralph Kiner, Vin Scully, et al., who have brought considerable wit and wisdom to the game and who encouraged me to consider it a topic for serious analysis. I know it is just a game, but what pleasure it has brought over the years. By my reckoning it's been time well spent.

BASEBALL
AND THE PURSUIT OF
INNOCENCE

Introduction

ENSHRINED as the "national pastime," baseball was offered to the public both as entertainment and as a barometer of American society. Because it "mirror[ed] the nation's soul," according to one observer, its influence would range well beyond the realm of athletics and entertainment. With its rich history dating back to the early nineteenth century, baseball could be anointed guardian of traditions and repository of values considered fundamental to the culture, could serve as the gateway to an idealized past. This it welcomed and, unmindful of the burdens, embraced the dual roles of an immensely popular and profitable sport and of a revered national symbol.

Baseball summoned us back to a simpler rural past, a timeless, unchanging era when life seemed manageable, youth more enduring, essential truths more readily discerned, an age of inner stability and innocence. "Baseball," the celebrated broadcaster Ernie Harwell reminds us, "has a history and tradition that other sports really can't touch." It represents, as Stephen Jay Gould observes, what "we wish we were (or as we imagine in our false nostalgia we once were)." Wilfred Sheed concurs. Much of the writing about the sport, he tells us, "isn't really about baseball at all but about how nice America used to be . . . or how great it felt to be young."[1] Baseball appeared, on the surface at least, uniquely suited to support such fantasy. A game of parks, green fields, sunshine, and summer days, it embraced potent symbols of purity and serenity. Moreover its unhurried pace, liberated from the restrictions of time, offered an oasis of tranquility and so reaffirmed its link to an idyllic past.

Its players, decidedly atavistic young men, hailed disproportionately from rural and small-town America, a setting where traditional virtues seemed at once more rooted and secure. Most, it was supposed, had learned the game at play in open pastures or rough sandlots, throwing stones for hours on end at imagined targets to establish arm strength and accuracy. The love of the sport they inherited from their fathers, while tossing balls back and forth with them or while

3

sitting together, exchanging heroic tales and indelible recollections and, more tangibly, precious bats and mitts.

Over the years baseball eagerly nourished and reinforced these mythic themes. Meanwhile, those who set their sights on becoming professional baseball players (and what youngsters didn't?) could expect to serve their apprenticeship in the "minors," leagues expressly layered to reflect the progressively advancing skills of young ballplayers. Fundamentals would in time be mastered and the more accomplished would eventually be dispatched to the big leagues, where they would appear all starry-eyed and innocent, willing (if asked) to play for little more than room, board, and expenses. And so the game, continually nourished from its grass roots, saw its fundamental ways and values reassuringly reinforced.

The above is of course an idealized portrait, a collection of comforting mythic elements consistent with the innocence and simplicity long associated with baseball. This portrayal, however compelling, has not gone unchallenged; skeptics have delighted in puncturing the game's pretenses, though perhaps not as eagerly as in recent years. Nonetheless the traditional view, for all its romanticized elements, attracts legions of loyalists, intrepid defenders of the faith committed to the sport's original purity and purpose. In the process they who have identified a mounting list of challenges and responded to a growing wave of threats. The minor leagues, they warn, are not what they once were, carefree playgrounds for budding talents. Many have withered away; others have become overly preoccupied with bottom lines, have lost their special allure or worse, failed to nourish essential skills. The joyful innocence of spring training is fading. Eagerly awaited and long welcomed for its relaxed atmosphere, for its primitive and exuberant celebration of spring, this much-heralded pre-season period has turned to elaborate training techniques and complex drills, become preoccupied with serious preparations and condoned progressively higher ticket prices. The charming, crusty old ballparks, full of idiosyncrasies and ghostly memories, are being leveled and replaced by efficient, though ofttimes sterile, stadiums and indoor domes. Natural fields too have been uprooted, lush grass yielding to seamed surfaces of exotic composition.

Today's ballplayers do not measure up or inspire confidence. Few acknowledge their links to the past, while individual preferences continue to erode a commitment to team and place. "We don't see kids hanging around clubhouses after games," laments former star Willie Mays, "or talking baseball much during the season."[2] Many, it is true, still chew tobacco, expectorate with zest (in 1989, a less-than-pleased viewer of a Cincinnati Reds–New York Mets ball game kept score and reported that batters alone spat 324 times during the course of the game), and routinely engage in childish pranks, but still the innocence seems strained, compromised by external pressures and priorities. Money has flooded into the sport, eating away at existing structures, severing ties and established loyalties (and threatening baseball's long-standing exemption from the federal government's antitrust laws). Expansion dilutes talent, mediocrity is richly rewarded; competence commands once undreamed-of wealth as agents ply their trade unrestrained and unrepentant. The bloated payrolls of lackluster teams stand in sharp contrast to others which play with gusto for a comparative pittance. The game of long summer days has been largely replaced by nighttime contests, the glare of floodlights substituting for the warmth of afternoon sunshine and the mystery of ever encroaching shadows. Fans at home or at the ballpark grow weary as one day passes into the next while the game drags on. Designated hitters replace pitchers in the batting order, aluminum bats threaten to invade the majors, statistical accounts and endless number crunching squeeze out drama and fond memories, while plans advance for an additional level of postseason play to satisfy the need for ever greater revenues. Innocence and simplicity struggle to survive amidst the complex changes and forces transforming the game.

In one way or another the essays that follow, those probing the symbols and subtexts of the game, others examining the way it's played and the manner in which it is viewed and interpreted, all explore the issues of innocence and sophistication, simplicity and complexity, inheritance and innovation, thematic conflicts long present in baseball and in its attendant culture. It appears when we investigate the matter of "time" as leisurely pace as opposed to "time" as a tactical maneuver. It surfaces when we contrast the orderliness and strict morality of baseball with the fear that stalks the game and its tolerance when the rules are bent. Baseball, perceived as simple, spontaneous, natural, and just plain fun must contend with the view that the mastery of fundamentals determines fitness to play the sport and that complex mind games, relentless battles of wits, and statistical reinforcement determine outcomes. Although baseball must contend with vitriolic and vengeful fans, it also enjoys adoring supporters. In 1993, *Baseball Weekly* invited submissions of essays and poetry on baseball for a contest sponsored by the magazine. Could one imagine such a competition for any other sport? Garrulous, folksy "old-time" managers rely on hunches and fond memories to win, while in the other dugout opposing field generals counter with detailed scouting reports and statistical compilations. A game mindful of past glories and heroes must face this reality—that the present generation of players feels more and more disconnected from baseball's bygone days and is less respectful of inherited tradition, less likely to feel pride in place.

And yet while we acknowledge the tensions, contradictions, and discontinuities and wonder about their impact upon the game, let us also consider the possibility that baseball could well succeed in incorporating these divergent elements without seriously compromising the sport and all that it has represented. Thus while other institutions retreat and falter before an array of pressures that undermine their vitality and integrity, baseball may not. Resilient and resourceful, it may instead rise above the conflict and move toward reconciliation and renewal.

And so we turn to examine a sport at once consistent and contradictory, ever rich in meaning and complexity, ever more convinced of this essential truth once expressed by baseball's preeminent bard, Roger Angell, that "always . . . there is something more to be discovered about the game."

PART ONE
Meanings and Memories

In the following chapters the case is presented for baseball's role as a symbol for an America now but dimly recalled. It is in this connection that the related notions of pastoralism, simplicity, and innocence, so closely interwoven into the sport, are identified and analyzed. The fields of green, the summer sun, the rural cadences, the initiation into the game of young sons and daughters by fathers all resonate with these themes. Not content simply to invoke the past, baseball lavishes attention upon and is ever respectful of its early days. Memories remain exceptionally vivid, statistical comparisons abound while the dialogue between present and past stays consistently rich, fresh, and rewarding.

Baseball's uncommon regard for order and regularity recalls a past in which formal structures reflected a world more rigid, more sharply defined. Baseball's demanding moral order appears suited to a traditional age, one that defined and enforced appropriate behavior, prescribed obligations and fixed individual responsibilities. Finally, baseball's grip on the popular imagination was enhanced, made more credible because the game in many ways appeared familiar, its players, strategies, and rhythms recognized extensions of the fabric and flow of daily, commonplace events. Thus baseball invites us to suspend our sense of time, delight in our youth, partake in an orderly universe, relish the natural freshness and hope of spring, and take comfort in the workings of the familiar. Baseball's therapeutic value cannot be underestimated.

ONE
Passion for the Past

MOST AMERICANS are inclined to dismiss the past as "old fashioned" and largely irrelevant, and despite occasional bouts of nostalgia, they acknowledge few ties or obligations to these "olden days." Dynamic and progressive, we celebrate the new, extol the modern, gravitate to that which is certifiably up to date. There's much truth here — but not when it comes to baseball. "In baseball more than anything I know," writes David Halberstam, "today is not merely today; it is yesterday as well." In its willingness to acknowledge and honor its past and to question innovation, baseball represents a most striking anomaly.[1] It deliberately encourages us to look back, invites us to return to a simpler rural past, a society secure in its inherited customs and enduring values. For many it serves as an anchor of reassurance, a link to a past scarcely remembered but fondly imagined. "Like everything else, baseball has changed but less," says writer Jon Margolis, "so it's pretty much the way it was when we were kids, which means it's better than things are now because things were always better back then." Baseball, John Thorn adds, "has changed less than any other American institution."[2] "None of us," Bart Giamatti once remarked, "can go to a ballgame, I think, without in some way being reminded of your best hopes, of your earlier times, some memory of your best memory. It's always nostalgic . . ." To best enjoy it, according to Wilfred Sheed, "You have to fill out the game you're watching with your own thoughts and memories and place it in the rich context of a season and a tradition." Summing it up best, perhaps, is writer Ralph Shoenstein. "Baseball," he notes, is "the one place where I have always felt safe and happy and young."[3]

Several factors are at work, some of which are discussed elsewhere in this volume and so warrant but brief mention here. Baseball's roots run deep into the countryside, a locale long idealized, regarded as special by Americans. Though the game achieved prominence and commercial success only when it entered the cities in the late nineteenth century, baseball's rural motifs were inescapable (and especially ap-

9

pealing to city folk recently arrived from the countryside). There was, of course, the ballfield, an expanse of grass, lush, green, fertile, seemingly endless. Consider also the baseball season itself, opening in the spring, ever the occasion of planting, of renewal, of hope, and concluding in the fall at harvest time before the winter freeze and silence. Because baseball rejected time limits and largely disregarded the clock, it recalled an older, task-oriented rural society where the time of day was clearly secondary to the completion of the job at hand. Though major-league teams emerged in the larger cities, baseball's proliferating minor league system extended across small town America, just as in the past when such modest communities defined a traditional America and embodied its essential values. Baseball also came to be regarded as the sport of youth, tirelessly pursued with irrepressible innocence, over countless days of summers gone by. Fondly remembered too were those occasions past when fathers playing ball with young sons reinforced these rites of paternity and passage, projecting them back to the past and assuring their continuation into the future.

Baseball's substantial stake in the past has not been ignored. Indeed its continued popularity, we are reminded, depends upon this vital link. Accordingly, baseball delights in outfitting current players in old-fashioned uniforms from time to time and in staging Old-Timers' Days (invented by the New York Yankees in 1947).[4] Old-Timers' Games have become popular fixtures at many of the ballparks. (In June of 1992 St. Louis celebrated its one hundredth anniversary with many former Cardinals present to participate in the festivities.) Inviting back retired ballplayers, allowing those among them still spry to cavort on the field in uniform in an abbreviated game is, of course, a boon for public relations. But at the same time it delivers an unmistakable message—that baseball, unlike most of the society, chooses not to forget, is respectful of its history, and is fully realized and properly responsible only when it reaches out to connect with its past (one that includes the Negro leagues which baseball, to its shame, once too easily ignored).[5]

Baseball's shrine, the Hall of Fame with its associated museum at Cooperstown, New York, links us to the past by celebrating the immortal heroes of baseball and by preserving the material culture of the sport. As an example, when Rickey Henderson in 1991 broke Lou

Brock's stolen base record, his uniform and shoes were promptly dispatched to the Hall of Fame. When Expos' pitcher Dennis Martinez pitched the fifteenth perfect game in major-league history in 1991, the Hall of Fame requested catcher Ron Hassey's glove, Martinez's uniform top and an autographed ball and ticket from the game. In memorable displays that delight the faithful who pack its exhibition galleries year after year, it exhibits these recent artifacts along with countless other significant objects of the sport that summon forth each era and testify to past glories. Elevating the Hall of Fame to so central a position in the sport reinforces baseball's ties to its past in yet another way. At any time, most members of the hall are "old-timers" whose accomplishments proclaim that past ballplayers were men of exceptional skill whose achievements equal or exceed the performance records of contemporary stars.[6]

Fans also maintain a lively interest in baseball's lore and legend, move eagerly and easily between the past and the present. Most can trace their entry into the mysteries of the sport back to their childhood and as adults can speak with authority about the intervening years. It is by connecting their own history to that of baseball's that the inevitable erosion of memory is slowed if not halted. "More than any other sport," Rick Lawes notes, "the mention of a year evokes memories of the accomplishments on and off the field." The poet Donald Hall concurs. "One of the magical ingredients in baseball occurs because the mere mention of a team or player can invoke an era." How natural it is for fans and observers to recall in detail and to relish heroic achievements and memorable moments of games long past. One baseball fan writing in 1992 noted that he could "recite from memory how every run was scored in every game in the 1975 classic" (World Series). When in the final game of the 1992 National League Championship Series the Braves, with two outs in the ninth inning, beat the Pirates, reporters felt obligated to turn to the history books looking for dramatic conclusions that might rival this one. In short order they uncovered spine-tingling finales in 1912, 1924, 1960, 1972, and 1976.[7] Earlier in the season, when Philadelphia's Mickey Morandini executed an unassisted triple play, the scoreboard promptly displayed the fact that the previous one had occurred back in 1927![8] How true it is when Roger Angell tells us that "Baseball is intensely remembered. Baseball memories leap over decades at a single bound and long flown afternoons return without effort, often in the heroic present tense."[9] For a recent illustration, recall the sequence from the 1991 movie, *City Slickers,* (in which the central character, Phil, played by Billy Crystal, appears throughout the film wearing an old Yankees' baseball cap):

PHIL: "So do you hate baseball?"

BONNIE: "No, I like baseball. I just never understood how you guys can spend so much time discussing it. I mean, I've been to games, but I don't memorize who played third base for Pittsburgh in 1960."

PHIL, MITCH, AND ED, simultaneously: "Don Hoak."

Statistical recollection is very much a part of this ready association with the past. Numbers long before committed to memory are summoned forth instantly. Most fans maintain a mental file on significant records of long standing. The numbers remain meaningful and comparable, for despite the passage of time, the game has remained fundamentally unchanged. Furthermore, which marks are threatened and which appear, for the moment at least, to be secure, tends to be common knowledge. Once a record of long standing is threatened, the challenge instantly rekindles interest in the existing mark.[10] Because in baseball loyalty lasts, the past is never without its defenders. Substantial numbers might wish to see the long established record stand. Certainly that was the case when Roger Maris broke Babe Ruth's home-run record. Furthermore, when it comes to awarding Gold Gloves for fielding excellence at each position, previous winners, still active, are almost always chosen over newcomers who are expected to be patient and await their turn.

Without doubt, the popularity of baseball memorabilia and the rapid commercialization of collecting has literally and figuratively strengthened fans' investment in the past. In recent years the ranks of collectors have swelled appreciably, while rising prices have prompted collectors to scour the land in search of collectibles. Bats, balls, uniforms, tickets, scorecards, baseball cards, remnants from defunct stadiums, autographs—these are just some of the items available to feed what has become a voracious high stakes market.[11] But it is not just commercial consideration that prompts this energetic rummaging through baseball's past. Present almost always is a love of the game as it once was, an appreciation of its heritage and hallowed memories.

Sports literature, whatever the field, tends to focus on current stars, recent championship seasons, record-breaking performers and revelations of eccentricity, even wrongdoing. It seeks to capitalize on yesterday's headlines by providing inside information and supposed insight from those directly or otherwise involved. By and large it represents literature at its most ephemeral — breathless, hastily assembled sweeps across the sports landscape. Baseball is in no way immune to this phenomenon, but to its credit it has encouraged another genre unmatched by any other sport in scope, perceptiveness, and often literary style. This is not the place to survey the already immense and ever-fertile field of baseball literature but to point out that a significant body of this work addresses the past. In explanation, sports columnist Steve Jacobson reminds us that "baseball is so good for looking back."[12] Biographies of former players and managers, team histories, statistical compilations abound while extended accounts of past seasons, notable pennant races, and overall surveys of bygone eras have attracted a wide readership. Because of this outpouring, baseball history remains a vital and compelling subject. One result is that many baseball fans are unusually well-versed in the rich traditions of the game and capable of maintaining a lively dialogue between past and present.

Because the past is valued and encouraged to speak for itself, baseball avoids a mindless presentism and welcomes repeated questions of how well the traditions and values of baseball are being preserved. What are acceptable levels of innovation for the sport? When and where should change be opposed? How does the game as played today compare to performance levels in former days? Was there in fact a Golden Age (variously located somewhere between the 1920s and 1950s)? Is "The Book" (the inherited wisdom and time-tested tactics of the sport) still accepted gospel or has it become, as Ralph Kiner suggests, "just the old-fashioned way of playing baseball"? (Indeed the very fact that there is a "book" and that it still commands considerable respect further reinforces baseball's ties to its past.) Such questions surface in other sports, but only in baseball do they provoke such serious and informed discussion and bear such emotional overtones.

Where else but in baseball do traditionalists enjoy such respectful attention even when they take lively exception to the way the game has changed? Criticism flows in several predictable directions. Most new ballparks are not to their liking. Too slick, too uniform, too cold and impersonal—that is their considered judgment. The closing of Chicago's Comiskey Park and the threatened demise of Detroit Stadium evokes deep and genuine sadness, a sense of irremediable loss.[13] Then too, today's players do not compare favorably with yesterday's heroes. A sense of dedication, the virtues of loyalty, both are declared lacking. Current ballplayers don't play as hard, don't care as much, and certainly are undeserving of their extravagant salaries. Most unforgivably, too many display bland personalities and utter comments riddled with clichés. This is in contrast to the earthy, frank, lovable "characters" who once populated the game.[14]

But are they on the whole better than earlier generations of players? They're not, or so a case, generally persuasive, might so conclude. Baseball is perhaps the only major sport where one may reasonably maintain that past performers were equal to if not superior to contemporary athletes. (A case probably could be made for boxing, as well.) Pitchers today, the argument might begin, lack the staying power that hurlers once displayed. Hall of Fame pitcher Bob Lemon offers his own wry explanation: "I'm just glad I pitched before they invented rotator cuffs."[15] Modern moundsmen require more rest, are injured more frequently, and appear reluctant to challenge batters with close pitches. Rarely do they complete games. Even the number of fastballers (a pitch of pure speed considered essential and fundamental) today do not, it is said, compare to the number of those who once "threw heat." Neither are today's hitters as productive. They strike out excessively, advance runners too infrequently, and bunt awkwardly and too often unsuccessfully. Ted Williams, the man who nearly elevated hitting to a science, finds today's batters wanting. "Hitting as a whole," he notes, "is not as good; the best hitters today are not as good as the best hitters I saw in my career."[16] Base running, the case continues, has progressively declined with modern players less venturesome, insufficiently alert on the base paths, and seemingly unconcerned with this aspect of the game.

Defenders of the contemporary game do not shrug off these arguments. Though able to fashion a strong case of their own,[17] they regard the opposition not as hidebound conservatives railing against change, but as dedicated fans, unduly nostalgic perhaps, but otherwise well-intentioned and well-versed. There's no denying past glories nor reason to question that the legends of the game could easily have held their own against today's stars.[18] The point is rather that baseball summons the past so as to cast a sharp spotlight on contemporary realities and as often as not invokes the present to illuminate the past in notably useful ways. It is a mutually beneficial exchange—a model of peaceful and profitable coexistence.

TWO

True to Life

ALL SPORTS in one way or another mirror life's realities, and offer us compelling dramatizations of the human situation. Baseball's surely no exception, as the many observers of the game are forever pointing out. "The game is so much like life," one of them reminds us. It is, Tom Boswell assures us, "not something outside our everyday world, but merely a heightened and focused form of our common experience." Accordingly it invites our attention, instructs us, appears wise in the ways of the world. "It reflects in countless ways the lessons of life," adds Thomas Heitz, librarian at the Baseball Hall of Fame.[1] When so many can identify with what is happening on that very public stage, perhaps they're watching more than just a game.

Why does baseball succeed so well in reflecting the twists and turns, the rhythms, the vicissitudes, even the banalities of life?[2] Consider the fact that baseball is of human proportions. How many folks imagine themselves strapping on skates and careening full throttle over the ice, or putting on pads and helmets, then confronting mammoth hulks on the gridiron? Those of average height have difficulty seeing themselves jockeying for position in the pivot against seven-foot giants. Baseball, however, demands fewer stretches of the imagination. No unalterable height and weight requirements exist to exclude the masses. Indeed, unlike the athletes in most every other sport, many baseball players are less than perfect physical specimens. "Where does it say you have to resemble a Greek god to play in the majors?" the always chubby Mickey Lolich once remarked. Though an accomplished hitter, John Kruk could, according to a teammate, easily "pass for a pretty good couch potato."[3] Whereas no power forward should be less than 6'7" and a defensive lineman fall below 270 lbs., no standard configurations apply to first basemen or centerfielders or even catchers. Idealized types may be suggested—the wiry diminutive shortstop, the squat, solid catcher, beanpole pitchers well beyond 6' tall—but performing equally well are catchers like Benito Santiago (6'1", 180 lbs.),

16

shortstops like Cal Ripkin (6′4″, 213 lbs.), and pitchers like John Franco and Scott Terry (5′10″), or a "midget" like Steve Frey (5′7″). Additionally, players do switch positions easily enough and some, like Jose Oquendo, can play them all (as he did during the 1988 season). So what does a baseball player look like—just like the rest of us.[4] That's why it's not hard to see ourselves out there.

Furthermore, what these players do, we too have done, men and women alike. Who hasn't thrown a ball around at one time, tossed pitches to someone waiting to hit, or stood bat in hand delighted at having applied some "good wood" to the ball? Who hasn't imagined himself out there on the field, the crowd roaring its approval? A fan letter in the *New York Times* described how it might feel. "I can look at Nolan Ryan and think, well, now there's not too much difference between him and me, a few years, a few pounds. When the box score tells me Ryan's strikeouts were in double figures, I can think to myself, man, we brought smoke yesterday."[5] Then too, baseball delights in the success of its "blue-collar" players, individuals who without exceptional natural gifts succeed by virtue of their hard work, dedication and sheer doggedness. The success of such people as John Kruk, Robin Yount, George Brett, and Wade Boggs would seem to confirm the fact that "ordinary" folks can make it in baseball.

Baseball speaks to us in familiar ways and often enough so as to appear "true to life": The similarities we find reassuring, the parallels significant. Baseball's almost a year-round affair. No other sport succeeds in maintaining interest, not only during the course of its regular schedule, but well beyond into the "off-season." "Baseball," Tom Boswell reminds us, "is always there when we want it."[6] Officially, the game is played for over half the year, but spring training and the exhibition schedule add well over a month to that total. Even when fall signals the season's end, baseball lingers and rewards its followers. It takes time to digest the World Series, to review the season's statistical harvest, relish the achievements and memorable moments and await news of the Most Valuable Player (MVP) and Cy Young Awards. Before long attention turns to the winter meetings, the rumored trades, the inclinations, then signings of free agents, and finally the decisions of arbitration proceedings.[7] The Hot-Stove League is in full swing and then, even as cold grips most of the nation, players are packing their gear and heading down to training camps while fans begin plotting their Rotisserie team picks. So baseball is almost year round: it doesn't leave us, it's never remote or inappropriate. We must be prepared to deal with it as with life, in different ways, at all times, in all seasons. Still, it must have occasioned some surprise when a discussion of baseball was made the principal topic at a gathering held late in June of 1990 at Central Intelligence Agency (CIA) headquarters outside of Washington. Indeed there was a reason, then–CIA director William Webster, an avid Cardinals fan, explained. Both baseball and national intelligence "could be called 'the sport of the long season.' Both demand the long view," he observed.[8]

Once "in season" baseball is always with us, day after day, week in and week out, month after month. There's no letup, no respite, no opportunity to get away from it all. You're in it for the long haul. "Nothing comes easily in this game," says Davey Johnson. "The game is a grind."[9] That's how the players experience it; it's not much different for the fans. Much like a job, you're obliged to stick with it, only here, weekends are included. No wonder an off day or a rainout on occasion is most welcome.

Baseball provides no instant gratification; it's enormously time consuming. Consider the fact that games routinely last upwards of two-and-a-half to three-and-a-half hours. Include pregame and postgame commentary, and at least another half-hour can be added to that total. (Notice that post-game commentary almost always includes a most detailed account of each threat and of every situation that led to a score. Even after watching the entire game, fans expect and enjoy such recapitulations.) Then there are the sports talk shows available in most major cities. What better way to sample fan sentiment and digest the latest developments? After that the sports pages must be consulted. Having watched the entire game does not eliminate the need to read all about it; indeed it probably whets the appetite if yours is the winning team, because you get the sweet satisfaction of savoring every detail of the victory. Beyond the account of the game, one looks to supplement the basic information with locker-room chatter, behind-the-scenes commentary by sports columnists, and news from elsewhere around the league. Baseball isn't in any rush; it doesn't come and go. Rather it envelops; it endures.

Baseball's an absorbing game, but a baseball game isn't consistently compelling or entertaining. Like many of life's experiences it may drag, be distressingly humdrum,[10] even be boring. Roger Angell calculates that "about half of all the ballgames played are not especially close or interesting; about a quarter are truly tedious."[11] A dominant pitcher on the mound and overmatched batters at the plate, and the result is likely to be a succession of foulouts, strikeouts, routine ground balls, lazy pop flies—little drama here. Sitting through a "laugher," your team behind and showing no signs of coming back, is altogether dispiriting. The slow pace, which in a tight game heightens interest and intensity, is now simply irritating. Nodding off is appropriate; so is considering alternative uses of your time. But then a rally, which seemed so very unlikely, begins to take shape; suddenly you're riveted to the screen. Your team now has a chance—it could win! The unexpected does happen; life's full of surprises. Sometimes it takes a baseball game to remind you of this.

Return now to the original situation for a moment—a dominant pitcher and overmatched hitters. On a given day with a Roger Clemens, Dave Stewart, David Cone, Jose Rijo, Dennis Martinez, or Tom Glavine out on the mound, one can expect to see batter after batter turned away, unable to make solid contact. Ordinarily, hitters expect to solve a pitcher as the game progresses. But these pitchers usually get sharper as the game wears on, especially if they're ahead. So the innings roll on, three up and three down. It looks so simple—batters way off in their timing, lunging, knees buckling, swinging awkwardly at bad pitches, guessing wrong, shaking their heads. The outcome is almost inevitable—perhaps a shutout, a one- or two-hitter, clearly an insoluble problem, a mismatch, decidedly unfair. What's the point here? Just a reminder that the world can seem just as overwhelming. Over the short run at least, certain problems simply can't be solved, repeated losses and setbacks must be accepted, and a sense of helplessness cannot be dispelled. For a time, particular individuals can effectively dominate others. Life's often one-sided and unfair. A well-pitched game can produce such dark thoughts.[12]

Dominant pitchers aside, it's common knowledge that even good hitters are retired seven out of the ten times they come to the plate. It's always been that way. No matter how keen their eye-hand coordination, how rapidly they pick up the spin on the ball, irrespective of how patient they are at the plate, how well they know the pitcher, how quick their bat and their ability to protect the plate, they're destined to make out most of the time. As formidable a hitter as he's been, Jose Canseco knows this well. "You have to remember," he reminds us, "that you are unsuccessful 70% of the time in this job . . . You play expecting to fail." It is instructive that the best-known poem in all of sports involves such a failure. In "Casey at the Bat," the hero, in the most critical of situations, strikes out.[13] Pro basketball players score on nearly 50 percent of their shots, quarterbacks frequently exceed a 50 percent completion rate, and field goal kickers well beyond that, while tennis players will succeed with well over half of their first serves. The comparatively poor record of batters seems consistent with the belief that hitting a baseball safely is among the most formidable tasks in all of sports. In 1987, National League hitters averaged .261 over the entire season, and batters in the junior circuit, thanks largely to the designated hitter, .265. The following year, batters took a turn for the worse, the comparable averages registering at .248 and .259. There's been little improvement since—in 1992, American League hitters averaged .259, while National Leaguers hit at a .252 level. Most major-leaguers manage a hit in only one out of nearly four times at bat. To take pride in being a hitter at the highest level of one's craft and yet be unable to perform with any degree of consistency cannot but produce a keen sense of frustration—and embarrassment. As each player comes to bat his batting average, however anemic, is posted on the scoreboard for all to see. No other sport evaluates individual player performance so objectively or so relentlessly. Who among us would appreciate having his shortcomings repeatedly exposed and publicized? But are any of us strangers to disappointment and feelings of inadequacy? Do we not sense that even at the height of our powers we are not sufficiently productive, altogether in control, entirely deserving? Sports writer George Vecsey understood that "baseball is largely about failure."[14] So did Bart Giamatti. "It was meant to break our hearts," he once said.

The foregoing would seem to confirm the belief of those who see missed opportunities, not positive outcomes, as typical of the game. Consider that your team has gotten the leadoff batter on. Next, a sacrifice bunt is mishandled and so there are now two on, none out, and the top of the order coming up. Surely your hitters will deliver in this scoring situation. Excitement builds, expectations skyrocket; the momentum is yours. But then in an instant there comes a double play, then a pop-up—the curtain comes down, hope is extinguished. Unusual circumstance? Hardly. Getting the two runners on in succession was itself exceptional. That more "good things" would follow thus becomes less probable, the notion of momentum, an artificial construct. An interesting case in point emerged on opening day, 1989, with the Cubs facing the Phillies. The game entered the ninth inning, the Cubs clinging to a 5-4 lead. But then the Chicago pitcher, Mitch Williams, promptly yielded three straight hits, loading the bases. Certainly Phillies' fans already could envision the runs crossing the plate, an opening day victory in sight. Williams, however, was not finished. Up to the plate stepped Mike Schmidt, who in his previous at-bat had homered. Williams struck him out. Chris James came to bat, then promptly sat down again, a strikeout victim. With the bases still loaded, Mark Ryal then fanned to end the game. For the Phillies, the pool of positive developments had run out with the third hit of the ninth inning, but who would have guessed it? Despair, delight, exhilaration, numbness—in one half-inning Phillie fans had careened erratically along an emotional roller coaster. As in real life, expectations outpaced realities; failures outpace fulfillment. Left-on-base numbers tell us just how often runners tend to be stranded and the batters branded for failure to deliver in the clutch. "Baseball," as Tony LaRussa sagely suggests, "is the all-time humbler."[15]

Naturally, there are exceptions. Baseball wouldn't be the absorbing game it is if batters repeatedly failed. They do manage at times to beat the odds. Baseball lore delights in tales of dramatic rallies, stirring comebacks, batters delivering at critical times. Already legendary are Bucky Dent's dramatic blow to left against the Red Sox in 1978, Dave Henderson's home run which propelled the Red Sox past the California Angels in 1986, and the improbable devastating smash by Kirk Gibson of Los Angeles in game one of the 1988 World Series against the Oakland Athletics. Nearly incapacitated with an injured leg which left him unable to run out a ground ball, Gibson faced a dominating Dennis Eckersley, two outs, one on, last of the ninth, the

Dodgers trailing by a run. Every youngster who has played the game
has imagined a heroic conclusion to such a scenario. Incredibly it happened. Gibson's swing propelled the ball into the right field stands
and put the surging Dodgers in a position to dominate the World Series. Though mere mortals play baseball, heroic deeds still occur, and
are remembered long after the failures have passed beyond memory.

Just as variety adds spice to life, so it is with baseball. In most all
sports, uniformity prevails. Field dimensions, playing conditions—
there's not much difference. Hockey rink sizes do vary, artificial turf
alternates with grass across the nation's gridirons, and Boston's an-
tiquated parquet floor is a rarity. But in general, there's not much that
would affect the flow of action. Baseball's different. Like life itself,
it offers a range of environments, demands flexibility and rewards those
able to adapt. No field is the same in size, playing surface and playing
conditions.[16] Places like the Metro Dome, King Dome, and Astro Dome
offer the consistency of indoor environment and artificial surfaces.
But the hallmark of baseball has been and for the foreseeable future
will be the unique shapes and conditions found in most all of the outdoor stadiums. Around all the infields you'll find matching dimensions prevail, but once in the outfield, sizes and angles head off in
different directions, from the green monster at Fenway, to the short
right-field porch at Yankee Stadium to the 420 foot center-field at Detroit's Tiger Stadium (and everywhere subject to alterations to suit
team strength and neutralize weaknesses.[17] One calculation lists sixteen changes over the years for center field at Chicago's recently demol-
ished Comiskey Park.) Then too, foul areas are mostly different. Just
look around Oakland's Alameda County Stadium and notice the generous dimensions of its foul territory, a sight always discomforting
to hitters, especially when compared to Fenway. That's not all. Unlike
carpets, grass heights vary, as does lighting intensity and consistency
and depth of coverage. Infield conditions differ,[18] and mounds incline
in distinct ways (Roger Clemens found it "strange but when you stand
on some mounds they seem very close to the plate, while others seem
very far away"), outfield fences and walls are high and low, padded
or ivy-covered, flexible or unyielding. (Basic dimensions like height
and slope of pitching mounds—including those in the bullpens—are
checked by the umpires three times a year in every ballpark.) Each

field requires getting used to. Pitcher Dave LaPoint preferred artificial surfaces because they brought more ground ball double plays. Most infielders prefer grass because it slows down balls hit their way. Hitting distractions vary. Keith Hernandez, for example, had the Mets paint the white 410 feet sign in the outfield black, after noticing that the pitched ball often was obscured by the white background. Home teams have a distinct, though not a decisive, advantage.[19]

The most notable variation in playing situations, however, involves not the fields themselves but the great outdoors. In no other sport are conditions likely to vary as much as in baseball. Wind, rain, sun, clouds, cold, heat, dry, moist—every element has a role to play—by itself, or in combination with the others, certain ones more prominent during the day, others affecting play more dramatically at night.[20] One writer notes that "no other American sport uses the changing sky as effectively as a visual overture." When Hubie Brooks played in Chicago he recalled that he "need only check the flag outside his hotel." That served as a pretty accurate indicator of what game conditions at Wrigley were likely to be. And if the winds were blowing—anything could happen. Don Zimmer certainly understands the vagaries of Wrigley. "When the weather warms up and the wind blows out" there's no cause for complaint but, "It's tough to hit when a cold wind is blowing in your face. Like I said you've got Wrigley Field No. 1 and Wrigley Field No. 2. . . . When it's blowing out, a lot of crazy things can happen."[21] Actual studies of wind patterns at Wrigley for several years challenge its reputation as a hitters' park.[22] They reveal winds blowing out for 194 games, while blowing in or across the field on 362 occasions. The swirling winds of Candlestick Park, San Francisco, are notorious ("For guys who don't know the place, it's tough to throw a breaking pitch," says Will Clark.), but wind direction at Fenway Park can become just as erratic. In Reggie Jackson's view, the wind blowing in there adds fifty to sixty feet to the outfield dimensions. Before he left the Red Sox, Wade Boggs conceded that these winds would probably keep him from ever hitting forty home runs in a season. "When the wind blows in during April and May I'm not," he admits, "going to hit any balls out to right field." For years Oakland's Jose Canseco carried a personal grudge against the wind at Alameda County Stadium. The villain in this case was the stiff night breezes that hold up balls heading into the power alleys. "I think," Canseco comments, "I can honestly say that Oakland is the worst power-hitting park in any league." For another view, listen to a pitcher. "I like the winds," says Greg Swindell. "You can just throw fastballs and see how hard they can hit them."[23] On the other hand, batters won't complain when wind takes hold of their fly balls, carrying them beyond the reach of outfielders, even over the fences. With fielders it's a different story—outfielders trying to track balls blown beyond their reach, infielders attempting to follow the tortuous course of a major-league popup on a blustery day, everyone trying to dodge loose paper blowing all about the field. On one occasion in Pittsburgh with paper being propelled by fifty-MPH winds, Mike Scott complained that "it wasn't easy to field because you didn't know what to pick up."[24] So like the navigators of old time sailing ships, ballplayers look skyward, wondering whether breezes and winds above will prove either a blessing or a curse.

The movement of air is not the whole story. It matters whether the atmosphere is dry or moist. If it's moist it will be lighter. And balls hit up into it will carry farther—at times even out of the ballpark (not uncommon at Atlanta's Fulton County Stadium). Dry, heavy air can be an outfielder's unsung accomplice especially when it operates to keep outfield fly balls in the stadium. But when the air becomes too moist and it rains, it's a whole new ballgame. Played during or right after a downpour on a slick outfield and sloppy field, baseball loses its crispness and controlled style and becomes a tricky, hazardous game of chance. Hitters clutch bats grown suddenly slippery, reluctant to dig in, knowing well the pitcher no longer has complete control over the moist baseball. Balls come to a sudden splashy halt in the rain-soaked outfield grass, pursued by infielders uncertain of their footing, unable to get off the mark, or outfielders diving, skidding, planing across a puddled terrain. Runners hesitate to steal in the heavy infield, tiptoe their way around the bases, thankful just to maintain their footing. Who can forget the sight of Keith Hernandez during the 1988 Dodger-Met National-League playoffs on his way to third round base paths made muddy by an earlier heavy rainfall? Short of third base he slips and falls, tries to get up, loses his balance, and decides instead to crawl toward the base as a throw heads in the same direction. Knees pumping, hands padding along, this stellar athlete turned quadruped by field conditions does not make it, is thrown out, a likely run the Mets would not register.

What better time to enjoy baseball than on a bright, sunny day? Certainly it's true for the fans in the stands; not so for the players, however. The sun may create problems that can change the complexion of a game. Have it reflect off the predominantly light-colored shirts of the fans, and it forces players to strain just to keep sight of the ball. Sometimes they can't find it, the ball obscured, temporarily lost in the sun-brightened background. A first baseman knows a ball's heading his way, but just where is it amidst the bright shirts he sees behind third base? A rising line drive heads toward an outfielder who stands frozen, waiting for the ball, hoping he can pick it up as it emerges out of a background that includes the crowd behind home plate. A pop-up is sent soaring high over the infield, the second baseman watches it disappear, looks for it in vain against the high, glowing sky, then lunges awkwardly as he catches sight of the ball at the last second. Outfielders tracking fly balls try to position themselves at an angle that will keep them from looking straight into the sun. (Trouble with the sun is most pronounced in April, September, and October.) They don't always succeed. Rafael Palmeiro, former Cub outfielder, knew it would not be easy out in left field at Shea Stadium on this one bright day in September several seasons back. Sure enough a ball came his way, and Palmeiro instinctively dashed to where he expected to snare it. Looking up, he became blinded by the sun. Instead of nestling in his glove, the ball crashed into his flesh hand and tore past his finger. It required seven stitches to close the wound. Once a fielder loses sight of the ball, it becomes a menace. He then has a choice. He can either stick his glove out where his sixth sense tells him the ball might come down and hope for a lucky catch, or he can choose the path of self-preservation, covering his head and face with his hand and glove and pray the bill misses him. Whatever the decision, it is not among the prouder or more graceful moments of outfield play.

The sun as it moves across the sky also produces a series of sharply etched shadows—of the roof, the light stanchions, the stands themselves—stretching across the playing field, seemingly careless of where they fall, as if an apprentice stage manager had been left unattended in charge of the lighting. Almost each inning the field plays differently as the alternate patches of light and shadow march across, until at last the shadows conquer all. The problems here are obvious: To catch or to hit balls going from light to shadow and the other way around won't be easy. "I'd rather have my wisdom teeth pulled," comments Andy Van Slyke, "than play a five-o'clock game." With a home-plate area in shadows and the pitcher's mound still in the sun, it's clearly advantage pitcher. Batters won't likely accomplish much until the shadows cross the mound. An already formidable pitcher aided by shadows becomes fearsome indeed. Certainly such was the case when Lee Smith pitched for the Cubs out at Wrigley Field. "You can't help but be a little scared," an opposing player remarked, "when he takes the mound in the ninth inning of a game that started at 3:00 P.M. in Wrigley Field and he throws pure gas from out of the shadows." But then even his catcher at the time, Jody Davis, found the situation unnerving. "The shadows are killers. I can't see Lee's ball any better than the batter or the ump."[25]

Let no one forget the sun is our source of heat. Ball-players are not likely to, especially during the dog days of summer and in such notorious hothouses as the old Houston Colt Stadium (where one day Colt catcher Hal Smith remembered losing fourteen pounds), Busch Stadium in St. Louis ("it holds the heat very well," the always obser-vant Casey Stengel once commented), Atlanta's Fulton County Stadium, or out in Kansas City's Royals Stadium. There on a hot day all look forward to game's end. Royals pitcher Mark Gubicza recalls how on one occasion he and umpire Durward Merrill managed to hurry a game along. "I was pitching on a hot day, and Merrill, who was be-hind the plate, kept telling me, 'Come on, Gubie, let's throw strikes. I want to get out of here. It's too hot!' I said, "Fine, just call me a few strikes.' And he said, 'Okay, I'll call a few. We both want to get out of here and have a beer, don't we?'"[26] When in the summer of 1993 temperatures spiked up to 100° for days on end, the games in nearly all the outdoor stadiums became an ordeal. Most directly af-fected are the pitchers, called upon to perform inning after inning. Changing their shirts throughout the game and applying cold towels (or cabbage leaves stored on ice) to their heads helps, but still the heat takes its toll. A complete game, though unlikely, exacts a high price.

"During a day game at Wrigley I lose anywhere from six to seven pounds," Rick Sutcliffe, then with the Cubs, once observed.[27] The Chicago Cubs had hoped that with lights installed at Wrigley Field the increased number of night games at home would yield more victories each season. Spared the wear and tear produced by the hot daytime sun (it was not uncommon for the Cubs to fade late in the season), the theory seemed plausible. Their divisional championship in 1989 represented an impressive piece of early evidence, but recent disappointments have cast considerable doubt on the proposition.

Heat's a problem, but so is the cold. Baseball and cold weather have never mixed well. It fits no one's idea of suitable game conditions. Still, because the season begins in April and ends in October, (just about everyone in baseball, excepting perhaps the owners, agree it ends from seven to ten days too late) expect frigid days and nights and legions of uncomfortable players trying to stay warm.

Still there are limits; baseball's about the only game that will be canceled on account of cold weather. Moreover, subpar performances from scores of players are generally overlooked and explained by the cold weather. In April and May the most common excuse for anemic batting averages among hitters is the weather. Once summer weather arrives, they assure us, their bats will turn hot. There was, for example, no love lost between Mike Greenwell and Fenway Park in early spring. "I hate it. I hate the weather. I want to go somewhere where it's warm. It's a beautiful park to hit in, but not the first two months of the year." Teddy Higuera was once scratched from a game in Kansas City in early May when temperatures dropped into the thirties. He was replaced by Bryan Clutterbuck who proceeded to pitch eight scoreless innings in a 1-0 victory. To pitching coach Chuck Hartenstein the substitution had made sense: "You have Mexican fellows who like to pitch in hot weather and you have big redheads with beards who like to pitch in cold weather." Baseball offers us scores of hot-weather players who peak only when the temperatures do, sometime in July and August. Except, of course, at San Francisco's Candlestick Park, which remains distressingly chilly almost the entire season. Still, for years the great nightmare of baseball was always the possibility of a World Series in Canada—Montreal (until it built its domed stadium) and Toronto in October! That this great showpiece of the sport might be played under winter-like conditions chilled the hearts of many a fan (who otherwise could accept frigid conditions for early season games such as the one in Chicago in 1990 when on April 9 the Cubs beat the Pirates with the temperature at 33° and the wind chill level at 8°. Worse, it had snowed two hours before game time). Perhaps it was their prayers that prevented such an "unnatural" event from taking place until Toronto, to its credit, constructed a new domed facility. So just as life must be lived under varying conditions ranging from pleasant to perverse, so baseball takes place in settings that defy consistency, that at times enhance the game and on other occasions detract from the ability to perform, demanding always flexibility and adaptation as the price of success.

THREE
Country Boys and Green Pastures

IN THE BEGINNING, baseball brought the country to the city.[1] By "enshrining its rural origins," as Bart Giamatti reminded us, baseball shrewdly capitalized on this aspect of the game and thereby attracted legions of loyalists. Gathered as most of us are in cities or their suburbs, we remain rural sentimentalists, readily associating the countryside with tranquillity and tradition, youthful innocence, enduring values, and down to earth, uncomplicated folks.[2] By evoking once-simpler times and allowing its rural roots to remain exposed, baseball remains ever seductive, generation after generation succumbing to its charms, while confirming its standing as the "national pastime."

Rural themes and symbols—baseball measures them by the bushel. Consider the baseball season itself—a spring awakening and a fall conclusion—a pattern countless centuries old, when planting and harvesting lay at the center of human activity and survival. Spring offered new beginnings, fall the opportunity to reap, to rest and look back, reflect upon what had transpired. Baseball delights in its association with the arrival of spring with its bright sunshine and moderating temperatures. How well it answers our most basic needs for revitalization and renewal.

Baseball's surface simplicity reflects its rural origins. "Hell, if this game was half as complicated as some . . . writers make out it is," Bucky Walters once remarked, "a lot of us boys from the farm would never have been able to make a living at it."[3] Baseball's often been served up country style, the cultivation of a certain pastoral pretense regarded as essential to its continued popularity. Even Robert Frost, esteemed poet of rural New England, admitted he always wished to be mistaken for an old-time baseball player. Surely the current veneration of Mickey Mantle as the quintessential good ol' country boy fits the pattern precisely (as did a contemporary, Bob Feller). The abiding appeal of Yogi Berra and his "innocent," "wise," "down to earth" Berraisms, even if few are directly attributable to him, reflects an appreciation of a folk wisdom assumed to have originated back in our rural past. But it's not all contrived insofar as your basic big league types still tend to hail disproportionately from the land of RFD by way of the "farm system." Some examples of small town origins or current residences are Tom Browning, Casper, Wyoming; Dana Kiecker, Sleepy Eye, Minnesota; Steve Howe, Whitefish, Montana; Bill Sampen, Hanover, Illinois; Kevin Brown, McIntyre, Georgia; Bob Brenly, Coshocton, Ohio; Tim Birtsas, Clarkston, Michigan; Nolan Ryan, Refugio, Texas; Otis Nixon, Evergreen, North Carolina; Kirt Manwaring, Horseheads, New York. Given this rural flavoring, it's no surprise that nearly a dozen Australian-born players are playing professional baseball in the United States. Australia, after all, is the site of one of civilization's last substantial frontiers.

When former Angel Greg Minton refers to fellow pitcher Bryan Harvey as "just a good ol' country boy," his characterization would also apply to scores of other ballplayers. Pitcher Lee Smith felt comfortable on the Cardinals because, he said, "most of the guys here are country boys sort of like me." Smith would, no doubt, have much in common with pitcher Ed Whitson, described by a reporter as "a country boy who was raised with a fishing pole in one hand and a can of worms in the other."[4] "Doc" Edwards, former manager of the Cleveland Indians, enjoyed the reputation of being a genuine homespun type, as are probably most folks from his hometown of Red Jacket, West Virginia. Then there's Tim Belcher from the small farming community of Sparta, Ohio, Mickey Hatcher, who makes his home in Apache Junction, Arizona, and John Kruk, formerly of the San Diego Padres, he a native of Keyser, West Virginia, two-and-a-half hours' drive from Pittsburgh. Tim Flannery, a teammate then, recalls a time when the team was playing the Pirates in Three Rivers Stadium and Kruk left fifty passes for his friends. "We look up in the stands behind the dugout and there's this big rowdy group of people with eye patches, no teeth, huge bellies. It looked like the cast from 'Deliverance.' I ask Kruk if they are from his home town and he says, 'Yeah, and those are just the women.'"[5]

Not surprisingly your basic rustic has succeeded in setting the tone for the game. How else could you explain the love of chewing tobacco, the constant chomping, the shameless, incessant spitting, the simple

tastes and the unstylish clothes? In what other sport do so many players eagerly await the schedule's end so that they can begin the hunting
season or head off for a little fishing? Ted Williams, it appears, has
done little else since retiring. Deion Sanders is forever trying to induce fellow ballplayers to accompany him on fishing expeditions. Atlanta catcher Greg Olson seemed genuinely conflicted in the fall of
1991 when he admitted that because of World Series responsibilities
he would, for the first time in his adult life, have to pass up opening
day of the Minnesota pheasant season. Mitch Williams has already
mapped out his plans for retirement. He is preparing a rodeo corral
adjacent to his house. Nolan Ryan already has his own "range" of
twenty-five thousand acres and fifteen hundred head of cattle.[6] Note
too, the preference for laconic, folksy types, especially among coaches
and managers (and their inevitable depiction in such films as "Bang
the Drum Slowly," "The Natural," and "Bull Durham"). What other
sport sets such a high value on palaver, or is the source of an almost
endless stream of stories? The old traditions, tall tales, reminiscences,
yarns of all sorts,—no one tells 'em better than baseball people, the
original cracker barrel bards (or sings them better in the off-season
than umpire "Country" Joe West).

Baseball's rustic roots may go deeper than anyone has yet imagined and back as far as the Old West when cowboy heroes plied their
trade and fired the imaginations of many an armchair adventurer. Numerous connections and a wide range of shared symbols suggest that
possibility. Remember that baseball emerged as an organized spectator sport for the general public in the late nineteenth century just
at the time the widely circulated dime novels were popularizing cowboy
legends. Could that explain why both cowboys and baseball players
roamed grassy pastures and held fences in special regard, or the obvious allure both of the West and baseball's playing fields as wide open
spaces thinly populated? Is there not at some level a connection between the cowboys' determined roundup of strays and the headlong
pursuit of stray foul balls by fielders? Surely the corral and the bullpen are not unrelated. The late baseball commissioner A. Bartlett
Giamatti suggested a further linkage, reminding us of the essential
connection between "home" and the range across which the cowboy
rode. "Baseball is," he suggested, "quintessentially American in the

way it tells us that much as you travel and far as you go out to the green frontier, the purpose is to get home, back to where the others are."[7] Then too, is it mere coincidence, the cowboys' "long drive" and baseball's long season, or that baseball's signs—reminiscent of Indian sign language—and cowboys' branding irons both communicated unmistakable messages? Does not the crack of the cowboy's whip and the "pop" of the fastball into the catcher's mitt both convey the same message of authority and power? Is it also just coincidence that the 1991 movie *City Slickers* featured a trio of baseball fans who decide to search for the true meaning of life by signing on for a western cattle drive?

Consider the confrontation between pitcher and batter ("usually they hate each other," says Toronto manager Cito Gaston), facing each other alone at sixty feet, six inches, each wielding a lethal weapon (the fastest slinger verses the quickest bat, or in baseball parlance, "strength against strength"). Does this not recall the most vivid of western encounters—the classic duel from which but one person came away the victor? That's exactly how Mike Krukow once viewed his confrontations with Darryl Strawberry. It is, he says, "like the old gunfighters in the West. Neither one of us will ever give in." Dennis Eckersley concurs. "It's just you against him out there." Perhaps because they once were teammates, Wade Boggs shares Eckersley's perspective. "Once you get out there," he says, "it's one on one. . . . When you get a hit you've won."[8] Observe a hitter about to face his adversary whipping the bat back and forth through the air again and again. It is an exercise designed to enhance his stroke and to augment bat speed prior to the encounter, an action precisely reminiscent of the gunman repeatedly drawing his six-shooter from its holster to enhance fluidity and speed in the event of a showdown.

In baseball, though it is not a duel to the death, each encounter produces a winner but also an awareness that there will be many subsequent confrontations between the two. Accordingly, triumphant gestures are either absent or deliberately downplayed. During the 1991 American League Championship Series, Toronto's Joe Carter faced Minnesota's Jack Morris in a prolonged at bat. As he awaited the twelfth pitch of the series, a smile appeared on Carter's face as if to declare he had now gained the upper hand. Sure enough, he hit Morris's next pitch solidly into right field for a single. Once at first Carter smiled again and exchanged several words with Morris—a compelling mini-drama complete with the promise of future such duels.

Is it mere coincidence that while the ten-gallon hat defined the cowboy, baseball became the only sport in which players were obliged to wear caps? Surely we can recognize the effort to "break" high-spirited horses as analogous to the need to "tame" wild young fastballers who, lacking such control, present a danger to themselves and others. Note the link between the tall tales told around the campfire and the heroic legends recounted at the Hot Stove League (or the fact that certain western "heroes" appeared on "Wanted" posters while the pictures of today's stars top the most-wanted lists of baseball cards). Recall also that, for a time, relief pitchers rode to the rescue from out of the bullpen in cars, symbolically reenacting the classic scene of western deliverance—the dramatic appearances of the United States Cavalry to save the day. Do not the spurs of our western heroes relate to the spikes of our starting nine? Do not both employ leather gear? What of the constant infield chatter so reminiscent of the cowboys communicating to the restless steers in their midst? Admittedly, horses do not roam baseball's playing fields, but surely some measure of the affection once displayed toward those beasts has, one senses, been transferred to the tools of the game—the bat and gloves (once "broken in," the bats often carefully customized by players with a fondness for whittling earlier displayed by the cowboys) regarded as personal life-like extensions of the players. (Kevin Elster and Howard Johnson of the Mets even took their bats to bed with them on several occasions some seasons back.) Are not batters continually digging in at the plate much like horses repeatedly pawing the ground, both a bit nervous and tentative, but intent upon establishing firmer footing?

Our authentic cowboy hero comes off the trail laden with dust. Has any baseball player truly performed without having his uniform encrusted with dirt and grass stains? Surely Lenny Dykstra is one who would consider a clean uniform shameful. What of the delicate balance in baseball between individual accomplishment and team cooperation? Does that not mirror life amongst the cowboys—personal pride and reputation second only in importance to cooperative action (to keep those steers from stampeding and trampling everyone in their path)? Anyone who still doubts the western connection should observe ballplayers leave the field then head for the food and drink awaiting them in the clubhouse, and remember when the men once gathered round for a chuck wagon feeding (and then headed off to shoot up a nearby town much as players took to carousing when on the road). While few cowboys remain to ride the range, their successors still "corral" flyballs, stir clouds of dust along the base paths, stride confidently in from the bullpen (recalling the cavalry rescue), and relish the telling and retelling of it all. And so it should be no surprise that one, both a celluloid cowboy and silver screen ballplayer, tapping powerful currents of nostalgia and pride, captured the hearts of the American electorate and managed not long ago to become president of the United States!

FOUR

A Regard for Order

B ASEBALL appears to be a most orderly sport. Highly structured and exceptionally tidy, it conveys a sense of simplicity
along with the promise of easy accessibility. Sports writer Jerry
Izenberg considers the game as "America's last law-and-order sport,"
while Roger Angell marvels at its "orderliness and constraint." "Nothing," concludes A. Bartlett Giamatti, "is more orderly and geometri-
cal, more precise than baseball." "Baseball fits America so well," he
adds, "because it expresses our longing for the rule of law."[1] Surely
some portion of its appeal relates to this feature. In a turbulent, wildly
unpredictable world, baseball represents a model of stability, an oasis
of orderly expectations. Admittedly, all sports share this characteristic. Everywhere there are rules and referees to enforce them; always
contests are resolved within a finite period (though baseball, unlike
football, hockey or soccer, rejects ties). Games are won or lost, teams
aligned strictly on their records, champions crowned, and then, right
on schedule, the process begins once again.

But baseball goes beyond other team sports in its elaboration of
rules, strict organization, and its adherence to orderly patterns. Each
game, for example, begins in a manner entirely predictable. Rejecting
the coin toss, jump ball or faceoff, baseball clings to a protocol long
established, follows a traditional etiquette.[2] As befits the treatment
of a guest, the visiting team is permitted to bat first. Not until it has
completed its turn does the home team then proceed to the plate.
When at bat each team must present hitters according to a prescribed
lineup — the batting order. Deviation is all but impossible since copies
of the lineup are presented to the officials and to both managers before the game begins. It must be followed; any departure, inadvertent
or otherwise, is disallowed and penalized. Number two batter follows
number one; number six, number five, and so on — without exception. Those about to take their turn at bat are required to leave the
dugout and appear on the field. There they are consigned to a well-
defined zone, the on-deck circle, as they await their turn. After ad-

vancing to the plate, they are then once more confined, this time to a batter's box—a carefully structured, highly formalized procedure reminiscent of the inevitable advance of the assembly line (evolving within industrial America just as baseball first gained wide popularity early in the twentieth century).

Because baseball prescribes the order of player appearance, the game unfolds in a singularly restrictive manner. At critical junctures this inflexibility becomes obvious and seriously limiting. Whatever the sport, it is precisely at such crucial times that the best players are expected to perform. Faced with an important "third and two," a football coach will dispatch his most elusive runner into the game. Down by three with ten seconds remaining, the team's best three-point shooter will most assuredly take the court and get the ball. In desperate need of a tying goal, a hockey coach will turn to his first line and may even augment it after removing his goalie. What these tactics all have in common is plain enough—when the need is greatest, the ablest are summoned. But baseball's orderly ways often preclude such an obvious strategy. It happens repeatedly that a team will put runners on base and threaten to score—only to face the inexorable fact that next in line are the weakest, least productive hitters in the order. Herein lies at once one of the supreme ironies and abiding frustrations, yet also compelling features of the game of baseball—soaring hopes instantly deflated by stubborn reality, possibility offset by mediocrity. Still, the inflexibility is not total; one can dispatch a more proficient batter to substitute for the scheduled batsman. But a pinch hitter is costly (and usually entails great risk given the generally substandard performances of most). Unlike the other sports which allow players to be shuttled back and forth almost at will, baseball exacts a severe price for substitutes—players removed from the game at a particular juncture cannot return under any circumstances. (Consider how baseball might appear were it played with freer substitutions so integral a part of the other team sports.) The batting order, with all its rigidity, thus represents a major factor, often the decisive element affecting the outcome of the game. It also offers an intriguing waiting game for fans, who are forever looking ahead to see who's coming up, and who patiently wait for the best batters to take their turns at bat. That's because baseball opts for a predetermined order over and above op-

portunity; it prefers that you play your cards as given rather than resort to an expedient sleight of hand.

Not until a team makes three outs is it obliged to "take the field"
and assume defensive positions. It can score repeatedly and still remain on the offense (quite distinct from football and basketball where
the ball is presented immediately to the opposition after a score).
Baseball's adherence to the three-out offensive opportunity allows a
team to score many runs and, in effect, put a game quite out of reach
before the opposition ever receives a chance to bat. In baseball, order
once more assumes precedence, this time over equilibrium.

In the other major team sports, being on the offensive and in possession of the ball or the puck is not always clearly defined, and often
represents a more fluid situation subject to instant alteration. A quarterback's pass is intercepted by a safety whose team, as a consequence,
assumes the offensive. It's much the same in basketball, hockey and
soccer—rapid unpredictable turnarounds. Not so in baseball; here there
can be no blurring. Baseball, committed to an orderly procession, has
established a clear distinction between offense and defense. No scoring is possible, for example, unless a team's at bat, on the offense.
Few other sports uphold such direct and distinct separation. A clear-
ing pass from behind the cage hits that player's own goalie sending
the puck rebounding into the net—score one for the opposition (which
was, at that moment, on the defensive). A running back crashes into
the line, fumbles the football, and watches as it's picked up by a defensive lineman, who then lumbers into the end zone for a touchdown. Almost any play can lead to a score for either team. Baseball
rejects such haphazard happenings, and limits opportunities to a single
prescribed procedure. Only when authorized to do so can a team score,
not otherwise.

In baseball, "position" players generally remain in position, a territorial base clearly delineated, their range well established. The pitcher
occupies the mound area; the third baseman is on patrol in the vicinity of the base, et cetera, et cetera. Simplicity resides in this fixity.
Compare the situation to other team sports and the differences are
striking. In football, the line of scrimmage—for a moment a picture
of repose and order—quickly dissolves into a chaotic snarl, safeties
blitzing into the backfield, ends sprinting down field on pass plays—

opposing linemen twisting, turning about—few positioned where they were but an instant before. Only with diagrams can one track and comprehend these erratic movements. In basketball, a guard may pinch in under the backboards and contest opposing forwards for rebounds while the center drifts outside of the lane to expose the middle. In hockey, defensemen may be seen bringing the puck up ice into the offensive zone, then directing a shot on goal. These sports offer us controlled disorder, assigned positions serving largely as points of departure.[3]

For additional evidence, consider the linear patterns of baseball runners on their way around the bases. No diversion, no curls, no broken field running, no lateral motion, nothing other than movement in a straight line is permitted. Runners who deviate, as some are prone to do on their way to first, or when trying to impede a fielder at second base, or when attempting to elude a tag in a rundown, are called out. Although not strictly defined (except from homeplate to first base), there are base "paths" along which a player is expected to run. (What other sport enforces imaginary lines?) The straight and narrow is how baseball intends to play it.

In all sports, the forces of order attempt to contain the aggressive elements embodied in the offense. In baseball, the former, represented by pitching and defense, are especially dominant. In most innings of most games no one scores. The pitcher is without dispute the team's defensive stalwart, charged with maintaining order. When his "control" is sharp, he remains entirely in control, repeatedly inducing batters to strike out, pop up, ground out weakly. Stability reigns when a pitcher retires the opposition "in order"—one, two, three. Witness a succession of scoreless innings and the impression of baseball as tidy, uneventful, and excessively disciplined is inescapable.

But disorder always threatens. It's up to the hitters to prevent one, two, or three innings. It is they who send fielders scurrying about for balls hit out of reach and enable runners to dash around the bases.[4] Compare a strikeout, the ball nestling snugly into the catcher's mitt, the batter shuffling back toward the dugout to a well-hit ball propelled deep into the outfield, fielders in hot pursuit, others scrambling to set up for the relay, the batter meanwhile speeding around the bases. The difference between order and disorder is unmistakable. (Baseball inclines toward order; witness the fact that there are usually twenty-seven outs per team in a game, but rarely more than one-third that number of hits.) Ordinarily when a pitcher tires, loses control, or retires few batters, the forces of disorder are unleashed and are at least momentarily in the ascendancy. Runs cross the plate and the score mounts. It is imperative that control be restored. Out to the mound strides the manager, and from there he summons a new pitcher, fresh and usually fast, intent on "putting out the fire" and restoring order.[5]

The disruption caused by hitters assumes a different form if and when they reach base. An aggressive baserunner, especially at first or second, becomes notably unsettling for it is precisely his task to resist control, stir up disorder, and confuse the defense. The pitcher's rhythm and his delivery must now be altered. Instead of concentrating on the hitter, he's obliged to divide his attention and watch the runner as well. Pitches that he might have selected may be set aside to reduce the chances of a successful stolen base. He may now throw more balls to first than to the plate in an effort to keep the runner close to the base. The rhythm of the game will, for the moment at least, be altered. So, too, the positioning of the defense. The first baseman must remain close to the bag while the second baseman "shades" toward second in the event of a steal. Meanwhile the catcher positions himself for a quick toss to second, anticipating such an attempt. When, for example, Rickey Henderson gets on base he always gives the defense fits. "You'd almost wish he'd hit it out every time," former pitcher Jerry Reuss explained, "so you can concentrate on the next hitter."[6] Without doubt, runners are the agents of disorder, notable nuisances intent on upsetting ongoing patterns, threatening to subvert the defense and frustrate its efforts to maintain control.

Baseball inclines toward orderly ways even when departing from its prescribed procedures. There is risk-taking in baseball but most always they are calculated, conservative risks undertaken, not impetuously, but with a clear understanding that such chances represent an established part of the game. If and when they backfire, there is generally no handwringing or recrimination but the realization that such chances are necessary and expected. With a runner on third and one out, many managers choose to walk the next batter, putting him on base and in danger of scoring, in the hope of getting a double play.

With the lead run on third in the late innings, managers will frequently deploy a drawn-in infield risking a ball getting through easily but hoping to cut down the runner attempting to score on a ground ball. Taking large leads, calling for pitchouts, walking the bases loaded, creating exaggerated shifts against particular hitters — all are designed departures from orderly play but are considered necessary risks, not reckless gambles. There has been a reduction in attempted steals of home, a resoundingly risky play, in recent years, although the "suicide squeeze," a play surely perilous, remains popular.

In baseball, everything is given a number, assigned a value, calculated and represented by an average. (In what other sport do so many fans sit in the stands inning after inning assiduously keeping score in a shorthand long established. Such scorekeeping allows for an orderly review and recapitulation of the entire game. Should a game become exceptionally lengthy and complicated, it is usually reflected in a dense and disorderly looking scorecard.) It makes for an orderly process, one that by defining and redefining, serves to minimize surprise. A career .260 hitter will, most of the time, perform like a .260 hitter. A switch hitter who bats 73 points higher as a lefty will, if he comes to the plate in the late innings, probably face a left-handed pitcher. Numbers imply limits. When the statistics on pitcher Frank Viola pitching in Exhibition Stadium once read three victories and eleven defeats, it suggested that he pitch elsewhere. Statistics make it possible to compare everything and everyone in the game, today or in past years. They embrace all, reveal much, indicate problems, suggest solutions, and establish limits — in short produce a pattern of orderly expectations. Amidst the euphoria of the Dodgers' glorious conquest of the A's in the 1988 World Series, Orel Hershiser, the principal architect of that victory, expressed little confidence in the Dodgers' ability to return. "I wouldn't pick us to repeat," he observed thoughtfully. "I'm a very statistical man and it would be tough for us to repeat."[7]

Order prevails in baseball even as far as uniform appearance. You'll likely see football players looking altogether disheveled with torn uniforms, exposed pads, towels hanging from belts, and shirttails draped over the pants. In basketball too a certain laxity is evident, especially with respect to exposed shirttails (although new regulations in the 1991–92 season saw an effort to have them tucked in). No such sloppiness prevails in baseball. Here the dress code is taken quite seriously, extending even to a cap. It must be worn; it's not a matter of personal preference. There's also little latitude about the appearance of the uniforms. When, for example, some players draw comments for wearing their uniform pants legs down it's a fair indication of the level of control that still prevails. It was not so long ago that umpires finally were permitted to take off their jackets on a hot day and to work in shirtsleeves. Consider the game when pitcher Zane Smith served as a pinch hitter and promptly singled. As was his practice, he called for his warmup jacket upon reaching first base, only to be told by the umpires that he would not be permitted to wear it. Why? Only pitchers could be indulged and allowed to dress inappropriately when they became base runners. Because Smith was not pitching that game, he was subject to the dress code commonly applied to the other players.[8] Even in minor matters, baseball insists upon a strict sense of order and propriety.

So it is when baseball must deal with those persistently troublesome. If a player continues protesting a call, ceaselessly badgers an umpire from the dugout or, disregarding a prior warning, pitches perilously close to a batter, he will be ejected from the game. It can happen in other sports as well, but normally with penalties less severe — a two-minute benching, awarding yardage to the opposition, or a chance for a foul shot and additional points are imposed. Baseball, however, is more unforgiving, choosing to maintain order, not by imposing mild punishments, but by banishing the disorderly. (Even baseball's onfield fights between members of opposing teams are usually quite orderly with a ritualized aggression substituting for free-for-all melees.)

Finally, baseball games almost always arrive at an orderly conclusion. This is because, unlike other team sports, the game has eliminated time as a factor. There need be no panic or the pressure of a frantic finish, no preoccupation with the clock. Absent is the necessity to rush players in for the final moments, to gesture wildly for a time out, or to complain bitterly that one has been cheated out of a few seconds of time. Ninth-inning dramatics there may be, but in baseball, even the drama is deliberate and orderly, yielding a conclusion always reached in due time.

FIVE

Judgment Day

EVEN the most cursory examination reveals that baseball operates under an exacting moral code that scrutinizes performance, holds individuals personally accountable, and expresses itself in a manner pointedly judgmental, with a vocabulary reminiscent of the ancient biblical prophets. Is it any surprise that Jim Struck, trainer for the Virginia Generals in the Carolina League, could in all candor suggest that "to people around this game baseball is a religion. The field is a cathedral. The clubhouse is a confessional."[1] What other sport has produced a body of rules so exquisitely precise? Armed with rule books, the umpires, ever the stern defenders of the faith, evaluate all, confidently pronouncing some "safe" and others "out," distinguishing what is decidedly "fair" from what is distinctly "foul."[2] And beyond the formal rules, one encounters an unwritten code that prescribes what does and what does not conform to established practices and the venerable traditions of the game. Baseball does not hesitate to pass judgment; from its verdicts there are few, if any, successful appeals.

Baseball insists that players faithfully execute the fundamentals, the basic game skills and acquired savvy rarely noted in the box score. Baseball wisdom declares that unless the routine plays are performed flawlessly and consistently, success will be fleeting. A deficiency here is judged sternly, variously attributed to insufficient preparation, bad habits, the failure to concentrate, or a questionable work ethic. When the entire team performs in slipshod fashion, or indeed, when in a particular contest, both teams do, observers do not hesitate to pronounce the game as decidedly "ugly." Such baseball fundamentalism frowns upon the erratic outfield play of a Pete Incaviglia or Chili Davis and was dismayed when Darryl Strawberry and Mookie Wilson repeatedly lost balls in the sun. Fundamentally sound players, on the other hand, earn praise for consistency and reliability. Willie Randolph, Carney Lansford, Terry Pendleton, Ryne Sandberg, and Bill Doran — their steady hands and sound instincts all are welcome models of acceptable

42

practice and performance. In baseball, basic skills define character.

Baseball gives due credit for hard work, hustle, and "all out" play while it frowns on those who "dog it," malinger, or seem less than completely dedicated. Performances judged successful need not be immediately rewarded. Observe, for example, the "good" at bat, a notably skillful turn at the plate in which the batter battles toe-to-toe with the pitcher—lays off unhittable deliveries, "protects" runners who may attempt to steal, fouls away and thereby "spoils" tough or "mean" pitches, and manages several lusty swings (preferably against the pitcher's "mistakes"). The batter, though eventually retired, has acquitted himself well and earned high praise. On the other hand, a hitter surely will be criticized if retired after "giving up" on pitches that bend back over the plate or after offering at a series of "bad" or "waste" pitches. A "free swinger" rarely serves as a term of praise. Expected to be "selective," to practice "bat control," to resist temptation, to avoid being "anxious" or "stubborn" and to swing only at "good" pitches, critics will now question his patience, self-control, and maturity.[3]

On the spacious baseball field, each individual stands alone, unobstructed, isolated, easily observed. This is especially true of the pitcher, who is evaluated more closely and continuously than anyone else. Judgments follow each and every ball thrown to the plate. He's rewarded with a strike call for a delivery properly located or charged with a "ball" for a pitch beyond the zone. Let his motion stray from the prescribed pattern or be judged deceptive and he's penalized with a balk. A deficiency of control produces a "free pass" for the batter who heads on down to first base. (If, however, the base on balls is intentional, the pitcher is exonerated.) A pitch well out of the strike zone beyond reach is derided as "wild," a reproachful term suggesting a lapse of discipline, a breakdown of mechanics, a moral dereliction. On the other hand it is high praise indeed when that fellow on the hill is rated a "control pitcher," implying order, precision, and discipline. It is also most complimentary when this same pitcher refuses to "give in" but instead entices hitters, "tempts" them with balls near the plate, away from their "strengths" and directed to their "weaknesses."

Pitchers responsible for neutralizing batters are also expected to restrict the activities of runners on base. They must be kept "honest," prevented from taking a big lead, that "jump" that enables them to steal or take an "extra" base on a hit. To accomplish this, a pitcher must not ignore or be indifferent to the activities and likely intentions of the runner. He must, moreover, have a pitching motion sufficiently compact and deceptive that the runner will have difficulty "reading" him and will, as a consequence, hesitate to stray far from the base. Pitchers who, either through negligence, insufficient attention or elaborate windups, cannot keep runners close "on a tight leash" are generally blamed for such derelictions. When, on a steal attempt the catcher's throw arrives "late," almost everyone is quick to find fault with the pitcher.[4]

Pitchers are accorded an elevated spot on the field—the mound—and from that favored position are expected to control the batters. Indeed aficionados insist that baseball, at its best, its purest, is a pitchers' game, a duel in which the batters are overmatched, their bats silenced, their aggressiveness kept in check, control maintained throughout, the preferred final score 1-0 or 2-1. That is, according to "purists," the way the game "should be played." Even so, a pitcher may yield many runs and still be held blameless. The moral sensitivity of baseball is perhaps most acute when expressed in the concept of "unearned runs," which exonerates pitchers for runs scored because of errors committed in the field. No pitcher's record need bear this blemish, he being liable only for *earned runs charged* directly to his account. It is also present in the question of "responsibility" for runners who eventually score. A relief pitcher will not be charged for the runs of baserunners whom he inherits. Since he did not permit them to get on base, he must, in all fairness, be exonerated. Neither is a pitcher altogether to blame for a losing record when his team provides him with little offensive support, scores few, if any, runs for him. He then becomes a "hard luck" pitcher, a victim not of faulty performance but of fate.

Consideration for pitchers is also evident on those occasions when their effectiveness slips and they are being manhandled by the opposition. Such times bring suffering and public humiliation, but also merciful managers, who will come to their rescue, (once it becomes apparent they will be unable to "settle down") sparing them any further embarrassment. Enter the reliever at this point, a fellow pitcher prepared to shoulder the burden of holding off the opposition and preserving the lead. If successful, this good Samaritan will be credited with a "save," and his predecessor with a "win" and a return to a state of grace.[5]

With the fall of Adam and Eve and their involuntary departure from the Garden of Eden, humankind has searched in vain for a return to perfection. Only baseball offers such an opportunity. Up there on the hill, atop the highest point on the field, miracles can happen. And they have. Not very often, (fifteen during the course of major-league history) but enough to suggest that the gods occasionally will tantalize man with visions of supreme excellence. Every once in a long time, a pitcher rises beyond his normal powers, becomes an inspired artist, and for a brief period seems capable of achieving total domination, and so immortality. Batters rendered helpless inning after inning sense they are in the presence of higher forces. All too often such feelings are an illusion, a devilish trick to lift expectations so high that they can come crashing down when the bubble bursts and the dream dies — as it all too often does in the eighth and ninth innings. In 1988, for example the gods apparently delighted in this scenario. Time after time, pitchers carried no-hitters into the eighth and ninth innings only to see them "spoiled," often by "the meek," by hitters of little repute, a further indication of how perverse these higher powers often are. But on those rare occasions when twenty-seven batters march up to the plate only to make out twenty-seven times in succession, we have a "perfect game" and we wonder at the magic and mystery of it all. Announcers in particular face a moral dilemma over the issue of when to declare that a perfect game is underway. The concern is that by mentioning it, the pitcher will be jinxed, the spell broken and the no-hitter lost. Generally the perfect game "watch" begins in the fifth inning, any earlier mention is deemed premature and morally dubious. In an early season game in 1993, Braves' announcer Skip Carey repeatedly made mention that Cubs pitcher Jose Guzman was working on a perfect game but denied he intended to jinx Chicago. "Nothing we say up here can affect what happens on the field." Nonetheless Guzman lost his bid and settled for a one-hitter.

Batters, like pitchers, are assigned clear responsibilities and are judged accordingly. The measure of each individual's burden depends upon his positioning in the batting order. The higher levels of accountability rest at the top of the lineup; as one approaches the bottom, the burdens and expectations diminish until, in the National League, at least, one reaches the pitchers, where responsibilities are reduced, and whose failures are forgiven. There is, for example, no confusion as to expectations surrounding the lead-off hitter (although, in reality, he may get to lead off an inning only once—at the start of a game). His job description reads—"get on base any which way you can." By so doing he gives meaning and purpose to those who follow him to the plate. The number two batter is expected to be focused, versatile, capable of advancing the runner to second, and hopefully, even third base. Of the many ways this can be done, one deserves special mention. He can move the runner on to second most nobly, one might say, by giving himself up, by "sacrificing." What other sport incorporates so magnanimous a gesture?[6] You can set your "pick" in basketball or "block" for a runner in football, but neither play is considered the moral equivalent of a sacrifice. Such nobility of purpose, however, does not go unrewarded. The hitter is not charged with the time at bat, that is, his batting average does not suffer for his willingness to forgo the possibility of a hit, and instead to bunt the runner over into "scoring position."[7]

It may be called the "heart" of the batting order but it's not emotions that are involved, but hit-and-run production. The "table has been set" by the first and second batters in the order, and numbers three, four, and five are expected to deliver them, that is, to drive them in.[8] The heaviest responsibility falls upon the number four man, the pride of the batting order, otherwise known as the "cleanup hitter." His runs batted in (RBIs) total must be substantial in order to justify his position in the batting order. If, instead, he strands runners on the bases with regularity, he has failed. A prolonged failure of this sort would probably lead to his removal as the number-four batter— usually a demoralizing demotion for an established slugger. Gary Carter, for years a proud cleanup hitter with the New York Mets, sulked much like Ulysses in his tent when manager Davey Johnson decided his productivity no longer justified the number-four position in the order. If, on the other hand, a clean-up batter succeeds in driving in runs he stands tall and proud, a dominant and feared figure in the lineup. Whatever other deficiencies he has as a batter may well be overlooked. No matter that he strikes out frequently or hits into repeated double plays. (Jack Clark might come to mind here.) If he delivers with some regularity, he is judged a success, having lived up to expectations and to his responsibilities.[9]

With two or even three men on base and the cleanup hitter at the plate, the stage is set for high drama. When in these circumstances he delivers a homerun, it is a magic moment. Baseball, to its credit, knows how to heighten such drama. No other sport builds in such a celebratory ritual. (A quarterback after a touchdown pass heads directly off the field. At least in hockey a goal is followed by some obligatory hugging and skating about.) Logic and efficiency might ordain that after a batter hits a ball into the stands over the fence or out of the stadium his team automatically gains a run as he strides out of the batter's box and heads on back to the dugout, mission accomplished. But that's not the way of baseball. He must circle the bases, touching all of them, including home plate in order for the run to count.[10] This triumphal tour is the payoff, a public award for achievement. Trotting from base to base unharried, unhurried, safe from tags or obstructions by the opposition—such moments are for him to savor. (Celebrating his one-hundredth home run, Jimmie Piersall ran around the bases backwards!) Still, even at such moments, players are expected to demonstrate modesty and self-control and a basic decency that keeps them from "rubbing it in" by lingering too long at home plate to watch the ball sail into the stands, employing triumphant gestures, or embarking upon too leisurely a tour of the bases.[11] No other sport accords a hero of the moment so much time to bask in the spotlight. Take a hitter who has, in the bottom of the ninth inning, just tripled in the tying run. Then he is stationed at third base—for the moment with no place to go—soaking up the cheers of jubilant fans. And he is likely to remain there for a time, his presence a clear reminder of his recent heroics.

Moral judgments, philosophers tell us, cannot be made out of context. In a crowded lifeboat about to capsize, is it wrong not to try and save everyone? Well, baseball, too, has its situational morality and encourages judgments based upon circumstances. Certainly this is the case with hitters. Hits are always welcome, but when they arrive in unpromising situations, they may not be much appreciated. Down six runs in the late inning a home run is hit. Two outs, no one on, the bottom third of the order coming up and the batter singles—neither are pressure situations. Players who collect hits at such times may even be criticized for such empty gestures. (Rafael Palmeiro, an accomplished hitter, was nonetheless traded by the Cubs in 1988, in part, because he failed to produce when it really counted. Palmeiro in 1988 had not one game-winning hit! After arriving in Texas in 1989, he mended his ways and became more "reliable" and "productive" in key situations.) When, however, hitters succeed in crucial situations, they can expect lavish praise, whatever their overall performance. They are now regarded as producers who delivered "clutch hits" under pressure, when the need was greatest. Teams that surge from behind and prevail are also deemed especially praiseworthy, the comeback win representing a most highly esteemed path to victory.

Judgments today are delivered in a manner most precise. Players can no longer find comfortable shelter under the category of overall batting averages or total runs batted in. Today's statisticians crunch numbers endlessly, pinpoint responsibility, provide undeniable evidence that one is a clutch or a chance hitter. (Some seasons ago Davey Johnson, to reinforce his point about anemic run production, calculated, then distributed to each Met player his batting average with runners in scoring position.) Measures of ability or futility are not hard to come by; available figures highlight production with runners on, with two outs, with two strikes, or in the late innings. Base hits are not the only form of productivity. Most welcome is the right-handed batter who "gives himself up" by grounding to the right side in order to advance a runner to second or to third. And of course there is, with a runner on third and less than two outs, the fly ball to the outfield, hit far enough to permit the runner to tag up and score from third. Here is yet another version of selflessness not unrelated to the sacrifice bunt. One could debate the issue of moral equivalency inasmuch as the sacrifice fly is stroked to the outfield, with some possibility that it will fall safely for a hit, whereas the sacrifice bunter essentially renounces any chance for a hit. Nonetheless those who hit sacrifice flies are doubly rewarded for their efforts, awarded a run batted in and not charged with the time at bat.

Hitters accept responsibility when they come to the plate. They understand game situations and know what they must do. When they fail to perform their disappointment is real and quite often their anger unmistakable (notwithstanding the fact that baseball accepts the likelihood of disappointment, understands how frequent are the squandered chances and wasted opportunities). In other sports, players rarely are as demonstrative in calling attention to their own shortcomings. The moral dimension of baseball is most striking here, with its unabashed admissions of guilt and its public confessions by players acknowledging their own shortcomings. It's not at all uncommon to see players gesture in obvious disgust and disappointment or to hear them moan, "I stink," after a dismal performance at bat or in the field, or their teammates or manager publicly acknowledge that "we were just awful," were overmatched by the opposing pitcher, or failed to take advantage of opportunities. After Kansas City began the 1992 season in dismal fashion, Royals Manager Hal McRae admitted, "This team stinks to put it mildly. I won't give a plug nickel for the ball club right now."[12] Baseball involves a long season where mistakes can be rectified. Such confessions and acts of contrition may help reduce burdens of guilt that might otherwise impair future performance.

Watch how often a batter who strikes out with runners on will do little to conceal his anger, disappointment, or even embarrassment. Ripping off his batting helmet, flinging his bat, kicking the dirt, shouting at himself—all this self-flagellation and incrimination while heading back to the dugout. Once there, we may see the start of round two—fists colliding with the wall, the bat rack assaulted, or the water cooler subjected to a shameful all-out attack. It was no surprise when former Angels' manager Cookie Rojas installed a punching bag in the runway leading from the dugout at Anaheim Stadium. It would, he hoped, deflect some of the abuse away from the walls and water cooler in the California dugout. And it might prevent players from getting hurt. Punishing themselves for "failure" was one thing; injuries was quite another. For years there was no fury worse than that of Kirk Gibson returning after a failure at the plate. Muttering, cursing, steaming, a volcanic eruption in the making, he stormed back to the dugout, prompting teammates to scatter in fear of their lives. An angry George Brett could probably challenge Gibson for title of dugout demon. Listen to him relate an incident of mayhem after a strikeout:

"I had just struck out for the third time in two days and I had to find a release, so I went to the dugout runway and threw my bat, then I saw a gallon paint can. First I kicked it, then I threw it up against the wall and it just exploded and paint went all over the place."[13] Compare these demonstrations to the impassivity of a Kevin McReynolds, whose expression rarely betrays what happened or did not happen at the plate. This study in contrasts became even more vivid after McReynolds, via a trade, became a teammate of Brett on the Kansas City Royals in 1992.

Baseball, to a surprising degree, offers the opportunity for redemption. With great regularity, players who early in the game have fallen short and wasted opportunities find themselves at a later stage of the contest in a position to turn the tide and become the architects of victory. When broadcaster Gary Thorne proclaimed baseball to be "a game of redeeming opportunities," he no doubt had in mind such striking reversals of fortune. In a game late in 1992 Jeff King of the Pirates suffered the humiliation of hitting into an unassisted triple play—only the ninth in major league history. But then came a chance to win the game in the thirteenth inning. Sure enough, King came to bat and singled, helping to erase the stain of his previous misadventure. In game three of the 1991 World Series a bad error by Braves' second baseman Mark Lemke appeared likely to result in victory for the Twins. Minnesota, however, proved unable to capitalize on the opportunity. Whereupon Lemke, at bat in the next half-inning, promptly singled home the game-winning run. Had he not done so, however, and had other opportunities been wasted during the game, observers would have been quick to conclude the team did not "deserve" to win, that it had forfeited any moral claim to victory. This theme of redemption and just desserts was very much part of the discussion at season's end in 1991, which saw pennants captured by two last place teams from the previous year. "The last shall be first" was a theme baseball found compelling and uplifting.

If, as many contend, 90 percent of baseball if pitching, then the man on the mound bears overwhelming responsibility for the outcome of a game. His job is that of pacification, thwarting the aggressors who stand ready and eager to wreak havoc out on the field.[14] He's permitted to use power and wile, speed and "stuff" to blunt their attack and send batters in retreat back to the bench. When he's operating quickly and efficiently, teammates on the field behind him have their burdens lifted, enjoy an easy time of it. If he's hit hard, however, he must watch as they chase after balls well out of reach and look on helplessly as the opposition cavorts about the bases. If he fails in his job to keep the opponents at bay or at least keep the game close in the early going, he will most likely be asked to surrender the ball and leave the mound. However much he protests this decision and promises to mend his ways, managers extend few if any reprieves. Instead, head bowed low, he slinks back to the dugout, then retreats quickly to the clubhouse. Not for him the humiliation of sitting along the bench (possibly infecting the others), having failed when so many had depended upon him. Rather for him there is banishment, then the ritualistic cleansing "shower" to help erase the stigma of defeat.

Out in the field[15] performance likewise is judged on a play-by-play basis. Ordinarily all goes smoothly: at the major-league level fielders are uncommonly skilled. Still, there will be balls that are dropped, grounders that pass through the legs, and throws that are misdirected. These miscues are committed out in the open; there's no overlooking or ignoring them. And of course they're not. When the "E" flashes on the scoreboard, it's official — an error has been charged to a particular player, who can only pray it will not be critical.[16] In 1992 Bobby Bonilla was upset because he considered the "E" for error sign on the Shea Stadium scoreboard to be overly large. Then there are the other kinds of errors that, though often damaging, are not flashed onto the scoreboard or noted in the box score. A runner who forgets how many outs there are, a fielder who overlooks the lead runner, an outfielder who throws to the wrong base — mental errors all, few of which go unnoticed, many of which prove costly. All too often they do. Craig Biggio, when an Astro rookie catcher, saw that as the principal difference between playing college ball and performing at the major league level. "You can get away with mistakes in college [but] here your mistakes are punished," he adds, "so you don't make them anymore."[17]

It is doubtless true that baseball players are judged more continuously and more severely than players in any other sport. Officially, there are the four umpires out on the field, and six in post-season play. They rarely, if ever, reverse their decisions, though they permit discussion of their calls. In no other sport do players and managers have such latitude in taking on officials, if one overlooks former tennis champion John McEnroe, that is. Then there is the official scorer of a particular game, whose job it is to rule on whether errors should be charged and hits awarded to players. The players themselves, as we have seen, are often the severest judges of their own performance, but this doesn't stop teammates from offering their own evaluations. Kangaroo courts have sprung up on many a baseball team, some of the more memorable in recent years being convened by judges Bob Brenly with the Giants, magistrate Andre Dawson with the Expos, along with such other honorable dispensers of baseball justice as Willie Stargell, Don Baylor, Steve Garvey, and Daryl Boston. These informal tribunals are designed primarily to relieve pressure on a team by providing comic relief and encouraging togetherness even as they mete out monetary punishments to transgressors for all manner of misdemeanors out on the field or in the clubhouse. Players are censured and fined (appeals are usually given short shrift) and a good raucous time is had by all. The underlying theme, however, is unmistakable and serious—misdeeds observed and swift punishment meted out. These exercises in self-censure serve to maintain standards, make certain that the game is played properly.

A manager's judgments are taken far more seriously, for although his authority has eroded in recent years, still, he cuts a formidable figure with the team. And one of his primary responsibilities is to evaluate talent, judge performance level, and reward and punish based upon his conclusions. This he does in a variety of ways—benching a player, platooning him with another, replacing him for defensive reasons in the late innings, pulling him for a pinch hitter, moving him every which way in the batting order, calling upon some and not others to come out of the bullpen, speaking his mind at team meetings, ordering additional batting practice (such as the one Hal Lanier of the Astros once called immediately *after* a game) or canceling such workouts. Each move communicates a measure of displeasure, and registers strongly with team members. So do the fines he may impose from time to time when he believes team discipline is being undermined or his authority challenged or a player has behaved irresponsibly. Carrots there are aplenty in baseball; so also, an occasional stick.

That fans stand in judgment of players is certainly no secret, it being one of the privileges accorded those who display such consistent team loyalty. That's what makes being a fan so much fun. There is among them never any hesitation or reluctance to evaluate players, their own favorites as well as those on opposing teams. Should any of the latter incur the disfavor of home town fans, they can expect the reaction to be vocal and vociferous when they take the field or come up to bat. On the other hand, local players may find themselves targeted by fans to the point that their ability to perform at home is seriously impaired. That fans can be harsh judges of talent is well understood. Sit in the stands and listen as players are singled out and subjected to withering criticisms. Observe the banners with their often unsportsmanlike and unsparing indictments of individual players and teams. Read the local newspapers, which frequently contain highly critical assessments of individual players, by columnists and fans. Back in the clubhouse, players may get the message in another way. Here they'll read letters, some vilifying, some praising, some offering advice. Fans seem to feel especially close with baseball players (closer it seems than with players of any other sport), and believe it vital to make their feelings and views known to them together with suggestions about how to field their positions and perform at the plate. Players, for their part, have no choice but to grin and bear it, to accept that as the price of fame and the consequence of playing the national pastime in the glaring spotlights of publicity.[18]

Finally, players are judged and subjected to the severest test of all along the statistical gauntlet. There's no escape from the verdict of their own numbers or the comparisons of these figures with those of others. Quite predictably, each season produces an abundant harvest of numbers, statistics which will be compiled, pored over, analyzed, then used for all manner of comparisons—one player with another, to evaluate two different teams, to determine player compensation in arbitration proceedings, to distinguish players and teams past and present. Each player is likely to know every pertinent number related to his performance—plus shifts, trends, even projections. A game, a month, and a season all produce numbers, some of which in the short term appear to be defining, but as the seasons pass and the figures accumulate, a more enduring and reliable picture emerges. A player is classified by his averages; the numbers tell his story. He cannot escape them or appeal their verdict. Actions speak louder than words or claims or press releases. A career .270 hitter, an 80+ RBI man, a consistent 20/20 producer, a .500 pitcher, a 200-plus–innings workhorse — all define acknowledged levels of accomplishment. There will be "career years" such as Dwight Gooden's in 1985, and as Dave Henderson had in 1988, and Andres Galarraga enjoyed in 1993; some players will elevate performance levels by cutting down on their strikeouts, making use of the entire field, learning to read pitchers better, and taking large leads or developing a new "outpitch." But by and large, the inexorable limits of their statistics and talents will remain in force, rendering judgment on what they've done, and signalling what is yet to come (and, if the numbers warrant, providing for the comparative few who are "deserving" — and it is precisely this issue that provides the grist for endless debate — entry into the Hall of Fame).

This has been a strange, and perhaps unexpected, excursion across the moral landscape of baseball, sounding more like prescriptions from the pulpit than a description of the national pastime. But that's because baseball, a game respectful of traditions, has managed somehow to retain at least the flavor and fervor of an era now long gone, one with fewer shadings, more stringent requirements, exacting standards and greater commitment to matters of individual responsibility.[19] To watch it and to accept its ways and judgments is to be drawn into a world both simpler and more certain of its truths. For that reason alone, baseball has its legions of true believers and faithful followers.[20]

PART TWO
Between the Lines

In this section we move out onto the field and discover that all is not what it seems once play begins. Established canon maintains that spontaneity and untutored talent are the principal ingredients of success, that victory depends on basic skills performed with regularity, and that the simple virtue of patience will be consistently rewarded. But further analysis reveals the presence of complexities and worrisome uncertainties quite at variance with the game's surface simplicities. The rules, so exquisitely precise, emerge upon close observation to be at times loosely enforced and occasionally arbitrary. The playing surface assumes added and uneven dimensions with the incorporation of foul territory, an expanse that serves generally to complicate play. That this game of leisurely pace and bright summer skies contains dangerous elements and produces fear among players surely represents a jarring, disturbing note. Also surprising is the unsuspected function of time in a ballgame. Elapsed time as leisurely pace is well understood and celebrated, but time serves a more calculated function when it becomes a deliberate device to delay proceedings, to upset rhythm, to allow for complicated interventions and managerial machinations. It also allows for talk in generous amounts — in the dugout, out on the field, and in the stands. Indeed, baseball is surrounded, almost inundated by talk. And too often that talk adds to the burden of the game in the form of rumored trades, badgering by reporters, and heckling by fans. But then consider the serious conversation that develops in the latter stages of a tight, tense ballgame. Here talk adds to the existing tension, helps produce the strangely static, but excruciatingly dramatic, situations that are the glory of the game. There is surely then, in baseball, far more than meets the eye.

SIX
Baseball Fundamentalism

T HE FOLLOWING is a sampling of what baseball players should know and what they must do in order to perform at the professional level.

On a rundown between third and home, always drive the runner back to third base.

On a fly ball with a runner on base, position yourself to catch the ball while coming in so as to be able to execute a quick, strong throw.

While bunting, hold the bat almost parallel to the ground and pull it back smartly upon contact to deaden the ball.

Be sure to hit the cutoff man on throws back to the infield.

When bunting with runners on first and second, lay the bunt down so that the third baseman will have to field it.

Against a left-handed batter, a first baseman should not become preoccupied with holding a slow-footed runner on.

With a runner on second, don't attempt a largely futile throw to the plate on an outfield base hit, permitting the batter to take second.

Always know how many outs there are, especially if you're on base.

An infielder back-pedaling into the outfield in pursuit of a pop-up or flare should always, by shout or gesture, let others know he intends to make the catch.

With less than two outs and runners on second or third, an infielder should always first "look" the runners back upon fielding a ground ball.

On a base hit into the alley in right center field, a runner on first should endeavor to go to third, especially if the right fielder is right-handed.

Backing up plays is essential; for example, a catcher down to first on a grounder, a pitcher behind home for a play at the plate, a center-fielder in behind second during a steal attempt at that base.

With no outs, whenever possible hit to the right side to advance runner(s).

Get behind ground balls; don't field them to the side.

On a pitched ball into the dirt, a catcher should avoid reaching for it with the glove. Smother it with the entire body.

On a high, pop foul behind the plate the catcher should hold on to the mask until he has sighted the ball and then toss it away from the immediate area.

With runners on, don't hold the ball in the outfield. Quickly toss it or run it back in.

Don't tip off a suicide squeeze by a premature break off third base.

On a double steal the runner on first should make certain the one on second has broken for third before accelerating.

When in a rundown, avoid being tagged as long as possible so that other runners can move up.

On a ground ball, try, as a runner, to time your advance so as to get between the ball and the fielder.

Try to break up double plays by upsetting the fielder down at second base with your slide.

Avoid taking too wide a turn at first after a base hit.

On a ball hit wide of first the pitcher must break immediately for first base.

On a play at the plate when the ball arrives first, the runner must attempt to jar it loose from the catcher.

On a ground ball to the right side fielded near where a base runner is advancing from first, the runner should slow down, avoid the tag, and force the fielder to throw to second base.

Whenever possible, on a shallow fly ball, the outfielder running in should take charge in preference to an infielder back-pedaling out.

Hold on to the ball. Be safe rather than sorry. Avoid throwing the ball when badly off balance or when there's little likelihood of getting the runner.

On a bunt play with runners on, a nearby fielder not making the play should shout to the one going for the ball which base to throw it to.

A pitcher should send a "calling card" to runners on first periodically to remind them that they're being watched.

Batters, after a base hit to the outfield, should be alert to bobbles or double "clutching" as an opportunity to take an extra base.

Leading off in the late innings with your team behind, make the pitcher throw strikes. Attempt to work out a walk rather than swing at the first pitch.

On a deep fly to the outfield, return to the base and tag up rather than advance halfway and then return when the catch is made.

Don't be diverted by excessive throws over to first base when the runner is not a base-stealing threat and a dangerous batter is at the plate.

A hitter should observe the positioning of the defense as a clue to the next pitch.

On a hit-and-run, a fielder must come in and then over to cover second base so as not to yield his position prematurely.

It's the established wisdom in baseball that winning over the long haul depends not on dramatic flourishes, strokes of genius, or even outrageous good fortune. Rather, the edifice of victory rests on a broad foundation of commonplace elements, basic physical skills and a tactical savvy that are the essential building blocks of success. During the course of a lengthy season, it is the cumulative impact of these elements that separate the winning teams from the also-rans. A fundamentally sound team, one that executes not so much the rare but the routine plays, will always be in contention. This belief has long served as a foundation principle of the game. Testimony is unanimous on this point. "Most games are won," George Will believes, "by small things executed in a professional manner." Writer Lee Eisenberg observes that baseball is a game of fundamentals. "By this I mean it isn't fancy. It isn't contrived. It isn't trendy." Darryl Strawberry paid the Dodgers the highest compliment in 1988 when analyzing the reasons for their unexpected success. "They're playing the game the way it's supposed to be played. You got to do the little things." Jeff Blauser explained why it was that the Atlanta Braves, pennant winners in 1991, had finished last the previous year. "We didn't always know how to win," he commented. "We didn't know how to do the small things that it takes to win." Lou Piniella, determined to improve upon the Reds' disappointing 1991 season, announced what it would take to get his team back on track in 1992. "We're going to work," he said. "We're going to stress fundamentals and have a lot of individual instruction."[1]

Those "little things" are to baseball what character is to the individual; they are the bedrock upon which all the rest depends, upon which judgments ultimately are made. They are also part of its link to the wisdom of the past, an inheritance, a cumulative savvy that would be costly to neglect. They may go unnoticed or may not always be acknowledged, but when they're missing or performed indifferently, the results are flawed, the prospects for long term success dim. "I'll take nine guys hitting .220," says former California Angels' manager Cookie Rojas, "who do the little things it takes to win over nine guys hitting .300 who aren't doing the fundamentals."[2] Just about every manager dissatisfied with his team's play will insist upon the need to return to fundamentals. For new managers in particular it will become a lodestone, an absolute article of faith. Most players will welcome such an approach, recognize its value, appreciate its rewards. "I get more satisfaction out of playing the game right," says Terry Steinbach, "than I do out of going 4 for 4."[3]

Baseball's fundamentals are not unlike the rituals of religion. Both provide assurance and stability, serve as a discipline that reduces the need to think and, because they produce a sense of well-being and accomplishment, are their own reward. When rituals lapse or are performed indifferently, religious authorities bemoan a decline in faith, an erosion of belief. So also in baseball. Guardians of the game are quick to sound the alarm, to warn of disturbing trends and threats that must not be ignored. In a 1991 survey of the game, *The Sporting News* declared that too many players were "Flunking the Basics," a conclusion that went largely unchallenged by the ballplayers. Conceding that today's players were stronger than ever, Rick Dempsey nevertheless agreed that, "fundamentally they are weaker," while Cal Ripkin, Jr., observed that "more fundamental mistakes [are] being made." Andre Dawson notes that most young players are getting along "because of their raw ability. . . . They're not in tune with the basics and fundamentals." Delino DeShields does not dispute this. "Most of us young players," he notes, "[are] not the students of the game the players were in the past."[4] What accounted for this decline in standards? An array of explanations were offered from a diminished pool of talent, inadequate minor league preparation, an overemphasis on specialized skills, a decline in the work ethic, to a structure of rewards that focused almost exclusively on offensive statistics. Whatever the reason the message was clear—the keys to the kingdom were to be found in the basics of baseball.

Other sports are not all that different. To be able to dribble the basketball with either hand, and snap the football briskly and accurately to the punter—such abilities are fundamental. An inadequate skater will not make a lasting impression in the National Hockey League (NHL). Still, in baseball, the emphasis on fundamentals is especially pronounced, involving not only the flawless execution of basic physical skills, but a mental awareness and acuity that instantly produce the right decisions. In team sports like football and basketball, a great number of plays are designed in advance, players assigned, and expected to concentrate upon specific and limited roles. Naturally, freelance situations and "broken plays" surface and spontaneity and creativity can be decisive, but the idea generally is to keep these to a minimum. In baseball, on the other hand, while "plays" are put on—hit and runs, infield shifts, decoys, double steals, and so on—mostly there's no set script, instead a reliance on well-honed individual skills and team savvy. In baseball we speak far less of *plays* than of *situations,* of which there are hundreds, each demanding a combination of inherited wisdom and improvisational finesse. This is where the "little things" often play a decisive part. A player must be well-schooled physically and mentally in the fundamentals, which is what the instructional leagues, the minor leagues, and spring training is all about (though some today question just how seriously all this is taken). Even so, lapses are common and "refresher courses" and drills even for the most skilled and experienced players go hand in hand with playing the game.

Fundamentalism finds persuasive expression in the offense when discussion turns to "building" a run. When a team is not hitting, or when the ball fails to bounce its way there must be a concerted effort to "manufacture" runs in the most prosaic of ways, capitalizing on otherwise unexceptional events to produce a score. There is tremendous satisfaction in baseball circles at this approach, and considerable pride taken in this minimalist strategy—a sense that baseball has not strayed too far from its roots (in the era of the "dead ball," when one could not rely on dramatic homers to post runs on the scoreboard). To appreciate this approach, listen to the words of former Milwaukee Brewers manager Tom Trebelhorn. "I'll tell you what I like. A Paul Molitor bunt for a base hit. A steal of second. A Jim Gantner take-it-with-you [drag bunt] to the right side getting Molitor over to third. A Robin Yount hard ground ball to the backhand side of the second baseman whose only play is to first. Paulie scores. I love that."[5] In this instance, the ball never left the infield and yet a runner crossed the plate. Other variations involving hit-and-run-plays, delayed steals, and sacrifice flies are part of this understated, quietly effective arsenal. When the long ball has gone "south," a back-to-basics approach can yield notable dividends.

Hal McCrae, reflecting upon the lessons taught by the renowned hitting instructor Charlie Lau, offered a similar perspective. "Charlie taught us," McCrae noted, "you can't be hot all the time. You come to the park with the idea . . . I'm going to do something today—score a run, drive in a run, have a base hit. He taught us that in the end these things will add up."[6] Perhaps the "Rickey Rally" known to fans of the Oakland Athletics best exemplifies this approach. It is simplicity itself. Henderson begins by drawing a base-on-balls. He proceeds to steal second base and then third. He then scores on an infield out. A 450-foot home run registers no more on the scoreboard than this mixed assortment of minor accomplishments.[7] The "little things" add up; often it is those mundane events that provide the margin of victory.[8]

SEVEN

A Surface Simplicity

"Baseball is not that complicated
but it is not easy to do."
—Yogi Berra

WHY IS IT so many people in and around the game insist there's not much to playing baseball? Consider some of that good-natured teasing by insiders, along with a certain disingenuousness from people who've been asked far too many questions for too many years. Who would, after all, accept a similar response from a conductor who claimed his principal task at the podium was to wave the baton, first to start up, then to stop the sixty-odd musicians before him? Certainly that's part of it, but so are several more intricate chores along the way. There is admittedly a descriptive simplicity to all games, baseball included, a basic objective that must be achieved—putting a ball through a hoop, a puck into a cage, a football over a line. There's no argument there. But accomplishing this more consistently than other competitors—that's when complications arise and why Roger Angell observes that "serious fans . . . know how hard this game really is." So enormously complex can it become or be made to seem that Tim McCarver cautions players to "keep the game as simple as you can."[1]

One can watch baseball and be taken in by the seeming artlessness of it all, the reliance upon obvious tactics and straightforward everyday skills that one assumes are at the disposal of most all red-blooded American males. "More than any other American sport," says sports reporter Tom Boswell, "baseball creates the magnetic, addictive illusion that it can almost be understood."[2] Complexities present in other popular team sports seem foreign to the game of baseball. What's there to compare with the intricate matchups and maneuvers that take place along the line of scrimmage in football? Where else but in basketball do you see players careening down court at top speed, dribbling a ball, while eyes rapidly survey an ever-shifting flow of bodies looking for a sudden screen or pick to develop shaking loose a shooter suddenly airborne? Where in baseball is there such an uninhibited continuous flow of free-form athleticism? Just talk about strapping on skates and flying around on the ice and you've convinced most of the population that the game of hockey is suited only to those few gifted with unerring balance and unyielding teeth. In baseball, you've got your feet on the ground, and everyone generally stays in place and then moves mostly in straight lines.

Most baseball people are inclined to keep it simple. Spokesmen for the "Aw, shucks, there's not much to it" school of thought have always populated the sport. The great Honus Wagner would have us remember that "there ain't much to being a ballplayer, if you're a ballplayer." Babe Ruth assured an admiring public there was nothing very complicated about what he did so supremely well. Hitting, he remarked, involved little more than "pickin' a good one and sockin' it." Onetime Red Sox shortstop Johnny Pesky, though he played years later, had little to add to the Babe's reductionist philosophy. "You keep your eye on the ball, you hit the son of a bitch, that's my theory of hitting." Hank Aaron's view was hardly more complicated—"Go out and get that pitch." Yogi Berra's "See the ball and hit it" was simplicity itself.[3] Neither is pitching much of a mystery if you listen to that former crafty veteran moundsman (all pitchers still toiling successfully past age thirty-five are almost always labeled as "crafty") Rick Reuschel. What it amounts to, he tells us, is simply "making them hit the first pitch at somebody for an out." And, of course, does there live a fan who doesn't believe he could manage a team with the best of them? There's nothing to it! You won't get an argument from any number of reputed experts in the field. Just ask Whitey Herzog, former skipper of the St. Louis Cardinals, and you'll understand why he generally appeared so relaxed in the dugout. "Managing is simple," he'll tell you. "You just put out your best players and try to get them out there in their positions as often as possible." Such modest demands would seem to leave quite a few people overqualified for the position. So maybe the job is overrated. Long-time *New York Times* sports columnist Ira Berkow would have us believe that "no one truly knows if a manager makes a difference. Or if he does, how much of a difference."[4]

A case can be made for baseball's simplicity, at least at first glance.

Without the clock, free of time restrictions, there's no reason to rush things, no need to prepare specifically for those pressure-packed waning moments of a football or basketball game when everything hangs in the balance. In a game of baseball the pace generally remains slow, relaxed, even casual.

Observe a team on the field and the impression is one of spaciousness and easy definition. Former Cleveland Indian manager Dave Garcia reminds us that baseball is "always happening right in plain sight. It's all visible, every part of it," while George Will agrees that it is "intimately observable."[5] Players have no difficulty discovering where they belong. Positioning changes during the course of a game but ever so slightly. The same applies to the offense. Players bat in order according to a predetermined lineup—a simple enough scheme to follow with the superior hitters bunched together at the top of the lineup, the less productive ones relegated to positions toward the rear. This established order, whether in the field or at the plate, means that at one time relatively few players are taking part in a play. On the offense, only the man at the plate, and whatever runners, if any, are on the bases, participate in the action. Often the bases are clear, leaving just the batter involved at any one point. On the defense, involvement may be greater, but not necessarily. If the pitcher is unusually sharp he may spend much time playing catch with the catcher, the batters unable even to put the ball into play. More likely they will hit it, but even here the degree of defensive involvement may be limited. On a ground ball to short, the shortstop will field it and throw on over to first, leaving the rest of the players on the field with little to do other than observe the play. On a pop-up or fly ball to the outfield, one fielder will almost always take care of matters. The point is, that unlike the other team sports where all the players out there participate in some way on each play, baseball's different. Most players are not involved. Baseball does not feature the full-scale scrambles and runarounds en masse common to the other sports (except perhaps during a brawl). Offensively, a player easily can wait for up to an hour between appearances at the plate and the opportunity for direct involvement. In between, there is little for him to do other than look on and encourage others. Out in the field, participation is likely to be more continuous, though not necessarily. An outfielder can, for inning after inning, patrol his territory and not come close to touching a ball. (Ralph Kiner remarks that at one time people would shout to otherwise stationary outfielders: "move around, you're killing the grass.")[6] That, in itself, can be troublesome and produce diminished levels of alertness. Ordinarily, unless on account of the heat, few players (pitchers and catchers excepted) work up much of a sweat playing the game of baseball. (A pitcher *works* a game; the rest *play* it.)

More than any other sport, baseball has an exceptional number of standard "routine" (a word rarely employed in other sports) plays that, taken together, make the game appear simple. Most times after the batter makes contact, the fielders have an easy time of it. Bouncing ground balls ordinarily do not pose much of a challenge. So routine are most of these plays that batters must be continually reminded to run hard to first base in the unlikely event an error is committed. Those who "hustle," who run out every ball, reserve special praise. Pop flies and fly balls are generally not a problem. And when ground-ball base hits reach the outfield they are usually quite simple to pick up. Gloves, vastly improved and notably more spacious than in years gone by,[7] make the fielder's job even easier. So simple are most fly balls that some fielders introduce slick catching styles, create a little flair, presumably to add interest and drama to what is otherwise decidedly routine. Difficult plays there are, as difficult to execute as any in other sports, but such challenges are few compared to the number of unexceptional chances that arise in the course of a game.

Among all the major team sports, baseball is the only one in which a player generally performs unhindered, unguarded by the opposition. In many others he has to operate effectively despite the fact that right alongside him, literally hanging on to him, annoying him, harassing him, obscuring his vision, is his opposite number. In the pivot, the opposing center does all he can to muscle his counterpart out of the area, to deny incoming passes and to block, deflect or alter any shot that is attempted. In football, the split end, for example, is likely to be bumped at the line of scrimmage and then closely guarded as he scampers downfield. Should a pass head his way, the defense will converge on him in an effort to bat it away. All will leap high for the ball, fall back to the ground, a mass of tangled bodies. Baseball involves no such encounters. No one is guarded or can be impeded. Interference is unacceptable. No one patrols the outfield to knock the ball away from the centerfielder about to catch it. A runner can't deliberately swipe at the first baseman's glove in order to dislodge the ball. Players therefore can concentrate on what must be done and not worry about anyone else. Simple enough, though not entirely. A runner on the bases will, on a ground ball, try to dart in front of the fielder to obscure his view and force an error. A runner coming home or into any base will attempt in his slide to dislodge the ball and thus assure his safe arrival. A right-handed batter at the plate will somehow find the means to get "in the way" of the catcher on an attempted steal of third. But these are minor encounters at close quarters compared to the ongoing pairing and one-on-one competitions and physical sparring that occur in basketball, football, hockey, and soccer.

Baseball is not a contact sport. There are no blocks, take-downs, tackles, bumping, spearing, or handchecking. Though unlikely, it is possible that an entire game can pass without members of either team touching one another. That's one reason size is not of any great significance in baseball. Bumps and bruises will occur, but rarely will they be inflicted by individuals from the other team; the wear and tear originates elsewhere. That's not to say complete physical separation has been achieved, but it has been largely confined to two specific situations. Most commonly, it develops in and about second base when a runner barrels in from first in an attempt to disrupt a potential double play. His objective is to trip up or upset the opposing second baseman or shortstop sufficiently to keep him from throwing on to first, or to pressure him into a weak or inaccurate toss. At times bodies collide and tempers flare, but, by and large, players accept such encounters as part of the game; unless injury results, there is grudging forgiveness, except when the hard slide and contact relate to other incidents in the game, and are in retaliation for earlier improprieties.

There is, however, the possibility of physical fireworks taking place at home plate, the final destination, the last and most sought-after stop on any trip around the bases. Because "home" is so supremely important, the only place where a team can score, it's no surprise that an all-out defense of this area is permitted. Guarding this territory is probably the most solidly sculptured player on the team, certainly the one most padded and protected. If there is to be a play at the plate it is expected that he will use the full force of his body to prevent the runner, charging in from third, from scoring. We have, then, the making of a full-fledged confrontation as fierce as exists in all of sports (actually quite out of keeping with the overall style of the game). If the catcher receives the ball on time, has the chance to position himself before the plate, the runner dashing in is likely to run into a wall and be stopped cold well short of home. (A classic example occurred in the 1991 World Series when Twins catcher Brian Harper withstood the determined charge of the Braves' Lonnie Smith.) On the other hand, a slightly altered time sequence usually produces different results. In this instance, the ball arrives somewhat late, forcing the catcher to reach out, preventing him from concentrating fully on the runner heading straight in his direction. The latter, for his part, recognizes that he and the ball are likely to arrive simultaneously and that his best hope to score lies in crashing full force into the catcher and dislodging the ball. In this instance, it's usually advantage runner with the end result a catcher, somewhat off-balance, sent sprawling (the quite predictable result when, for example, Bo Jackson ran into catcher Rick Dempsey). Because collisions at home are fully a part of the game, only rarely do they provoke bad feelings no matter how resounding the blows.[8] Here is baseball at its most macho—players slamming fiercely against one another, then trying to walk away as if but a casual greeting had been exchanged. There's other physical contact possible at first base, indeed at all the bases, and during rundowns, but none is central to a game in which opposing players largely keep their distance, and perform free of interference (a principal reason why Atlanta Braves fans directed their wrath toward Minnesota's first baseman Kent Hrbek after he appeared both to have lifted and pushed Atlanta runner Ron Gant off first base to record an out in the 1991 World Series).

With players not interfering with one another, and for other reasons as well, the skills needed for baseball seem simple, less formidable than those required to play football, hockey, and basketball. Behind-the-back dribbles, breakneck speed fast breaks, blind passes, open field tackles, broken field running, hitting receivers on the run, controlling the puck while hitting the boards, instant decelerations— the maneuvers and motions of baseball don't appear to be in the same league. Neither is the same strength needed. What in baseball compares to the "power forward" muscling in toward the basket against bodies bent on stopping him or the raw forces required to stand up and stymie a three-hundred-pound defensive lineman? Baseball's skills appear less specialized and by contrast less dramatic—everyday and everyman abilities that seem within the reach of mere mortals—were we only to practice them. And as kids, didn't most boys and some girls do so, spending many an hour on many a day tossing a ball, hitting it around, simulating real game situations? Running from base to base in a straight line—we've all played our share of tag games. Is there that much more to the game of baseball aside from learning to chew tobacco? That it is, in many respects, a simple game is true; that it is an easy game is quite another matter.

Baseball's difficulties start with the fact that it is a long season, officially opening amidst the chills of early spring and concluding in the lengthy shadows and falling leaves of autumn. And since it is mostly played outdoors, the various seasons leave their mark, provide an ever-changing setting for the game. Because the baseball season is, in the words of Doc Edwards, not a sprint but a marathon, it must be approached and handled in a special manner with adjustments made all along the way. Little wonder then that Don Baylor sees baseball as, "all about staying power and endurance."[9]

On opening day all teams are tied for the lead and optimism abounds. The chase is on, though the road to the pennant is long, hard, and strewn with obstacles. Often debated is the question: when are pennants won? Decide that and one can determine which games are really important and which are merely preparatory exercises preliminary to the critical phase. One could, of course, declare that all games count equally and all are important, but how convincing would that be? Traditionally, the pennant chase has been compared to a long-distance race—teams running together in a pack in the early going, then a gradual thinning out as the contenders separate themselves at a certain point from the also-rans. This makes the first half of the season, up until the All-Star break, appear to be a warmup phase, an opportunity to work out the kinks, establish continuity, and size up the opposition. After that it becomes serious business, the occasion to dig in for the stretch run. Opinions vary as to when the race actually begins. One school of thought has established the "dog days" of August as the critical opening phase. Teams that "have the horses" will at this juncture display their mettle and demonstrate their character during these trying days. If teams can survive August intact and remain in contention, they've positioned themselves for the stretch run that follows. ("If it ain't September, it ain't crucial," Sparky Anderson proclaims.) This is when teams drive for the finish line, or, if they've expended their energies, their pitching staffs have worn thin, or their early phenoms have sputtered, fall off the pace. "The cream rises to the top in August and September," Jack McKeon tells us. The pennant drive is when veteran players demonstrate their "stuff," maintain their concentration, establish their leadership, and steady the rookies, even while as Reggie Jackson observes "the ball grows smaller and the outfield fences move farther away." All this, writer Tom Boswell remarks, makes "baseball in September perhaps the richest treat in sports."[10]

Downplaying the stretch drive, some point to the importance of winning early on. After all, games do count equally. "If you win in April, you don't have to win them all in September," Tom Lasorda assures us.[11] Besides, early victories establish a winning attitude, boost morale, convey a message to the rest of the league. There is nothing inevitable about a pennant race late in the season. It can be decided much earlier. Recall the 1988 season. With the exception of the American League East, which turned into a free-for-all at the close, the other three divisions saw the Mets, Dodgers, and A's establish early leads and never once relinquish their top spot for the remainder of the season. The same was true of the Pirates in 1991. In these instances early victories paved the way. What followed was icing on the cake. The absence of serious pennant races in all four divisions was a disturbing feature of the 1992 season.

Late-season pennant drives are an essential part of baseball lore. The notion of taking charge early on, then remaining steadfast and unyielding lacks the allure and drama of a race heading down to the wire. But then it all depends on who you ask. Teams lagging behind, those who have yet to "put it together," naturally will downplay the importance of the early going. Instead they'll point to hopeful signs and areas of progress, all the time denying the race has begun. When it does, "We'll be ready." Those who've taken the early lead will concede, "There's still a long way to go," but will take comfort in a winning habit already established. All this talk is just that, usually to appease the press and comfort fans, but it does relate to the inordinate length of the season. With a schedule that stretches on and on, it's not always clear if all is already lost, or when it's time to get serious.

Were the pennant drive to begin in earnest in April, more players and most teams would be hard pressed to complete their schedules. A pennant chase is pressure packed, a daily grind replete with high anxiety. No team could possibly sustain such intensity over a seven-month period. It's helpful, then, to segment the season and move from a relaxed attitude in April and May to a serious mood in June and July, and to high gear in August, and into the stretch run in September. This produces one of the enduring challenges of baseball's lengthy season, the need to combine relaxation and intensity so as to get through the season yet maintain the will to win up until the end. "What you want in baseball," Davey Johnson suggests, "is 80% over six and a half months."[12]

Players able to relax will perform better in the field and up at the plate day after day, and will have something left in reserve as the season heads into the final weeks. Without question, baseball lends itself to a relaxed style. Observe the leisurely pregame patterns, the pace of the game, the absence of time limits, teams remaining several days in each city, pitchers starting once every five days. Is there a more leisurely sight than a starting pitcher who has won the previous day, sitting in the dugout during a game, seemingly without a care in the world? He will, after all, not be called upon to work again for several days. But the intensity is never far below the surface, influenced by the need to win, the ever-present competition for jobs, the pride in professional performance, and the pressures of a pennant race. Still it's not something that automatically sustains itself, especially over a long season, nor is it an element naturally associated with the game of baseball itself. Can a player remain intense when he's mostly a spectator—at bat for a total of only a few minutes of a two- to three-hour game, uninvolved in a majority of the plays in the field? Furthermore, because baseball lacks physical contact with the opposition it cannot count on the high energy levels generated by such encounters.

Players who manage to remain relaxed day in and day out usually receive high praise for what is considered the appropriate response to the daily grind that is the baseball season. Such individuals, it is assumed, will not expend their energies needlessly but can maintain their strength for those times when they are needed. Still, what of the possibility of becoming too relaxed, too nonchalant? A fine line must be observed here, though most recognize when relaxation crosses over into lethargy, when a casual approach produces complacency. "I don't get too high or too low," says Dave Henderson, but how many players are able to so fine-tune their temperaments?[13]

But players and managers do also admire the high-intensity types, those who remain all business, are always "in the game," able to grind it out over the entire season. In 1988, manager Tony LaRussa deliberately cultivated this attitude among the frontrunning Oakland A's, "If you can tell me where it makes sense to allow yourself a little comfort I'd like to know," he insisted. "I don't see the benefit of it. The premium is the ability to push every day. As soon as you back off you are vulnerable." Still, intensity has its problems. Can one turn it up a notch when the situation demands even greater efforts? Might it be self-defeating during those inevitable slumps and down periods when recovery usually depends upon relaxing and introducing fresh approaches? Can intense individuals be made to loosen up from time to time? "You can't stay wound tight as a clock for six months," Tim Belcher observes. Bo Jackson tells us that he "learned in this game the more you press, the more you screw up." Even Kirk Gibson had to learn to relax a bit, not his customary approach to the game. So the game continues to search for the perfect blended baseball personality, calm but committed, temperate but tenacious, genial but gung ho. It may have found a model of control in Kevin McReynolds, although as Ralph Kiner reminds us, McReynolds "doesn't have an attitude problem. He doesn't have any."[14]

Given the lengthy season, one fully expects many surprises along the way. A team may get off to a fast start, thanks to good pitching and timely hitting, then inexplicably hit the skids. Suddenly play turns sloppy and the pitching staff falters. In truth, a team may experience several "seasons" during the course of a single campaign. Consider the California Angels in 1988. They began in dismal fashion, then, midway in the season, suddenly hit their stride and produced a 31-15 record. But a sweep by Kansas City sent the Angels into free-fall; they never recovered. They concluded the season with twelve straight losses, twenty-nine games out of first place. A team seemingly well-balanced and deep suddenly unravels when a rash of injuries hits key position players or pitchers. As the disabled list (DL) fills up, an em-battled manager hopes he can stay in contention until his regulars re-turn to the lineup. But sometimes they don't, and if they do, they're not quite the same. Or they return, are reinjured, and the patching and filling process begins once again. In 1988, the San Francisco Giants tried to stay in contention despite countless lineup changes. They didn't. In 1989 the St. Louis Cardinals' pitching staff was intact only briefly. With pitchers falling like leaves all about him, even the wizardry of Whitey Herzog was unavailing. The race often goes, not to the swiftest, but merely the healthiest, the team that escapes serious injuries and fields the same group of players day after day. Contrary to opinion, it doesn't always even out. "To win a pennant," former Dodger coach Bill Russell says, "you have to have a lot of things go right."[15]

The long season exacts a price, even if players manage to avoid the disabled list. Healthy is, of course, a relative term; it may mean little more than slightly shy of incapacitated. Playing hurt is simply part of the game. Darrel Evans at the end of the 1987 season probably spoke for most players. "I'm not just tired; I hurt. I come out here every day and the first thing I do is run sprints. Well, it hurts. It hurts to run those sprints at this time of year. I'm on aspirin all the time." In late August and September there's not much expectation that the body can bounce back. It's no longer a friend. It stays sore, the stiffness remains. It's tired all the time. The bats feel heavier, and as Chris Chambliss reminds us, a "slower bat speed is pretty common at this time of the year for a lot of the players."[16] The bangs and bruises have taken their toll (and with the cooler weather, feel even worse). But that's precisely when the body must perform, grind it out. By late in the season, players have slept in too many hotel rooms, enduring too many uncomfortable beds and too much unpalatable food. There have been too many hurried trips to the airport to catch waiting planes in the middle of the night. Half their games have been played in relatively unfamiliar surroundings, often before hostile fans. The disruptions of family life have now added up to several months. (For those in the chase, the flow of adrenaline masks most of these aches and pains as well as the loneliness. The home stretch allows little time for such distractions.) For all those out of the running there is only the pain. A day here and there out of the lineup may help, but still the end of the season begins to look like the promised land. "The closer October 4th comes the better I get," John McNamara once remarked.[17]

Besides an endless season, baseball is a difficult game because of tension between team effort and individual achievements. That's what made baseball the "most unique game in the world" for Ernie Banks. Baseball's a team sport; considerable energy and thought is applied to creating team feeling and group cohesion. But teams win without it (consider some of the combative Oakland teams of the early seventies) and by itself, it's not enough (recall the 1988 Tigers, a team where players were "tight" but unfortunately also somewhat short of talent). Still team spirit and togetherness can go a long way. That was the view of Dodger Mike Scoscia a few years back. "We ain't," he conceded, "the most talented group in the league. We're probably third in our division as far as talent. But we're the best team." Don Zimmer admitted that unusual unity amongst the Cubs in 1989 accounted for their exceptional season. "I used to think it was a bunch of crap," but then, "I learned about team chemistry. I never saw a team that played together and stayed together like this team did last year."[18]

Not one, but many, elements must be present to produce the synergy that turns a collection of twenty-five players into a spirited determined group. The ingredients may include rookies who played together in the minors, a balance between veterans and younger players, a smoothly functioning and relentlessly vigilant kangaroo court, a practicing prankster to dispel tensions, a peerless captain to lead the way, and a manager who plays no favorites. But teams are made, not born. True groups emerge out of the day-to-day struggles on the field. Unselfish play sets the right tone. Winning helps, especially when a different hero emerges each day. Adversity too has a part to play—a losing streak that players endure without finding fault, without recrimination. (Take note that streaks and slumps tend to be catching. When the team starts hitting, everyone hits. When it slumps, the contagion spreads to all players. So what an individual does often reflects current levels of team performance.) A rash of injuries permits substitutes to see action and encourages everyone to pull together to replace missing bats and strong arms. Nothing, however, helps cement a team more than the prospect of winning—the possibility of going the distance and capturing the glittering prize—the pennant. About this, the feeling is unanimous; nothing could be grander, nothing more worthy of pursuit. Such a prospect pushes all else aside: winning is everything. No other theme permeates the conversation of ballplayers so completely as the need to win.

A group generally forms in the clubhouse and dugout, not so much out on the field where group involvement is limited. Without teamwork, no basketball team can win consistently. On the gridiron it requires a machine with all parts finely tuned to push aside the opposition. It's not much different in hockey. In all other sports, players must mesh well for plays to succeed—all players at the same time. For example, if ten men perform but the eleventh, at left tackle, fails to block his man, the play unravels. Baseball can work this way but usually doesn't. We've already noted the large number of plays where perhaps half the team will simply stand around as interested observers, at most. No one denies how dominant a pitcher can be; though he needs people behind him to record many of the outs, almost alone he can control a game and turn it into a one-man show. Out in the field a spectacular catch can take place in which absolutely no one but that one player can assume even the slightest credit for the deed. At the plate the situation's much the same. It's the batter alone who makes contact, supplies the power, and guides the ball the best he can for a hit. "It's an individual game," says Wade Boggs. "When you're in the batter's box, no one sets a puck for you, no one throws a block for you."[19] In truth, an individual hitter can carry a club on his back at least for a period of time. Jack Clark did it for the Cardinals in 1987, Andre Dawson for the Cubs in 1987, and Joe Carter for the Blue Jays in 1991.

But the importance of individual effort can be exaggerated. So many plays for their success depend upon exquisite teamwork. Take, for example, a ball hit solidly toward the outfield wall. The pitcher, as it is launched, immediately points out its direction of flight to assist his outfielders. One of them finally catches up to it on the warning track,

75

then hears the centerfielder shout out the location of the cutoff man, who has run toward the outfield to receive the throw (backed up by a trailer should the throw elude him). Once the cutoff man gets the ball, he wheels and prepares to release it, exactly where, determined by the trailer, who tells him that the runner is heading home. So the throw heads there, the catcher (backed up by the pitcher) prepared to catch it and apply the tag to the sliding runner. Altogether, six out of the nine players on the field worked together to complete the play. Were we to detail the rotation play or the defensive efforts to thwart a likely steal attempt, the element of team play would again be highlighted. Still and all, the level of teamwork expected in baseball does not match that required for most other team sports.

A player's numbers speak of individual achievement. Like school grades they reflect his yearly performance, they represent his credentials and constitute his bargaining power at contract time. The numbers, although not always an entirely accurate measure of worth or accomplishment, are concrete statements of fact largely unrelated to team performance, though they are subject to differing interpretations. Bob Woolf, when negotiating a contract for pitcher Bob Stanley, noted that "we had statistics showing he was the third best pitcher in the league. They had a chart showing he was the sixth best pitcher on the Red Sox." Players talk about their numbers all the time, set target levels for themselves, and compare theirs to those of others. Despite this preoccupation, every player, to a man, will insist his numbers are insignificant compared to his team's standing. Certainly all managers agree. "When you start thinking about individual numbers," Cookie Rojas noted, "you're going in the wrong direction." Kirk Gibson some years back preferred not to talk of his MVP chances. "It's not a priority of mine. I'm not going to lose sleep over it. I want to keep focused on the real goal and that is to win." Greg Maddux, after winning thirteen games in one season, was clearly pleased, "but we're trying to get into a pennant race," he insisted, "and I don't want to get caught up in personal achievements." Certainly Bruce Hurst would agree. "Whenever you start pursuing personal goals in the game, it seems to me you get on the wrong track."[20] Endless statements from players leave no doubts here. There's no joy, little sense of personal accomplishment when the team's not winning. The year 1987 represented a fine season for Dwight Evans, but not one for the Red Sox, and that's what disturbed him. "I've said this again and again. I'd rather be hittin' .260 and be in the race. I've never had a better year, but I've never been so disappointed." Even when a player establishes an individual record, he realizes the need to share the spotlight and credit his supporting cast. After Roger Clemens' extraordinary twenty strikeouts performance in 1986, he was careful when "being asked one question after another about yourself" to emphasize that "It's a team game and I can't win without my teammates." "You have to be careful," he added, "to deflect some of the glory back to the team."[21] This subordination of individual achievement to team standing is an effective device, even if at times a useful fiction. In baseball, where team play is not always critical to success, the rhetoric of team priorities serves to fill in whatever gaps exist in the game itself.

There is one set of statistics that rivets attention and becomes the stuff of fantasy for players. Having battled furiously to make it into the major leagues, another plateau now awaits. It is the season that they hit their stride, put it all together, realize their potential, fulfill their most optimistic dreams. It is their "career year," the year that their numbers add up to one glorious awesome season never to be forgotten. For pitcher Bob Gibson, it came in 1968 when he compiled a 22-9 record, recorded an astonishing 1.12 Earned Run Average (ERA), and climaxed it all with a seventeen strikeout performance in the World Series against the Tigers. For pitcher Ron Guidry, it arrived in 1978 when he went home to Lafayette, Louisiana, after posting numbers which read twenty-five wins and three losses. In 1985, Doc Gooden experienced the thrill in only his second year in the majors, amazing everyone by finishing 24-4. Career years are wonderful, especially when they coincide with new contract negotiations, and when they produce radical reevaluations of "worth." They tend also, often indelibly, to fix a player in the public eye, cause people to remember him mostly for that year of glory, no matter that such a level of excellence does not recur. But career years have their drawbacks, not recognized perhaps until some time has elapsed. There is, of course, no way in the short run to determine whether, in fact, there has been a career year. Has a pitcher developed an additional pitch that will keep him dominant for years to come? Has a batter gained new confidence at the plate, lifting him to and maintaining him at a new level of competence? (That's certainly possible. Did not Jose Oquendo, Harold Reynolds, and Ozzie Smith, once journeyman batters, find their stride and become much more complete hitters?) Note what Dave Stewart accomplished after he moved over to Oakland after unspectacular years with the Dodgers, Phillies, and Texas. The likelihood of pitchers gaining new, and consistently high, plateaus is greater than hitters achieving new performance levels (which opens up a new and fascinating subject for discussion). Still and all, observers in baseball seem able to distinguish those who've had "monster" years and will likely return to earth, from those heading for new and higher ground. So do certain players. Dwight Gooden, for example, has acknowledged on many occasions that for him there will never be another 1985.

A certain sadness is inevitable (especially in the case of someone like Gooden who seemed to have peaked at the age of twenty-one) when one concedes that his best year is behind him. How can it not produce a sense of loss, of disappointment? Also, an air of mystery, as well. How could a star that shines so brightly lose its luster, a brilliance never again to be seen? But consider why this is plausible. A career year generates attention, causes the opposition to take notice, to plan more effectively so as to neutralize such threats to the established order of things. Batters start laying off first pitches, stop offering at those out of the strike zone; pitchers bear down harder against these hitters, stay inside or paint the outside corners. In this way, the pressure intensifies after a career year; repetition becomes difficult, the standards too high to take hold. The career year becomes an albatross around the neck, opponents discuss it as "a freak of nature," an aberration that won't recur. That is why most players will concede that while the career year was indisputably thrilling, much more rewarding would be a reputation for consistency. That player who year after year remains reliable, who "puts up numbers," who is rarely spectacular but always solid, who though he may not scale the heights, steers clear of the depths—that is the model; that is what they wish for themselves in their careers.

For most fans, memories of the game are there to savor for the sheer pleasure of it all. Players, however, are obliged to take them far more seriously. The past is important to them not for its own sake but for the light it may shed on future happenings. Recollections, more than curious tidbits, serve as guides, even limits on what is likely. If *they* don't recall the past, others will, and that may prove their undoing. Baseball players, one assumes, are of ordinary intelligence, probably no brighter or less intelligent than the norm. Yet at least in one area they excel: that is in their ability to perform feats of memory well beyond average competence. Listen to a ballplayer, and you'll discover him capable of impressive levels of recall, easily able to summon forth details from specific games and seasons past. It's no surprise that a batter can tell you how he's performed against a specific pitcher, in a certain ballpark, in particular circumstances. He senses the pitches he can expect in different situations. He can recall what he's done against righties and lefties, at night and during the day, in the late innings and with runners on base. Pitchers for their part can describe every pitch thrown to every batter during the course of the game. The pitch that accomplished the job, those that were hit hard—they remember them all. (Pitchers who can hit also recollect in exquisite detail their heroics at the bat. Here, for example, is Don Robinson recalling all his "dingers." "There was one off a Phil Niekro fastball. Then Ed Whitson, breaking ball; Joe Sambito, fastball; Warren Brusstar, slider; Scott Sanderson, slider; Lance McCullers, breaking ball, and Mike Scott, fastball.")[22]

Pitchers rarely forget those who have hit game-winning home runs against them. Some may choose to wait patiently for an opportunity to even the score. John Candelaria, for example, admitted hitting Juan Samuel, a teammate, in a Dodger intrasquad game in 1991 because of a home run Samuel hit off the lefthander six years before! "It is unbelievable but it is the truth," Samuel commented. "Candy told me that he finally got even with me after hitting me with that pitch. I said, 'Why do you need to get even with me?' He told me about the home run, when I was with Philadelphia and he was with Pittsburgh. I didn't even remember the home run. But now I got a bruise to prove it."[23]

Not all players trust to their own memories exclusively. Catchers will help pitchers recall, managers will also. Some will resort to keeping their own records, books brought to the ballpark and reviewed before and sometimes during the game. So when teams face each other and batters and pitchers begin the personal one-on-one duels, it represents merely another insert in a very long book familiar to both. Each player contends both against the past and the present; both admit it complicates matters. That's where certain mind games begin and perhaps why pitcher Bob Ojeda insists that, "baseball is not incredibly physical; it is incredibly mental."[24]

Memory also operates in another way to reduce surprise, to both limit and enhance performance. Baseball produces a collective intelligence and maintains a grapevine through which it is disseminated. Advance scouts reconnoiter and report back useful short-term information about who's been hot and who's not and whatever else may be of interest in the enemy camps. *The Sporting News,* which players sometimes read, provides capsule views of developments around the league, and local baseball reporters attuned to the broader picture toss twice-told tidbits into the general palaver. But it is the players themselves who communicate with one another, sharing what they've seen or heard about their favorite subject—other ballplayers. It happens when they meet on the field for pregame warmups; it goes on when friends get together socially for a meal or drink once the game's over. The whole process accelerates because players move about so much from team to team, and in their stopovers get to know, certainly get the chance to watch many other ballplayers. In short order intelligence is gathered and passed on. "What's he throw?" "What's he got in certain situations?" "What's his 'out pitch'?" "Does he rattle?" "Is he strictly a pull-hitter?" "Does he shorten up with two strikes?" "How's his arm?" The evidence mounts; the dossier grows thicker—there's no escaping what you've done or what you're capable of doing. As the Astros' Craig Biggio discovered, "There's a book this thick on you up here."[25] The possibility for surprise diminishes.

The first time around the league a player can enjoy a free ride. He's an unknown, a partial mystery—he has the upper hand. Second time around, the balance begins to be restored. Weaknesses surface and are passed on, patterns are perceived and are exploited. On the other hand, the legend may grow. "Abbott's for real"—"Justice is no flash in the pan"—"Watch out, Jack Morris is on a roll." The collective wisdom of baseball accumulates and is added to the statistical flow and the personal experience of individual ballplayers. Much is known, much is expected, and there can be few surprises in baseball. But remember, whatever the history, whatever the statistics, whatever the potential, it is, of course, the execution now that counts.

Some of the pressures of the game we've seen—the travel, the slumps, the threat of injuries, the drive to produce "numbers," to maintain team togetherness—but there are others as well. There is the need, also, to maintain self-respect as a professional, to avoid abject failure. Pitcher Jack Morris noted that he was essentially motivated out on the mound by the fear of embarrassing himself. Hal McRae concurs. "Players," he notes, "earn a lot of money, but this is a humbling experience. Nobody wants to be embarrassed in front of millions of people."[26] At the major-league level, nothing that happens on the field escapes notice, by teammates, opposing players, the press, or fans. It's all out in the open; always the "big show." It's not the time to blunder or provide any indication that you don't belong. It's painful when the "E" sign goes up on the scoreboard, signaling you've misplayed the ball. It's unsettling when a ball sails over your head in the outfield. Better to play deeper and avoid being embarrassed. Looking awkward at the plate, being fooled, swinging futilely—it's distressing. Above all, players don't want to be shown up in public. Having pitchers like Pascual Perez or Juan Berenguer punching out hitters with their fists after they've taken a called third strike cannot be pleasant. Pitchers want no part of the slow home-run trot (by Mel Hall or anyone else) or of any other triumphal gestures. (The 1986 Mets were labeled arrogant and resented by other National League teams, in part, for the curtain calls players took after home runs at Shea Stadium.) No batter wants to be called back from the on-deck circle and replaced by a pinch hitter. When Joe Morgan did it to Jim Rice in 1988, it led to a pushing incident and to a suspension and fine for Rice for shoving his manager. A pitcher resents what he considers to be a "quick hook," and will often make his displeasure quite obvious before stomping off the mound. Who amongst us enjoys having one's limits, weaknesses, or failures on display, exposed to the public eye? Certainly ballplayers don't, but unlike any other sport, it happens in baseball all the time.

The pressure of having to perform, to compete, to win, makes players more conscientious than ever when it comes to year-round conditioning, extra batting practice and studying videotapes, but it also produces a variety of other behaviors easily viewed as unreasonable, even irrational. On the other hand, if baseball itself is partially mysterious, occasionally unfathomable, the unconventional approach may not be entirely inappropriate. Whatever the reason, a majority of players are superstitious, accept the fact that performance is not just mechanical and mental, but is guided by inscrutable forces that must be appreciated, recognized and appeased. ("I guarantee that every player is superstitious about something," says Roger Clemens. Bucky Dent was even more emphatic. "There are certain things guys do," he commented, "that you can't take away. Some guys have superstitions. You try and find out what their little things are and respect them." Superstitions, according to Wade Boggs, are a way of promoting a sense of stability and confidence amidst circumstances that too often produce anxiety and repeated uncertainty. "All superstition is a positive framework for your mind," Boggs observes. "It takes the edge off worrying. . . . Any time you can relax and play this game it makes it easier. A lot of people play this game uptight, tense. Everything I do is for mindset, to relax me to the point where I don't have to think about what's going on. You form a routine. It makes everything flow. Everything is serene and flowing."[27]

Superstitions originate when players supposedly "discover" a connection between seemingly unexceptional, everyday events and on-field performance. The process usually begins, appropriately enough, in the aftermath of an outstanding performance, a great game. To be able to maintain that level—the thought is intoxicating. But that will depend, so the view goes, upon discovering some element that might be related to this exceptional exhibition. It could involve anything from taking a multivitamin to forgetting to wear an undershirt, arriving at the ballpark sixteen minutes early, or driving there by way of a different route. Still, there are guidelines that suggest one concentrate on those activities that were on this day outside normal patterns. What time did one wake? What did one wear? Eat? When did one get to the ballpark? Who greeted you? What exercises did you follow? The choices may be many, but invariably the "key" is discovered, and promptly accepted as the source of the much sought after magic. It may be a lucky bat (often one borrowed from a teammate) that will now be used, day in and day out, or a tee shirt worn now with regularity and pride, whatever condition it ultimately assumes, or it could be a cap such as that displayed by Tony LaRussa every day through the 1988 season ("If anyone touches it, I'll kill him," LaRussa warned)[28] and into the playoffs and World Series, or the chicken that Wade Boggs consumes each day with the passion of a religious convert (along with a host of other superstitions discovered when Margo Adams revealed the details of her travels with Boggs. It included lucky hotel rooms, lucky seats, lucky automobile routes, and lucky colors. All in all, Adams was a lucky charm for the Boston third baseman. When accompanying Boggs, he batted .341 as opposed to the lackluster .221 he hit when his wife joined him.)

The failure or progressive impotency of certain superstitions does not in any way undermine the integrity of the enterprise. Powers weaken, circumstances change, the time comes for a reappraisal. Other behaviors suggest themselves, a linkage is "established," a new commitment made. One just doesn't go about the game of baseball unprotected.

What makes these superstitious behaviors appear necessary is that the game of baseball, difficult as it is, becomes even more challenging when one is forced to contend with jinxes and other mysterious circumstances labeled "hard luck." Jinxes are low-level conspiracies directed at individual players and teams that undermine performance and produce frustration and failure. There's not much understanding of why these occur, but few deny their power or perversity. Certainly teams like the Chicago Cubs and Boston Red Sox understand that it's been more than just the opposition that has kept them from winning a World Series all these many years (eighty-six years for the Chicago Cubs, seventy-six for the Sox). The sophomore jinx haunts, though it doesn't strike, all second-year players. In Dale Murphy's first full year, he batted only .226 but then added fifty points to his average in his sophomore year. Players like Jon Hayes, Rickey Henderson, and Lance Parrish all beat the jinx and enjoyed solid sophomore seasons. Many pitchers sense "hard luck" is not an adequate explanation for what happens to their won-lost records when the bats of teammates strangely cool each time they're on the mound. Losing on the road they can accept, but not the fact that no matter how well they pitch, they're not winning anywhere! Hitters have their own burdens to bear. Battling opponents, contending against a jinx, the odds against success are formidable indeed.[29]

They don't take the field, negotiate contracts, or shout epithets from out of the stands, but the reporters exert unique pressures. For most new players the ever-present press is an entirely novel experience. It wasn't around in college and only rarely during their years in the minors. But there's no mistaking its presence now — newspaper, magazine, radio, TV people, they're all about. And in the big media cities — New York, Boston, Philadelphia, Chicago, Los Angeles, San Francisco — there's no escaping them. "The press is," according to former baseball commissioner Fay Vincent, "the connection between the game and the fans."[30] They're on the scene before, during, and after games; some beat reporters follow a team all season long. These reporters like sports, enjoy being around athletes, but it's also their job. They need to follow and photograph the action out on the field, obtain background information and quotable comments before the game, and reactions once it's over. Whether the team wins or loses they need this information, and because of deadlines, often in very short order. The press thrives on lively statements, controversial opinions, and inside information. Individual reporters can be relentless, at times openly provocative. What effect does all this attention have on the players? Many can't help but enjoy it — they're courted, made to feel important, offered "inside" information, their words taken seriously, their opinions respected. But it doesn't stop there — often they're hounded, badgered, and asked the same questions repeatedly. If the team has lost and they're depressed, still the TV lights glare. A thicket of mikes sprouts before them in their lockers; the questions come. Tired, perspired, half-dressed, often dejected, they're obliged to explain the obvious, forced to host an open forum. But all this is bearable, sometimes even fun. Besides, players are not helpless victims of aggressive reporters. They can say "No," refuse to respond to questions, beg off, request a "rain check," escape to the training room, or send reporters packing. "I know it's up to [reporters] to dig," Dave Righetti noted, "but sometimes we've got to take the shovel away." But many a player will talk, accept it as part of his professional responsibility. To Ellis Burks, doing so "tends to

84

take you away from your job, but then they got a job too. I got a job, they got a job." Many do a decent job, according to Phil Niekro. "The majority [of reporters] give you a fair shake, if you are fair and honest with them." Still, many players would agree with Robin Yount. "I'd be happy," he says, "if I didn't have to talk to anybody."[31]

Problems develop when reporters do more than reconstruct the game, but write "opinion" columns or articles, second-guessing decisions out on the field or taking players to task for various shortcomings, real or imagined. Kirk Gibson believes some of the discomfort he experienced playing for the Tigers (before he returned to Detroit in 1993) came from the fact that "What I did . . . in Detroit was never good enough and never could be good enough. The only thing," he adds, "I was ever guilty of was not living up to other people's expectations." Darryl Strawberry, while in New York, echoed similar sentiments. "I just want to go where thirty-five homers are appreciated, where I don't have the pressure of always living up to someone else's expectations, where if I hit thirty homers, the fans and media aren't asking why I didn't hit forty." George Brett believes the success he had at Kansas City came as a result of his being left alone by the press. "I think one of the reasons I've had the seasons I've had is that there hasn't been the big media blitz around me. You can just go out there and play."[32] Reporters explain it as part of their job, contend it's what fans speculate about and want to read. Players resent negative judgments as breaches of trust, unwarranted criticisms by folks unfamiliar with the complete story, who haven't been "there" themselves. Reporters are also the prime movers in the rumor mill, publicizing, lending substance to, even originating some themselves. Most trade rumors, it appears, germinate in the fertile minds of reporters. A rumor, after all, becomes a story.

Many players are by nature reserved, shy, distinctly uncomfortable in the spotlight. Davey Johnson tells us about players "who are more private" for whom "the microphones and all the attention can be smothering, suffocating." More and more players, it seems, have chosen not to play in New York, aware of the intense media scrutiny they would likely encounter there. Though they soon learn to offer stock standard answers, they would rather say nothing at all. Others become distrustful, and maintain their words too often are twisted, taken out of context, that reporters are rooting against them, against the team, singling people out for the sake of headlines. Pedro Guerrero worries about reporters because "sometimes they write what I say, not what I mean." Chris Sabo prefers to skip the sports news because otherwise "either you're too up or too down." New York is a "tough town," Kevin Elster notes in explaining his refusal to read the papers. Roger Clemens, on the other hand, once observed that Bob Stanley "reads everything that's in the papers" but as a consequence, "I think he worries too much about what's written or said."[33] Many a player has come to this conclusion and has gone incommunicado, refusing to talk to reporters whatever the situation. But even for those who maintain good relations, the press represents for them yet another element of uncertainty, one thriving on disharmony and controversy, pretending friendship but simultaneously preparing the long knives.[34]

The difficulties surrounding the game thus far outlined have related to developments off the field. But it's the game itself that's difficult, frustrating, never mastered. To begin with, the skills required for the game are many and formidable. Pittsburgh pitching coach Ray Miller compares baseball to ballet with "its agile, subtle, quick moves." No other sport demands so varied an array of abilities. Fielders need to be fleet of foot, also quick, with superb reaction times allowing movement to begin with the crack of the bat. Only the highly trained eye can pick up the ball right off the bat and follow its path against a background that too often obscures its flight. Judgment as to its speed and point of descent must be made instantly so that a rapid pursuit may begin. An instinctive ability to dive for a catch, crash into a wall, rush headlong toward an incoming teammate must be present. Then the arm comes into play, one capable of making a strong, accurate toss with one quick, fluid motion.[35] Up at the plate one must be able to set aside fear of a speeding ball often inches away, and instead with exceptional eye-hand coordination and impressive bat speed, interrupt the ball in flight with a round, thin, somewhat unwieldy piece of wood. Then, a burst of speed is required to get down the first baseline (ninety feet) in about four seconds. Once on the bases, it takes acceleration, speed, judgment, an ability to reverse direction, and to slide, headlong if need be, to enjoy any degree of success. This bare outline, just of the physical skills that baseball demands, should give pause to those who might claim the game is one-dimensional and relies on a cluster of very ordinary abilities.

Baseball's especially difficult because each play begins with almost everyone stationary, nearly motionless. Then within a split second players are set in motion, off in full flight pursuing a ball or speeding along the base paths. "Compared to the kinetic frenzy of basketball or the punishing impact of football, baseball," sports writer Steve Jacobson tells us, "looks like a leisurely picnic except that its periods of apparent inactivity are broken by bursts of activity demanding precision. Day after day after day."[36] In the other sports there is a far greater degree of fluid continuity, men are already in motion when called upon to perform the critical phases of a play. Compounding the problem is the fact that a fielder is handicapped because he never knows when he will be called upon, and indeed may experience lengthy periods of inactivity. But then it will happen. Suddenly he is required to expend tremendous energy, attain top speed, exercise instant judgment. Indeed, the challenge is formidable. Dave Magadan addresses this precise point. "I think the biggest obstacle at third is keeping your concentration for periods of nonaction. You can go three games without getting a ground ball there, then all of a sudden in that fourth game you get six ground balls. So you really have to stay on top of your game, staying ready. That's probably the biggest challenge I have—keeping my head in the game."[37] To offset the obvious complications here players will, as each play begins, start into motion, produce some movement so as to ease the transition. A pitcher, of course, winds up slowly, and a batter begins to crank up, putting the bat in motion above his head. Out in the field players crouch low, then bodies begin to sway, while runners look for moving starts in order to gather momentum. All are trying the best they can to overcome inertia, trying to cope with baseball's standstill to full-flight patterns.

Though he need display few physical skills (other than the ability to avoid sharply hit foul balls speeding his way) the infield coach, especially the one at third base, must evaluate an impressive amount of information before he makes the critical decisions that at times determine the outcome of a game. The not uncommon scenario involves a runner on third with less than two outs and a fly ball hit to the out-field. The runner can "tag up" and score after the catch, but if he's thrown out at the plate, a most promising opportunity to score will have been wasted. Thus the coach must decide, and very quickly, whether or not to send the runner (and he'd better make the proper decision far more often than not). Flashing through his mind are the following considerations: How deep has the ball been hit? (This deter-mination must be made even before it descends.) How strong and ac-curate an arm does the outfielder possess? Will his forward momen-tum enhance his throw or will there be an instant's delay while he repositions himself before releasing the ball? What is the score? Is it late in the game when few additional scoring opportunities can be expected? Is the runner a speedster who can fly home or a plodder who will struggle through this ninety-foot dash? Is the next hitter a reliable batsman likely to deliver in a clutch situation or a slumping hitter, an almost certain third out? What is the condition of the field? Will the ball bounce true or are erratic hops likely, thus giving the advantage to the runner coming home? The third base coach doesn't seem to make much of a difference in a game, but his correct process-ing of the above information on most occasions should give pause to anyone suggesting that he could easily be replaced with a standard traffic light.

Elsewhere we've addressed some of baseball's other complications. Moving from city to city, from one stadium to another, the game plays differently. The sizes and shapes of the ballparks vary, as do field con-ditions, prevailing breezes, and shadow patterns spreading across the diamond. Then too, night games and day games both involve special adjustments. Always there's the challenge of executing the fundamen-tals, holding one's own against pitchers despite their decided advan-tages, and hoping all the time that a slump will not rear its dreaded head, or if it does it will prove but a mild case. It would be hard to take issue with Ivan Rodriguez of the Texas Rangers when he admits that "no two days are alike. Baseball is not easy. It's learning eight hours a day."[38]

As difficult as the game is, there is also the unsettling feeling that some of what happens is simply unjust, spiteful, or the work of fates most unkind. Baseball offers no guarantee of fairness. "There's not," says Tony LaRussa, "a lot of justice in this league."[39] Certainly pitchers wonder about that when, having completely fooled the batter, the ball hits the bat as he ducks away at the plate, then manages to land just over third for a base hit. Or a titanic swing is followed by a dribbler down the first baseline that goes untouched for a hit. Certainly the nine pitchers in 1988 who entered the ninth innings with no hitters had to ask why they were "victimized" when the prize was within their grasp. How can you explain why in two successive outings Dave Stieb saw no hitters vanish in the ninth inning, one on a "hit" (the ball actually hit something in the infield) by Julio Franco, the other a "bloop" by Jim Traber. It was, Stieb admitted, "a heart breaker. It's hard to put into words. I'm just wrecked."[40] Hitters, for their part, have to mutter when a succession of solidly hit line drives head straight toward fielders who need do nothing more than stick their gloves out for them, or watch a "sure" home run get held up by the wind at the wall. Fielders know well the injustice of it all when balls easily handled hit pebbles and become unplayable or when they bounce against bases ands skitter off beyond reach. It's just not fair: there's no predicting what may happen out there. This uncertainty is present, day in and day out. Often enough, defeat is the result. And as Bruce Hurst reminds us, "It hurts a lot more to lose than it feels good to win."

In response to this abiding complexity what is the advice nearly everyone in the game freely dispenses? Almost always it is the same, ever simple and enigmatic. The solution one hears is to "have fun." But just what does it mean? Obviously it is what every employee hopes to find on the job—satisfaction and enjoyment. But can everyone have fun? Ryne Sandberg feels it's not quite right for him. "I try to have a game plan so I'm prepared when the game starts. There've been a few times in my career when I've tried the other approach; you know, try and be a little more relaxed, laugh, have fun, play the game. Let my abilities take me through it. It didn't work out. It just didn't feel right." Certainly it's not easy when things are not going well, a point emphasized by Dan Pasqua while in the midst of a hitting slump in 1992. "Ron (General Manager Ron Schueler) came walking through the clubhouse and practically yelled, 'Have fun out there!' Hey I'd love to, but it's kind of hard having fun when you're not getting any hits."

There's another problem, according to Bob Gibson. "I've always thought that you only really enjoy baseball when you're good at it. For someone who isn't at the top of the game—who's just hanging on somewhere down on the totem pole—it's a real tough job every day."[41] Still, for most ballplayers there is fun, especially when they get out to the ballpark early enough to enjoy the pregame rituals in leisurely fashion—browsing through fan mail, joking with reporters, playing cards, staging clubhouse pranks, taking batting practice (BP), standing out in the field, alternately catching balls in the neighborhood, or chatting with teammates. Who could deny it was fun for Al Nipper, Jody Davis, Greg Maddux, and Les Lancaster several years ago when the Cubs' first night game at Wrigley Field was postponed on account of rain. The four of them proceeded to engage in a series of bellyflops on the wet and slippery infield tarpaulin, the sight of which left manager Don Zimmer fuming: "I think it stunk!" But a surprised Jody Davis disagreed. "He's been telling us all year to have fun and we did."[42] Having "fun" also means remembering that baseball's just a game, one most major-leaguers began playing and enjoying when they were just little kids. "Fun" is trying to retain that original feeling of happiness and excitement. It was a feeling of lighthearted innocence, of pride in growing powers, of learning about the little things that one day would make a big difference. "Fun" came with increasing confidence in one's powers—when one's competence reached the point where tough plays could be made and the impossible ones attempted. But above all, as Davey Johnson succinctly put it, "Fun is winning." Suddenly it's all so easy. "The game seems so complicated when you're going bad and so simple when you're doing well," says Jack Armstrong.[43] Winning makes hitters confident and pitchers dominant, a team loose, and a manager congenial. Then the smiles come easily, the dugout stays alive, the fans appreciative, the reporters respectful. The postgame clubhouse becomes an ongoing celebration, drinking, nibbling on food, congratulations all around, an easy camaraderie, overflowing optimism, with few, if any, clouds on the horizon. Then there's nothing better in the world players would wish to do. So when players, amidst the pressures and disappointments of the game, remind each other of the need to have "fun," they're conveying not a trite sentiment but a meaningful message, offering advice that experience suggests can make the difference.

Before being traded to the Dodgers, Darryl Strawberry, often the center of attention and the focus of intense pressure, spoke longingly of sometime escaping from the pressure cooker that is New York. "I just want to go somewhere where I can be happy and have fun."[44]

EIGHT

A Question of Balance

IN ITS IDEALIZED FORM, baseball presents us with a most engaging scene of men playing at what in essence is a little boy's game, cavorting across a pastoral landscape during leisurely summer afternoons, reaffirming a tradition extending back generations. The skills required — running, catching, throwing, and hitting a ball — involve motions and movements considered altogether natural. Baseball rejects complexity. It depends upon no elaborate game plans or intricate plays. It is not complicated, nor does it demand complete concentration. Certainly that is the impression one gets when, during a game, players seem preoccupied with chewing tobacco, cracking open sunflower seeds, retiring to the water cooler, swapping stories, perpetrating pranks, and expectorating in all directions. Simple, transparent, deliberately paced and mindless, baseball is largely about having fun — a testament to more innocent and carefree times.

To this day many practitioners of the sport, professionals included, would accept such a characterization. Few would question the commonsense notion that in baseball, success depends on little more than the ability to pitch, hit, or catch a ball with a certain degree of efficiency. Accordingly, when the San Francisco Giants found themselves in last place early in the 1991 season, Manager Roger Craig, a baseball in hand, offered the classic explanation for his team's disappointing start. "See this?" he said. "We're not hitting it, we're not pitching, and we're not catching it."[1]

As for Craig or any other manager, this same school of thought downplays managerial influence and minimizes its impact on the game. Some managers, whether out of modesty or the need to neutralize outside pressures, readily accept such limits. Frank Robinson refers to managing as "a piece of cake"; others express surprise at the inordinate amount of attention they receive. "I don't think a guy should be lauded or applauded," observes long-time manager Gene Mauch, "for knowing a lot about a game that little kids are playing out in some park." One-time Milwaukee Brewers manager, the late Harvey

Kuenn, appears to have concurred. "All I do is write their names on the lineup card and let them play. It's not a tough job. I haven't mis-spelled one name yet." For Cookie Rojas, former Angels leader, it was no different. "I haven't done a damn thing," he observed. "All I do is sit there, make out the lineup and put it on the wall." Question the players and you'll discover them looking to their managers for something other than penetrating thought or technical ingenuity. According to sports writer Tom Boswell, "When ballplayers talk about managers they're far more likely to discuss the man's soul and psyche than they are his preference in tactics. A manager embodies qualities, not ideas." Given such minimum requirements and restricted responsi-bilities it's no wonder, as Gene Mauch observes, that "everyone in the world thinks they can manage."[2]

Subscribers to the philosophy of the natural and the simple tend to discredit the value of thought in baseball, and indeed perceive it as a hindrance to optimum achievement. Thinking inhibits perfor-mance, or as is commonly heard round the game, "analysis produces paralysis." Mel Hall would agree. When with Cleveland he remarked that "the Indians don't pay me to think. Computer analysts think . . . [but] baseball players do not," a philosophy he apparently shares with John Kruk. One sports reporter characterized Kruk as the major league's "leading hitter and foremost authority on the art of not thinking too much." (That this all can become somewhat contrived is reflected in sportswriter Mark Purdy's account of Mark McGwire's unwilling-ness to talk about his hitting success in 1992. "This is a wonderful quality about baseball. By not thinking—and by not talking about not thinking—Mr. McGwire is demonstrating that he is thinking pro-foundly.") According to Chris James, "Everybody knows that the less you think in this game, the better off you are." Scott McGregor would agree. "I don't want to think too much," he once admitted, "because I get confused." To one-time reliever Sparky Lyle this was entirely self-evident. "When you start thinkin'," he tells us, "is when you get your ass beat." Former Texas reliever Jeff Russell shares this view. Even in a tight situation, "the less time you spend thinking about it, the less trouble you get into," he insists.[3] Whatever thinking is necessary, some pitchers would prefer it be done by their catchers. "You're allowed to be your best when you don't have to think as a pitcher because the catcher is doing the intelligent thinking for you," according to Frank Viola. "When I start thinking," Viola added, "that's when I screw myself up." John Smoltz concurs. Explaining a successful outing several years ago, he observed that on prior occasions, "I was thinking way too much. This time I didn't think. I just listened." Many hitters will express similar ideas, explaining the absence of thought as crucial to their success. Could anyone have put this more succinctly than Yogi Berra? "How can I think and hit at the same time," he once inquired.[4]

That a naturalistic rhetoric persists within baseball is undeniable, but it is being challenged by the point of view that accepts a more cerebral approach to the game. In truth, baseball has long enjoyed a following among thoughtful observers attracted by its intricacies and subtleties.[5] But only in recent times have major-league players acknowledged this dimension of the game. That more and more of them have attended college over the past decade or so, institutions where serious thought is accorded occasional respect, may not be unrelated. Furthermore, new and far more sophisticated training techniques and analytical schema have been introduced that elaborate upon and dissect many hitherto unacknowledged aspects of the game. Additionally, more than a few teams are staffed with specialized trainers and psychologists to assist players with the inevitable difficulties that arise over the course of a lengthy season. Predictably, many more players are talking about the game in new and unexpected ways, accepting its complexities, pondering its mysteries. Former reliever for the New York Mets, Skip Lockwood, is not alone in recognizing this feature of the game. "I don't think you could think too hard. Baseball, when you really analyze it, is a game within a game within a game." "They like to say the game is played between the white lines," says sports columnist Steve Jacobson, "but so much of it is played between the ears." According to former catcher Ted Simmons, "If you stay with this game and really watch it, your appreciation goes much deeper. It rewards you."[6]

So it is that accompanying the physical contest are baseball's mind games, where the powers of observation and mental dexterity offer their own rewards. Hitters, for example, can obtain a distinct edge if they can decode the pitching sequence being employed against them. Watching the pitcher from the dugout may yield vital information if one detects certain telltale motions that unwittingly signal the upcoming pitches. "I don't know," says former star Mike Schmidt, "how many pitchers know that I'm sitting here in the dugout all through the game thinking about what they're doing. But I am. I don't mind if they know it. I'm watching." "You're always watching," admits Kirk Gibson, "with a pitcher out there. I'm trying to time him, get his release point." Tony Gwynn recalls how skilled Graig Nettles was at detecting pitches. "He'd look at a pitcher and know from the way the pitcher gripped the ball in his glove what was coming. Puff (Nettles) was great at spotting little things like that and relaying them to the rest of us." Batters at the plate are also scanning the area, noting the positioning and movement of the fielders, almost always an indication of the upcoming pitch, and of related defensive maneuvers. "You watch the infielders," Bob Boone notes. "Do they tip the pitches by moving or leaning? If we have a hit-and-run on, does the second baseman and shortstop tip which one will cover second base? If so, I'll know which side to hit the ball on."[7]

While the batter watches intently, he must also be thinking about pitch sequences, that pattern of deliveries that reflects the strategical thinking of the opposition. Mike Schmidt observes that, "A lot of times a pitcher will change his pattern against you if you happen to hit his best pitch ever . . . but you try to pick up on it if it's happening. Pitchers' patterns are what you have to keep studying—how they are thinking about you." Atlanta Braves' pitching coach Clarence Jones noted that Ron Gant's improvement as a hitter could be attributed to enhanced mental alertness. "Last year if the pitcher got him out the first couple of times he'd be finished . . . last year and the year before he refused to grow mentally. He was going on raw ability alone. Now he's figuring out what the pitcher is trying to do with him and he's sticking with it for four at bats." Of course, pitchers are thinking too, hoping thereby to offset batters' expectations, frequently looking to the past for guidance. Keith Hernandez recalls one such incident when he faced Dave Smith of the Astros. Hernandez entered the game with a career .600 average (9 for 15) against Smith, and with a chance to tie the score in the ninth inning. Instead, Smith's pitch broke his bat, resulting in a feeble grounder hit back to the mound. Smith triumphed by employing the element of surprise, throwing Hernandez a hard fork ball inside. "He threw me something he's never thrown in ten years," Hernandez later admitted, "I will log that; I'll remember that. He's got away with it once. He won't get away with it again. It was a good pitch. I tip my cap."[8]

To succeed in the mind games, to win these battles of wits, requires constant adjustments to an ever changing set of circumstances. Howard Johnson understood that need after his exceptional year in 1987. "I think they'll probably try to pitch me different. That happens when you have a good year. So I've tried to formulate an idea of what they'll do." "Great hitters adjust daily," Davey Johnson comments, but adjusting is no simple matter, as Wade Boggs reminds us. "People want one secret. They want to say, 'It's like this.' Well, it's not . . . hitting is never the same two days in a row. It's intangibles, so many intangibles. Is the wind blowing in? Where are they pitching you? With me it's here, there, and everywhere. Never a pattern. Where is the defense? If there was one way [to hit] then everybody would be great."[9] Don Mattingly is acknowledged to be an exceptional hitter, physically gifted, but also mentally acute. Observe his thought processes as he faces the redoubtable Roger Clemens.

Against Clemens, you try not to commit yourself. You're trying to see the ball first, look for hard stuff, then make the adjustment if it's a curve ball or split-fingered fastball.

Next I'm looking for a pitch to hit. You try to get a ball down in the strike zone. You try not to chase the high fastball, the ball that starts out at your belt and winds up at your chest. You try not to chase the breaking ball or the other pitch in the dirt. He really doesn't throw those other pitches as strikes a whole lot. A slider he does.

Let's say the first pitch I'm looking fastball. I get a strike. Then I'm looking fastball, thinking about hard slider, lay off his low one, lay off the off-speed pitch, the fork ball low. Really, I'm looking for the fastball again. If it's a ball, it's 1-1 and back to the same situation. Now I'm looking for the fastball, but I'm thinking, 'Don't chase the slider in and off the plate.' I've got to make the adjustment on the slider. Let's say it's another ball, so I have a strike and two balls. Now I'm looking fastball.

I figure he'll give me a fastball here, but where? Again, don't chase the high one. He's going to try to keep the ball away from me. Or he wants to get inside, right on the corner. So I'm looking basically away, thinking about taking him away if he comes there. If the situation is a ball and two strikes I'm gonna look in and take the ball away to get to 2 and 2 with him.

If I get to two balls and a strike, I think I'm gonna get something pretty good to hit right there, because he's not gonna get me 3-1, where he knows I can just look dead red. He has to come in and throw a strike, or especially the situation is where he doesn't want to put the winning run on. He's not afraid. He's going to come right at you. He's going to throw it on the outside half of the plate or the inside half of the plate, but he's not gonna try to nick a corner on you.[10]

Underway here is a complex mind game of remarkable subtlety instantly performed; a dynamic encounter whose outcome is as much dependent upon mental acuity as physical prowess.[11]

Doc Gooden, reflecting upon his upcoming comeback from surgery in 1992, talked about a dream in which he faced Philadelphia's Lenny Dykstra and the first sequence of pitches he would throw. Notice that even though a dream, he expected not simply to throw "heat" but to use deception to get his man. The first pitch is a fastball, a good one, thrown with ease and too much for Dykstra to handle. Take note of the sequence that followed:

Breaking ball misses low. Ball one.
Breaking ball, Dykstra buckles at the knees, but it just misses. Ball two.
Fastball outside. Foul ball. Strike two.
Fastball over but higher in the strike zone. Dykstra fouls it off.
Another fastball, another foul ball.
High heat. Strike three.[12]

Even the most overpowering pitcher eventually concludes that continued success still depends not on overwhelming batters but on outthinking them.[13] Accordingly, he must employ pitch sequences that will confuse hitters, throw them off balance, and keep them guessing. Sportscaster and former catcher Tim McCarver considers this to be a bedrock principle. The specific "outpitch," he proclaims, is not that critical; its success rather rests upon the prior sequence of well-conceived, carefully varied, and disguised pitches that pave the way for the batter's demise. The pitcher must remember what's worked for him in the past, have a memory retentive enough to provide such specific information. Without this capacity, some pitchers may be critically handicapped. "A lot of guys don't get into the big leagues," Tim Leary reminds us, "because they don't use their recall."[14] The better pitchers, however, are remarkably adept at this. According to Elrod Hendricks, pitchers Jim Palmer and Mike Cuellar could "remember darn near every pitch they've thrown in 10 years." Roger Clemens' success, according to Rich Gedman, is related to his ability to outmaneuver hitters by repeating successful pitching patterns recalled from past encounters. "He has an uncanny memory for hitters. I don't know how he does it." Orel Hershiser admits that his success has rested as much upon his mind as his arm. "I wasn't blessed," he concedes, "with a lot of tools . . . they asked me, 'What's your game?' and I say, 'Whatever is out there tonight!' I go out and try to find a way to win it. I play a game within a game. My game is thinking."[15] Here's an example of Hershiser's thought process while on the mound: "If a guy is a good first-pitch fastball hitter, I know it and he knows it, and I throw a fastball right down the middle and he takes it, that tells me his thinking is different this at bat. He thought I was going to throw him a curve because he knows that I know he's a first-pitch fastball hitter and he was sitting on a curve—he took a pitch he normally swings at. He's looking for something else, and that gives you a clue to his thinking."[16]

Giants pitcher John Burkett adopts a similar approach. Asked to explain the central element in his pitching, he replied unhesitantly, "My brain. I think I only have four average pitchers. . . . I can't blow it by anyone so I have to change speeds and move the ball around. I have to use my head." For pitchers, a lapse in thinking can spell trouble. David Cone discovered this in a 1990 game when after running the bases the previous inning, he lost concentration and subsequently was pounded. "I didn't get myself ready to pitch," he admitted. "I wasn't mentally prepared." And as pitchers age, more and more the mind, not the arm, becomes the key to winning. Ron Guidry in the waning years of his career came to recognize that fact. A home run by Pete Incaviglia forced him into such an epiphany: "I didn't sleep for two nights after that. I made the mistake of challenging him. Ten years ago he wouldn't have hit that pitch. Now I find myself having to think more. Five years ago I didn't have to think." Willie Randolph, before he retired, reached the same conclusion. "As you get older you start to think the game. By that I mean you get to the point where your body stops reacting automatically so you have to do more anticipating at the plate and in the field, more planning ahead." "Baseball is not incredibly physical; it is incredibly mental."[17] These words of Bobby Ojeda, an aging pitcher, should now be readily appreciated.

When pitchers think, it's usually in collaboration with their battery mates. Right along with them, hopefully operating on the same wavelength, are their catchers. They will signal one another repeatedly and, if necessary, meet together at the mound to share their thoughts. Catchers must know hitters as well, or better, than the pitchers. Many keep notebooks on hitters to be reviewed during the course of a game. Mike Stanley is among those keeping such logs. "I treat it," he says, "as if I'm studying for a test."[18]

The catcher is generally acknowledged to be in control of a team. It is his "heads-up" thinking that can make the difference. "Behind the plate, Carleton Fisk observes, "you have every part of the game running through your fingers." It is without doubt "the thinking man's position," according to Rick Cerone. Just what kind of thinking occurs may be glimpsed by this description of catcher Bob Boone's behind-the-plate activities.

> He rearranges his pitch sequence strategy, planning three or four pitches ahead, checks the positioning of his fielder, and dictates any necessary shifts, glances into the opposing dugout, studies the third base coach and the first base coach, chats with the umpire, chats with the hitter, (does he sound tired, eager?) studies the runners, (they'll tell you when they're going to run) sneaks a peek at the hitter to see what foot or hand adjustments he has made since the last pitch, thus ascertaining what pitch the hitter is expecting, checks his own dugout for any special instructions, scans his pitcher for signs of fatigue, flagging concentration or athlete's feet, and flashes a signal; all this while sweating under 15 pounds of plastic armor in 95 degree heat and chewing tobacco.[19]

This sequence will likely be repeated well over a hundred times in a game.

The catcher must be actively involved in the game, in a position to control developments.[20] But aside from the pitcher, the other seven members of the team, when out in the field, often have little to do, and must work hard at times maintaining concentration. "You tend to doze off there," admitted Bobby Bonilla when he played in the outfield. It is imperative that the mind stay focused, concentrating on the situation at hand, recognizing that circumstances usually change with each pitch. The challenge for fielders begins even before the ball is put into play. Thought comes before the action. The field itself is extensive; only nine individuals are on patrol. It's nine against one (the batter), except that none of the nine knows where the ball is going. It could be launched in almost any direction. But not quite; means exist to reduce some of the uncertainty. Batters are normally pattern hitters, that is, they hit the ball in the same direction most all of the time. Scouting reports, statistical surveys, and general baseball intelligence provide this kind of information. Pull-hitters essentially abandon large portions of the field. Such right-handed hitters as Chris Sabo, Jeff Kent, and Brian Hunter will, when they make contact, engage the third baseman, shortstop, left fielder, and center fielder much of the time. Ordinarily, right fielders will then play somewhat shallow, understanding that should pull-hitters go to the opposite field, it's usually with less than their customary power. One must also know that someone like Wade Boggs prefers hitting to the opposite field with two strikes. Understanding this allows left fielders to be prepared for this likelihood.

Pitchers, to a great extent, determine where a ball will be hit. Pitching inside to a left-handed hitter should result in a ball sent to the right side. A pitcher with an overwhelming fastball will usually cause batters to swing late and hit balls to the opposite field. A left-handed batter will, in such instances, often hit a ball to left field. Certain pitchers like Sid Fernandez ordinarily induce batters to hit the ball in the air, so outfielders had best be on the alert. Others like Tommy John, Rick Reuschel, Roger McDowell, all former sinkerballers, produced many a ground ball — the responsibility of infielders. Fielders can observe the stance of a batter, usually a signal as to where he hopes to hit the ball. Likewise his swing often will convey a similar kind of message, as will the sound of a ball coming off the bat (unless crowd noise drowns it out). So will the batter's immediate reaction. If he accelerates rapidly toward first base it is because he senses the potential for a hit. A somewhat lackadaisical exit from the box suggests the batter anticipates making out.[21] Clearly then, despite appearances, fielders are not simply standing around. At the major-league level, they're engaged in thought, processing information of all sorts, preparing mentally for any action likely to follow.

Though the most popular image of the manager remains that of an instinctive, naturally affable, blubbery, tobacco-chewing good ol' boy given to philosophic musings and occasional aphorisms, in the real world of baseball, there is an understanding that modern-day pressures require specific analytical abilities along with an imaginative grasp of the levers of leadership. According to Jeff Torborg, "The decisions you make still come from the gut but it's nice to have something to base them on. You want to make sure there are no surprises out there." There is, moreover, a greater appreciation of the decision-making responsibilities of the manager (in cooperation with a dependable and committed staff) as he attempts to keep a team competitive on a day-to-day basis and in contention for the entire season. Al Campanis, formerly with the Dodger organization, estimated that in a typical ballgame a manager could be expected to make approximately two hundred decisions. "Anyone who knows this game understands," Roger Angell calculated, "that there are a hundred ways to push those buttons in every game."[22]

Even before the game, managers must be well prepared for the encounter, having devised an effective rotation of starting pitchers for the upcoming series, considered, and finally constructed, a batting order that matches up well against opposing pitchers, and produced an overall game plan based in part on the assessments of advance scouts who have observed and evaluated the strengths and weaknesses of the opposing team. Certainly a manager has more to do before a game begins than idle about the batting cage and chat amiably with the press. George Will in his book, *Men at Work,* marvels at the degree of preparation A's manager Tony LaRussa undertakes before each game. According to Carney Lansford, the A's third baseman, LaRussa prepared better than anyone in baseball. "We go over the opposing hitters before each game. We know before we take the field how we're gonna pitch everybody, how we're gonna defense them. There are no weaknesses in Tony's game preparations." LaRussa explains why. "I'm sure there are still a few managers and staffs that think preparation is a waste of time, that either your players are good or they're not and either they play good or they don't. But as a manager you have a responsibility to put your player in the best possible situation for him to succeed. And your homework helps you do that." Other managers are not far behind. Tom Kelly of the Twins pays strict attention to every detail while former Mariners' skipper Jim LeFebvre admits, "There is no such thing as being over-prepared. I'm a grinder."[23] Preparations today involve scanning computer printouts, absorbing mounds of statistical data, consulting personal logs, and evaluating and rummaging through the past for insights and tactical hints upon which presumed hunches will later be based.

Managers do remember. When former White Sox manager Jim Fregosi played Mark Salas in a game against the Orioles' pitcher Jay Tibbs in 1988, it was because of something he recalled. "He hit a home run off Tibbs in spring training and I remembered that. That's why he played tonight. But tonight he hit a slider instead of a fastball." Tito Landrum recalls how "Whitey [Herzog] came up to me one day and said, 'I should've started you today. You hit the ball hard against this pitcher three or four times the last time you saw him.' I was impressed because the game he was talking about was a year and a half before. Even I hadn't remembered it." Charley Fox praises the same talent in Dallas Green. "His concentration is exceptional. Months later, he remembers what a pitcher threw to his certain hitter with two strikes. He remembers tendencies."[24] Managers today, it is clear, have much to think about.

The idea of baseball as natural, simple and spontaneous still has its charms and its adherents, notwithstanding the greater recognition now accorded the cerebral and deliberative dimensions of the game. Baseball wisely realizes that these two schools of thought are not mutually exclusive, that both are needed. Thus the challenge becomes that of understanding when each approach is best employed.[25] The players themselves are aware of the need to strike a balance. Analyzing techniques and dissecting performance is essential, but it can, they acknowledge, stifle spontaneity and yield diminishing returns. Hitters, for example, report that focusing upon swing mechanics can become self-defeating, and may inhibit their natural abilities. Some time ago a slumping Chili Davis admitted, "I'm not aggressive. I'm thinking too much up there." Bobby Murcer once described the connection between ruminating and reacting. "As the ball starts toward the plate, you think about your stance. And then you think about your swing. And then you realize that the ball that went past you for a strike was your pitch." It happens to pitchers as well. Mike Witt, off to a poor start one season, admitted, "I started dissecting everything I was doing instead of just sticking with it. . . . You like to keep things simple and I think I complicated things by trying to do too much too early. I'm thinking about too many things out there and it's just gotten out of hand. . . . I've maybe started to dissect things too much." According to one baseball writer, a similar affliction plagued pitcher Atlee Hammaker. "He's a thinker, a ballyard Hamlet. When he misses he walks around the hill dissecting his mechanics." Kelly Downs admits he's been "labeled as the type of pitcher who squanders good stuff because he isn't thinking out there. For me," he concludes, "the biggest battle is with my mind."[26]

Early in the 1990 season, the Orioles' Mickey Tettleton, shackled by a terrible slump, tried every imaginable remedy to regain his batting form. Finally he burst out in dramatic fashion, then offered this explanation: "I got off by myself and told myself to stop thinking. Relax. Enjoy the game. . . . I just hacked. 'See the ball. Hit the ball! Nothing else.'"

Writer Tom Boswell's comment on this episode aptly summarizes our discussion: "Baseball's a craft to be sure. But sometimes it helps to keep it simple."[27]

In our idealized portrait of baseball, little emphasis is placed on hard work. Sunny days, green fields, simple skills, leisurely pace — together these seem to suggest that playing baseball is altogether natural and largely effortless. Certainly one has to practice, but a quick observation of pregame warm-up sessions suggests that most players are just going through the motions, loping after lazy flyballs in the outfield, swinging easily against "batting-practice fastballs" in the batting cage. Nowhere in sight are strenuous drills, serious blackboard sessions, or the tedious repetitive honing of skills. How could baseball be hard work when most players patrol the field with little to do most of the time, when each batter appears at the plate for but a few minutes during the course of a two-and-a-half-hour game, when time outs are readily obtained and rest periods frequent? To be sure, pitchers and catchers work, but can the other seven men make such claims?

It was not by accident that George Will's recent survey of the contemporary game was entitled *Men at Work*. Will was not the first, but he is the most insistent, in observing that what happens out on the field during a game, and the preparations beforehand are serious business, demanding full attention and often exhausting efforts. The average fan may not see it, or may be inclined, out of habit, to disregard it, but it is an indisputable reality.

No one questions the fact that pitchers work hard. It is possible, of course, to "breeze through" a lineup, at least for several innings, but that's not typical. Each pitch requires strenuous effort, taxes the arms, the legs, almost the entire body. On a warm day pitchers sweat profusely and shed many pounds. With a runner on, a pitcher now finds his attention divided. He will strain to keep the runner close to the base and to do so will throw over there frequently. Upon releasing a ball toward the plate, a pitcher that instant becomes a fielder, having to assume a position of readiness, prepared always to charge a bunt or dash to first base in order to receive a throw. The demands on a pitcher are such that he must rest for several days before returning to the mound.

Truly the catcher is the team's workhorse, his sturdy build suggesting the punishment he can be expected to absorb. Indeed, the alleged decline in the quality of catchers today has drawn considerable attention and is viewed not as a chance occurrence but emblematic of a deteriorating work ethic in America. Youngsters, it is asserted, reluctant to work hard, are drawn to positions other than that of catcher. This reduced competition then results in less-talented athletes behind the plate. In truth, it is difficult to be a catcher. No one else on the team is required to strap on thick padding, don a mask, and try to flag down well over a hundred high-speed pitches each game. The catcher, moreover, is constantly at risk of being nicked by bats, hit by foul balls, and crunched by runners barreling in toward home plate. He must position his fielders, advise his pitchers, humor the home plate umpire, be prepared to pounce on bunts, stagger after towering foul pops, and attempt to keep the opposition from running wild along the base paths. That a catcher earns his pay is never in dispute.

Not as well understood is how hard everyone besides pitchers and catchers may be working. Only on a particularly hot day will outfielders work up a sweat, but they will be far more active than one normally assumes. The better ones will "play the count," that is, change their position continuously depending upon the probable pitch (which will affect the likely direction the ball when hit). Moreover, they will prepare for each pitch, bodies tensing, leaning, already in motion. Peerless Joe DiMaggio, centerfielder extraordinaire, considered the conventional phrase, "Off with the crack of the bat" to be a "romantic" notion essentially deficient in describing what must happen since "the outfielder should be in motion long before he hears the sound of the ball meeting the bat."[28] A given outfielder will have relatively few plays to make over the course of a game. But it is precisely this relative inactivity that makes concentration difficult. It is easy to lose touch in the outfield, for the mind to wander, for the body to relax. Outfield play requires a persistent mental toughness that keeps players alert to every pitch, that engages the mind, that forces it to consider proper positioning, the direction throws may take, in short, to encompass the total situation. Stationed alone ("You're all alone with no one to talk to," says Robin Yount) on a large field in the blazing sun during a slow game, ("lonely, tense . . . desperate solitary atoms" according to Thomas Wolfe) one must certainly work diligently at staying "in the game."

By contrast, the infield is a beehive of activity—fielders moving about with every pitch, rocking forward to anticipate the direction of the batted ball, hustling over to back up plays. "There's so many things in the infield to do," says Ron Gant. With runners on, first basemen and, more especially, second basemen and shortstops are ever on the move, before each pitch dashing toward the base in order to keep runners close and rushing back into position as the pitch is delivered. Such repeated efforts take their toll. In bunting situations infielders will scramble with each pitch, some charging furiously toward the plate, others heading over to cover the bases. A few bunt attempts constitute a serious workout for the men on the infield.

The case for hard work can be made during the game itself, but the argument holds as well for the behind-the-scenes activities. Practice sessions can be demanding and exhausting. Infielders will take hard ground balls by the score to improve timing and sure-handedness. Batters will stay in the cage for extended periods, swinging at pitch after pitch. ("Quality batting practice can lead to better at bats," says Mets hitting instructor Mike Cubbage.)[29] For slumping hitters it could involve extra hours of batting practice followed by demanding sessions with a videotape in an effort to analyze and correct mechanical flaws.[30] For injured players (and there are few who escape), the road to recovery is grueling and painful: after the physical therapy, heat treatments, and whirlpool baths come the tentative steps back onto the field, forcing the body back into shape, playing in some pain, and haunted often by the fear of reinjury.

Come September, even those who have escaped injury are hurting. There have been too many practice sessions, too many games (day and night), too much travel, too many hotels, too many hastily consumed meals, too few days off and far too little sleep. Beyond dispute, baseball is an exacting, exhausting, extended grind.

It may be a boy's game, and it may at times be fun, but without doubt it is work.

NINE
Patience Rewarded

BASEBALL COUNSELS PATIENCE, often demands it, and frequently rewards it. That should come as no surprise given the deliberate pace and style of the game and the general dominance in most games of the pitching and the defense. Patience applies almost everywhere in the game, takes precedence over anything that is premature or precipitous. "The rush to judge," Tom Boswell reminds us, "is the most certain sign of a baseball outsider."[1]

A long season puts a premium on patience. A team is better served over the long haul by calm direction and unflappable leadership. Injuries in May do not suggest ultimate disaster. When a divisional rival spurts into an early lead there is no cause for panic. Early rainouts, and therefore unexpected changes in the pitching rotation ought not be unsettling. Hitters and pitchers off to slow starts need not produce despair, nor should skepticism greet their assurances that warmer weather will bring them around. Rookies must be handled with patience and understanding, inserted into the lineup at the appropriate time, taken out when clearly they are overmatched, and benched when they encounter rough sledding. Walt Weiss admitted that his first benching early in the 1988 season was a most valuable experience, allowing him time to watch the game without pressure and reflect upon what had to be done. Weiss would, at the end of the season, be voted Rookie of the Year. A few tough lessons are to be swallowed, then taken in stride. "The breaks will even out" over a long season—such is the considered wisdom of baseball.

The players who sit on the bench, the utility men, the pinch-hitters, the second-stringers (proudly called "stunt men" on the last World Champion Los Angeles Dodgers team) must learn patience, however impatient they actually are to get into the starting lineup or just into a game. They're not likely to appear with any regularity (barring injury to a starting player). Some, of course, will sulk and complain and speak darkly about wanting to leave, ("Play me or trade me") but most come to a realization of what their role is, just how they fit in and how they must prepare themselves for those times when they are thrust into a game and expected to perform as if they were regulars.[2] It's a difficult challenge, but those who are patient generally persevere and are highly valued for it.

A patient hitter is a superior batsman. The batter intent upon chasing every ball sent his way will produce some hits, but too often he's earned himself a return trip to the bench. Pitchers generally thrive on free-swingers. There's no reason to throw them strikes or pitches close to the plate. The discriminating batter, the patient batter, the one who eschews first-ball hitting represents a serious challenge to pitchers. He will hold up on the screwball or split-fingered fastball that dips down and out of the strike zone. He will resist the eye-level fastball, which, seen so clearly, is so enticing. He'll foul off the tough ones and lay off the bad ones. And once he gets deep into the count his patience is rewarded. The pitcher must make the next one pretty good or yield a walk. The patient batter will study the pitcher's patterns during the course of a game. By the third or fourth time at bat, he will be better prepared and more likely to succeed.

Fielders, especially outfielders, must, given the nature of the game, be uncommonly patient. A game can go by, two to three hours pass, with their direct involvement limited to ten or twenty seconds of playing time. Indeed, it's possible that most of their exertions are directed to trotting on and off the field. ("Outfielders should pay to get into the park," notes former infielder Joe Morgan.)[3] The gaps can be immense. Still there are things to do—change positioning, follow the count, back up plays, call them for other players, but sometimes these are simply not enough to sustain an edge, to maintain alertness. Outfielders at times may appear to be asleep. Several years ago Bobby Bonilla welcomed his move from the outfield to be Pittsburgh's third baseman because "you tend to doze off there."

Patience generally improves pitching performance (although an argument certainly can be made about the advantages of being a fast worker). A pitcher needs the time to "settle in" out on the mound. Often he will start slowly, find little that is working in the early innings. He is having trouble with his curve, there's no bite to his slider, his control is elusive. Then he's back in charge, in the groove. Why? Because he stayed calm, waited patiently for it to happen.

Pitchers must remain patient with umpires. (Do they really have any choice?) Certainly there are ways of questioning calls and expressing their displeasure, but by and large, they are probably wiser to stay calm, remain patient, and hope the calls even out. Steve Bedrosian believes that is the wisest policy. "I found that if you keep your mouth shut on most of the calls the umps have a tendency to give you the benefit of the doubt on a pitch that could go either way simply because you kept your cool."[4] Pitchers need to grant umpires time to lock in on the strike zone and hope that instead of pinching in, they have allowed it to expand. Indeed, it may require an inning or two before they learn the kind of calls to expect.

Pitchers must also be patient with batters who deliberately attempt to unsettle them, to break their rhythm. Digging in, stepping out, calling time, demanding a new ball, going back for the pine tar—through all this, patience must be maintained. Even after a hitter has fouled off pitch after pitch, a pitcher must remain composed and not give in to him. A pitcher cannot afford to become rattled. With a runner on base stretching his lead, threatening to steal on every pitch—that's precisely the time for the man on the mound to maintain his cool and composure, not speed up unnecessarily or get "outside" of himself. A pitcher must also be patient with his own hitters. If they're not delivering and he falls behind in the game, he can do little but wait and hope they'll come to life, pitch even harder to keep the team in contention until they do. And if they don't, he must be patient with himself, understand it's part of the game, that he's done what was expected of him. Of course if this pattern persists—he pitches well, the team doesn't score much, and he loses—he then slips unhappily into the category of "hard luck" pitcher, a designation that could last an entire season. To remain patient under such circumstances is no easy task.

Managers must, of course, be paragons of patience. Indeed, the archetypical manager is often portrayed as infinitely patient, reflective, understanding all, enduring all. (It helps, of course, if his position is considered secure.)[5] A manager must keep his cool because the season is long and the crises will be many. There will be pressure from the upper levels of management to play certain players, bench others, consider trades, and call up minor-leaguers. The press will be a constant thorn in his side, calling for comment in his darkest moments, second-guessing his tactics, repeating the same questions endlessly, lending credence to the slightest rumors and disruptive comments. Utility players will complain about the lack of playing time and relievers about the length of time between appearances. He will be tempted to return previously injured regulars to the lineup. Temperamental stars will need to be coddled, grumblers neutralized, and team morale maintained. Losing streaks will have to be endured and resistance mounted against growing cries for drastic lineup changes. And all this takes place even before the cry of "Play ball" sounds each day.

During the game itself, managerial patience is often a virtue. When a starting pitcher flounders there is a temptation to replace him and keep the game from getting out of hand. Those steady at the helm usually wait, hoping the man on the mound will work his way out of trouble and regain control of the game. When the team falls behind early in the game, a manager must guard against a defeatist mood as well avoid trying to get all the runs back at once. Reducing the margin one run at a time is usually considered the wisest course (as opposed to having every hitter swinging from the heels). Effective pinch-hitters should be kept back in preparation for the "right spot" and other key players held in readiness for opportunities likely to arise. Meanwhile the opposing managers and coaches can be studied, their signs scrutinized in the hope of unlocking their secrets and gaining an edge. Some managers, like Roger Craig, will devote a good deal of time to just this enterprise. Frank Robinson when coaching with the Orioles patiently stuck to this task. At that time Mike Flanagan commented, "It's a very boring thing to do," but also conceded, "It's a very important thing to do. Obviously he's very good at it because he's helped us many times."[6]

After losing a game it's up to a manager to uncover silver linings, counsel patience and the philosophical acceptance of defeat, and remind everyone that tomorrow is another day, yet another chance.[7] Winning, on the other hand, leaves managers decidedly impatient. Tomorrow can't come soon enough; momentum must be maintained.

Finally, fans need also to be patient and, for the most part baseballs fans are, to a remarkable degree. True, some are prone to rush to judgment, to hail the Joe Charboneaus and David Clydes as sure-fire superstars, to have their heads turned by fast-starting "pheenoms," their patience tested by veterans slow off the mark, but, by and large, there is a remarkable maturity about baseball fans. Most understand that consistency is the hallmark of greatness in the game, that career statistics tell the story far better than any short-run spurts. Baseball, they have learned, requires patience as promising young players work their way up through the farm system and a positive team chemistry eventually produces a winning attitude. Trades can help, but hasty swaps of talented but untested minor-leaguers to fill immediate needs must be avoided in favor of more long-range considerations. It takes time, they realize, to strengthen a team and turn it into a legitimate contender. They know that each pennant race is akin to a marathon, that slow starts and early breakaways will doubtless fade into insignificance by the time the season's over. They are, more than the fans of any other sport, willing to "wait till next year," when their team falls short and accept the status of "long-suffering," even as they endure losing records year after year. They're patient, recognizing they're in it for the long haul, and find sufficient the satisfactions along the way, long before harvest time arrives.

TEN
Foul Play

THE RULES PRESCRIBE precise angles and measurements on the playing field and establish minimum distances for outfield walls and fences, but they are silent about the space beyond the lines—foul territory. It can be present in abundance, as in Oakland's Alameda County Stadium, or in San Francisco, or Atlanta, or there can be scant acreage, as in Fenway Park (or the old Ebbets Field). And just how much there is has considerable bearing on how the game is played.

The idea of foul territory is in itself intriguing. The very term denotes something dastardly, unacceptable, beyond the straight and narrow. Still nearly all sports depend upon boundaries to set off the field of play, but none of them intentionally create a secondary subsidiary surface which, though clearly not on a par with the playing field itself, still occupies a crucial part of the game. In football, nothing can happen out of bounds. In basketball, there's occasionally a problem putting a ball in play from there, but otherwise it's simply a place to seat more spectators. Same with hockey, except on those occasions when players charge into the stands in pursuit of overly belligerent fans. But baseball's foul territory is quite exceptional. Within these borderlands, important events can occur because it is an integral part of the field of play. What happens between and beyond the lines determines the outcome.

Most significantly, foul territory is the area where batters are often retired. A foul pop just outside of third base, for example, is one of the most inoffensive events in a game. The hitter can only lose. The ball will doubtlessly be caught to put him out, but even if it is dropped or falls without being touched, the batter has no chance for a hit. It represents the height of futility, clearly evident from the look of frustration on a batter's face. There is, in this instance, no reason for him to run. He must stand helplessly at home plate and hope, against all odds, for a miracle and a new "life" back at bat. Consider the fact that a large percentage of balls hit in any given ballgame are hit foul.

(In one recent year, the figure was 45.4 percent.) Foul territory must then be registered as a clear advantage for the defense, the explanation for many a sputtering offense. But it's not so simple. In foul grounds lie many snares and obstacles for the defense as well.

It stands as one of the more unnerving aspects of the game. First, there is the pitcher throwing a small ball nearly ninety miles per hour, a ball which must be caught repeatedly by a catcher crouched behind the batter and relatively immobile. Failure to catch a ball (unless it has been hit) will result in its heading away at a brisk pace from the plate into a broad expanse of foul territory behind the plate, where it may even be "lost" until the catcher discovers its whereabouts. It is a tribute to the skills of both pitcher and backstop that relatively few balls escape in this fashion.[1] But when they do, there's trouble. If, for example, the batter swings and misses a third strike and the ball gets away, he's free to run down to first, where he usually arrives safely. If there are runners already on the bases, they can move up quite easily. A passed ball or wild pitch are among the more demoralizing plays in the game.

On a ground ball to the infield, whoever "fields" it must throw it to first for the out. But sometimes those throws go astray, and when they do, more likely than not they skip into foul territory, where tracking them down and retrieving them is no simple matter. And while the fielders are giving chase, the runners are having a "field" day scampering ahead unchallenged. This also happens when throws, especially to third base, elude the fielder and bounce into foul territory. (Once a play is in progress, the fielders can position themselves in foul territory to back up throws and guard against what has just been described. On a ground ball you'll often see the catcher dashing down toward first so that if a throw goes awry he'll be on the scene to prevent additional damage. On a play to third or home the pitcher will very often scamper over into position to retrieve an errant throw.) The defense has an additional problem on a ball hit fair past first or third base, but which then heads into foul territory well out of reach of pursuing players. Not only must they close on the ball as rapidly as possible, but they must be alert to erratic angles and caroms should the ball slam into the rolled-up tarpaulin or bounce off the field boxes. Foul territory can give the defense fits.[2]

Foul territory is not the unremitting enemy of batters, though foul flies will send many of them back to the bench. Foul territory provides a protective mantle for some of their more feeble efforts. A slow ground ball hit fair will ordinarily mean a put-out, but one hit foul is harmless, a reprieve. A batter behind in a count and protecting the plate will swing at any questionable pitch to avoid a strikeout, and when he hits it foul he has achieved his purpose. Many an accomplished hitter will deliberately foul off difficult pitches and "stay alive" until he gets one he can handle. And the baseball sages also tell us that the more balls a batter fouls off the likelihood increases that he will make solid contact on a subsequent pitch, (1) because his timing of the pitches is progressively improving; (2) because the pitcher out of frustration or mental error may at last deliver one that can be hit squarely.

Balls hit foul consume time, often large amounts of it. The ball will have to be retrieved, inspected, and more than likely tossed out of the game (necessitating that a new one be put in and rubbed up by the pitcher before play resumes). At critical moments of a game, foul balls temporarily relieve tensions while simultaneously heightening the drama of the moment. With everyone looking on intently, the pitch is delivered, an apparent turning point of the game is now at hand. But instead, the ball heads into foul ground, causing a false start; spectators and players all enabled now to draw another deep breath just before the pressure mounts once more.

Some final thoughts on foul balls. What endless delight they are to spectators when they drift into or bounce up into the crowd. No other sport is so generous with souvenirs.[3] What youngster or oldster doesn't dream of going to the game and latching onto a foul ball? How many kids take their mitts to every game they attend? Even if the game is uninspiring, the hope of catching a foul ball and getting to take it home and showing it off is enough to keep many a fan lingering in a ballpark beyond all reason (and staying alert throughout. A line drive sent crashing into the stands represents a serious menace. A baseball spectator is in far greater jeopardy in this sense than a fan attending a football, basketball, or hockey game.)

What's the difference between a fair and foul ball? Sometimes just a matter of inches or even less. Who makes the call? Well, just about everyone does, but the only one that counts is that of the umpire closest to the spot. The difference between foul or fair may be just an inch, but that distance represents a world of difference. A foul ball is often a nonevent when another inch could have meant a happening of epic proportions.[4] What more dramatic sight in baseball than a deep fly ball heading straight down the line? "It has the distance, but will it stay fair?" The crowd leaps to its feet, necks stretching, eyes straining to follow the flight of the ball. Meanwhile, the umpire dashes out toward the outfield, better to position himself for a call on the ball. Players on the field watch helplessly. Matters are now out of their hands, while those in the dugout jump onto the steps, ready to call it themselves. Meanwhile, the batter likely remains at the plate, either knowing full well the ball will hook foul (he's hit enough of them to sense in which direction his ball will turn) or straining his torso employing every manner of "body English" to coax the ball into staying fair. (Who can forget Carlton Fisk of the Red Sox in 1975 applying such "controls" to his dramatic World-Series home run against Cincinnati in game six?) Foul ball! Foul ball! There is no uncertainty in the umpire's call. The pitcher takes a deep breath and walks from the mound and gathers up the resin bag. The hitter kicks the ground in utter frustration. Still, his foul ball has delivered a resounding message. And now the gods owe him one.[5]

ELEVEN
Bending the Rules

"A GOVERNMENT OF LAWS, NOT MEN"—our society has long been committed to this principle. Baseball, too, offers such assurances. "Baseball has," observed A. Bartlett Giamatti, "the largest library of law and lore and custom and ritual . . . in a nation that fundamentally believes it is a nation under law." It has rules, scores of them, all written down in over one hundred pages, governing all aspects of the game.[1] This "law and order game" then places four powerful individuals on the field of play to enforce the rules and, if necessary, to eject any and all of those who object too strenuously to their decisions or contest their authority.[2] But then, in the face of all the meticulously crafted regulations and in the presence of these all powerful figures violations occur. The reasons vary, but the fact remains that such lawbreaking occurs even in as conservative a game as baseball. It's not advertised, and it's not blatant, but that's no reason to ignore this relaxation of the rules.

Just what violations might we witness in a given day? They begin, alas, even before the game starts. There are rules against fraternization. Opponents are not supposed to be regarded as confederates or confidantes—familiarity breeds contentment, not competition.[3] But that's not what usually happens in the pregame period. Watch the Dodgers' Darryl Strawberry and his friend, Eric Davis of the Reds (before he was traded to Los Angeles), running windsprints together in the outfield, or observe Lenny Dykstra, once a Met, passing among his former teammates, talking of matters personal and professional. In fact, see knots of players from both sides milling around, talking with each other and to reporters and media representatives, while opposing managers and executives converse amiably. It's quite sociable— a garden party, a convention, a family reunion—it's all of these.

Now observe as the game begins, rule book in hand, and take note of the violations.[4] How frequently are hitters reprimanded for flagrantly rubbing out the lines of the batter's box? How often do plate umpires notice that the pine tar has been applied on too great a portion of

116

the bat? Why is a player not worried about hitting with a foot out of the batter's box? In fact, strict positioning is not something umpires generally are inclined to enforce. There may be no one awaiting his turn at bat in the on-deck circle, or there may be not one, but two, people present. Instead of remaining in the circle, some players inch up near the plate, better to observe the pitcher and determine what he's throwing. First- and third-base coaches rarely are confined to their rectangular boxes. They're permitted rather to run free along the base lines, shouting encouragement and transmitting signs and gesturing energetically to runners in motion. Then there are those first basemen, most notably Keith Hernandez in years past, who with a runner on, sets up on the bag with one foot in foul territory. That will help them take a throw from the pitcher, except that the rules do not permit fielders to position themselves in foul territory. While on first, it should be noted that first basemen are, with some regularity, permitted to come off the bag before receiving a throw, though the rules require that they remain on first base. Courtesy, convenience, concern over collisions, whatever the reason, it happens. Neither are phantom tags from second basemen uncommon. Note how often a second baseman or shortstop will be "in the neighborhood of the bag" without actually touching it. Still, they'll be credited with a putout.[5] This is also true on a steal attempt at second. If the umpire concludes the ball has "beaten" the runner he will often signal an "out," though the tag was not actually applied.[6]

On the mound, you'll never find a pitcher cited for failing to deliver the ball within twenty seconds, as required by the rules when the bases are empty. It's just not enforced. Nor is the home-plate ump inclined to call batter's interference when the hitter, following through in a swing, impedes the catcher in a poorly disguised attempt to thwart a putout at second. Neither will he notice when a batter fails to make an effort to avoid a pitch that hits him, although the rule states he must take such evasive action. He won't signal a violation when the catcher leaves the area behind the plate too soon in the course of an intentional walk. This is not the place to examine the issue in detail, but few will deny that umpires take the rules on the strike zone rather casually, impose their own individual ideas and inclinations, and generally refuse to call high strikes. The upper part of the strike zone is defined in a most nebulous fashion (midway between the waist and shoulders), introducing a broad area of discretion and individual diversity. ("So, just where is the strike zone anyway?" inquired *Baseball Weekly*'s editor Paul White in 1992.)[7] When several years ago the order went forth to extend the strike zone above the belt, the directives went largely unheeded. And certainly the crackdown on pitchers committing balks, which did occur for a time, signalled the fact that umpires had, up to then, been inclined to overlook the situation.

Thus far we've talked about nonenforcement of rules, but what of the issue of selective enforcement, of baseball being governed not by rules, but by men free to assert their authority? "It ain't nothin' till I call it"—umpire Bill Klem's assertion of unilateral authority put it best. Naturally, players talk and, being human, are inclined to blame certain of their misfortunes on others, namely malicious umpires, allegedly biased against them. They're not always wrong. A rookie can expect to be "disciplined" by a veteran umpire. "Umpires break rookies to balls and strikes the way cowboys break horses to the bit and bridle," says Tom Boswell.[8] A batter who has provoked an umpire will probably pay the price. Taking a close pitch on a 3-1 count, the batter without hesitating tosses away the bat in cavalier fashion and heads down to first. Few umpires will abide such presumptuousness, and instead will likely summon the hitter back to the plate with the resounding strike call. That batter had best swing at the next pitch whatever its location. On the other hand, certain hitters can expect favored treatment from umpires.[9] When a Wade Boggs or a Don Mattingly lays off the pitch on a 3-2 count, most umpires will be inclined to ratify their decision and award them first base.[10] Not that inconsistency is absent from football, where intentional grounding seems never to be called, or in hockey, when the penalty whistle grows silent in the last few minutes, or basketball, when referees at their own discretion may penalize or overlook handchecking or extra steps and in general tighten or loosen the reins on the players. It's just that in baseball, more rules seem to be bent or ignored. But then we noted elsewhere just how much baseball mirrors life.

TWELVE
Fields of Fear

A T FIRST GLANCE it doesn't seem possible. A pastoral setting, a leisurely pace, average-sized players, a limited amount of physical contact—how is it that gnawing fears lurk in such an environment? Nevertheless, they do, and always will. Consider some portion of it similar to that which appears in every sport among athletes competing intensely. But some are unique to the game of baseball. Here, there is the normal stage fright associated with every public appearance, except that in baseball, the stage is uncommonly large with every actor in clear view of the crowd, isolated, exposed, easily scrutinized. "Here," as Greg Gagne says, "you do or you don't and everybody sees what you do or you don't." Drop a fly ball, mishandle a routine grounder, and there's no place to hide. Thousands of witnesses are prepared to offer testimony against you. And because hitters often are the focus of attention, many play scared, bat defensively, afraid of embarrassing themselves. "The big fear hitters have is striking out and looking bad," pitcher Dan Plesac remarks.[1] Still, it happens all too often. Clutch situations become fearsome events. The pressure's on, it's up to them, there's no second chance. Observe their facial expressions at such times. The apprehension is unmistakable.

Rookie jitters are all but universal. There's no sleeping, the food usually won't stay down, there's little ability to relax, doubts outweigh hopes. Hear Scott Bailes's recollection of the event—first day in the majors, sitting out in the bullpen: "I thought to myself, 'Man, I'm going to get nervous when that phone rings.' So I turned to Jamie (Easterly) and said, 'Do you get nervous when you hear the phone ring?' And he said, 'Naw, I've heard it a thousand times!' Then he looked me in the eye and said, 'No matter how many years you play you can bet the first time you hear it ring in the new season, you have to check your pants.'"[2]

Indeed, nearly all pitchers no matter their level of major-league experience, grow anxious and fearful before their scheduled starts. "I wish," Roger Clemens observes, "I could tape every pitcher's 'game-face' on the day he's scheduled to start." Most can't eat, few can sleep the night before. Dave Stewart admits that, "I eat my last meal the night before I pitch. To eliminate throwing up on the mound I just don't eat." Concern is heightened when the pitcher's previous start resulted in defeat or was otherwise disappointing. After a notably poor outing, Clemens described the period leading up to his next appearance. "I was anxious to get out there. When you have an overall [bad] performance, it's hard. The hitter can go out the next day and redeem himself. I've got to wait four days. I can't stand myself for four days when I know I didn't pitch well." Bobby Ojeda spoke to that same sense of frustration that follows in the wake of a loss. "I hate it," he said. Now "I'm going to have to sit and wait."[3]

Consistency of performance is the ever-elusive goal of most ballplayers. Every player expects to be victimized by slumps. There's no way to avoid them and certainly no comfortable way to live with them. It's a fearful prospect. Back and forth from the plate—feeble swings, awkward lunges, weak grounders, lazy flies. The player looks wretched, he's hurting the team, and there's no obvious way out. Futility reigns, personality changes, the fun disappears, replaced by depression, anger, frustration. One becomes the target of endless boos, the subject of relentless press chatter, the recipient of a torrent of well-intentioned but insistent advice, much of it contradictory. It's ghastly . . . but it's part of the game. One searches in vain for signs of recovery.

Always there is the fear of injury. It can happen at any time; there's rarely any warning. A nagging injury generally won't keep a player out of the lineup. It will, however, be bothersome. Excuses won't be offered but it will hinder performance. It may, however, become serious, forcing him out of the lineup, maybe even onto the DL. Pitcher David Cone expresses a fear common to every player. "One minute, I'm flying high, on a streak of pitching that's about the best I can pitch, and the next I'm leaving a game because of shoulder stiffness. It makes you realize how fragile it all is, how your livelihood can go in an instant."[4] How long will he be gone? Will he be able to play at full strength when he returns? Could he be out of action for the season? Is it career-threatening? Playing careers can be distressingly short, usually the result of nagging injury. But even if he returns after but a week to ten days of inaction, there's fear all will not be the same. What if his replacement has performed well? It will be hard getting back into the lineup. A manager ordinarily prefers a hot hand. What if . . . ? At the highest professional levels, every player realizes there are others ready and able to take his place, talented athletes who, if given the chance, could present a serious challenge, younger guys, hungry and exceedingly eager. So every time a regular gets injured, he fears the consequences, understands he's become vulnerable. It's likely he'll make it back, but what about the next time? There's no way of knowing.

Injuries arrive in all manner of ways far too numerous to catalogue here. Certain situations, however, produce them with regularity. Some second basemen and shortstops are reputedly fearful or "tender" around second base, suggesting that they tend to shy away from contact with oncoming runners. That they do so is because such runners may pose a menace, barreling in with reckless abandon, attempting to upend the fielder. A runner sliding in with spikes raised surely creates a hazardous situation. Curiously, one's own teammates can also pose a problem. In no other sport do members of the same team collide with such regularity and with such damaging consequences. Because players are positioned apart from each other they are often unaware precisely where teammates are stationed. That they knock into each other (especially in the outfield) with distressing frequency is thus not entirely surprising.

What is to compare to the physical risks posed by a baseball speeding toward the plate perilously close to the batter or smashing into a runner along the basepaths? Do such dangers lurk in basketball? Stepping in front of a Charles Barkley on a drive is not a recommended strategy, but still apart from swinging elbows, pushing and shoving in the pivot, or occasionally a stray finger in the eye, the chances for survival are good. The same is generally true in football, despite the rough and tumble built into the sport, although a quarterback blindsided or a halfback met squarely and dropped by an onrushing linebacker may differ. Getting hit with a hockey puck is not pleasant, but helmets and pads do work effectively to soften the blow. Being hit directly by a speeding baseball must stand as a uniquely fearsome experience. (Certainly it is for fans, who look on with dismay when, for example, balls have hit batters squarely or smashed against their batting helmets.) Runners are struck on occasion by hard throws directed toward second or third base (while second basemen, by threatening to strike incoming runners with the ball, force them to give way and clear the flight path to first base). Outfielders can even be struck by balls either when they lose sight of them in the sun or via an occasional bizarre happenstance, as when Cubs outfielder Doug Dascenzo in a 1991 game tripped, fell, and was subsequently hit in the head by the flyball he was tracking.

Hitters would much rather avoid the subject of getting hit, though it's clear most have trouble banishing such thoughts from their minds. "Of course fear comes into it," former major leaguer Ken Harrelson reminds us. "The players won't admit it because it diminishes their macho. . . . Anyone who says he's never scared up there is lying. I played nine years in the majors scared to death." The greatest obstacle in hitting, according to former player Jerry Coleman, has always been the "fear factor."[5] That many players display "jelly legs" or "bail out" while at the plate suggests that they are not unmindful of the damage a speeding ball can produce.

Pitchers and batters don't much like each other. They are natural adversaries; each is prepared to do all he can to prevail. The pitcher aims to intimidate (and may even cultivate a reputation for wildness and erratic behavior to reinforce the threat), and with a hard ball in his hand, certainly has the means of doing so. This was certainly the point of Bobby Bonds's criticism of pitcher Mitch Williams in 1992. "Sometimes," Bonds noted, "he's out there trying to throw 100 miles per hour instead of trying to throw it over the plate. If he throws that hard and hits somebody in the head it's going to end someone's career. He better start thinking about that before he gets his own (career) ended."[6]

The area on the inside of the plate represents a principal battle zone, batters resenting pitches thrown in close, pitchers insisting on their rights there. "I'm not vicious by any means," Todd Stottlemyre observed. "That's my game and that's the way I'm going to be." Listen to Roger Clemens on this point. "I don't think a pitcher should ever try to hurt a batter, but you have to pitch inside. A hitter must realize that a part of the plate is mine. And if he leans in too far, then I'm coming inside. That has to be done to be a successful pitcher." No doubt pitchers would like to be feared, and realize this provides them with an edge. To onetime great Sandy Koufax, pitching was "the art of instilling fear." Dave Stewart credits Koufax with teaching him this. "He told me, 'pitching is making a batter fear you. Put one inch of fear in a man and you've won the battle.'" This is especially likely with newcomers. "If pitchers can intimidate a young player," Doc Edwards tells us, "it can last his whole career."[7]

Throwing at the batter was for a long time considered a legitimate part of the game. Former player and manager Bill Rigney recalls complaining to National League commissioner Warren Giles that Reds' pitcher Bob Purkey continuously threw at his star, Willie Mays, fully expecting the commissioner to consider disciplinary action or, at the least, issue a warning. Instead, to his surprise, Giles told him that, "we all know that isn't in the rules but it's part of the game, isn't it?"[8] And it's still a part of the game despite efforts to curb the practice. Throwing at the batter delivers a message and is unequivocally a "purpose" pitch. One such message is directed at supposed "showoffs"— cocky hitters pitchers instinctively dislike. "Pitchers don't like hot dogs," Wallace Johnson observes. They "won't bean them but they'll throw way up and in at those types of players."[9] Pitchers may also throw at batters to express their displeasure toward a previous hitter. It's not unusual to see a pitcher yield a home run, maybe even two, and in consequence take out his frustration and anger by throwing at the next batter, however "innocent."[10] He may also do it if he considers the batter guilty of improper behavior. When in 1986 Devon White attempted to bunt and break up a no-hitter being pitched by Danny Jackson in this manner, Jackson then thought it proper to pitch at him. "If a guy's got a no-hitter going you don't bunt," explained Jackson. "He's got to go down."[11] (He ended up with a two-hitter.) He may also "go down" if the pitcher believes it will be unsettling. Mel Stottlemyre saw that happening to the former Met Darryl Strawberry on occasion because he "gets very emotional and angry any time there is a ball thrown inside to him. Some pitchers try to use that to break his concentration." Sometimes no particular explanation comes to mind. To Don Baylor, John Denny "was a head hunter. He tried to deliberately hurt people."[12] (A batter's revenge being to pretend not to be hurt or to respond with a hit.)

Pitchers serve as a team's bodyguards. Given their ability and opportunity to throw balls at opposing players, they can exact swift revenge for indignities or bruises suffered by their own teammates. For example, when Dan Diego pitcher Eric Show beaned Andre Dawson, Scott Sanderson, the Cub hurler, took matters into his own hands. He threw at Chris Brown and brushed Tony Gwynn back three times before being ejected. Gwynn admitted, "I was scared to go to the plate." It's rare that players will admit to such feelings, but all know that up at bat they're in a war zone and that every hitter is a likely target, potentially a casualty.[13]

Pitchers are not immune to this kind of fear. Certainly they risk being assaulted if and when a batter's been hit or believes that a close pitch was intended to do harm. But these occasions and the always dramatic confrontations that follow are comparatively rare. What is a constant menace is the fear of being struck by a batted ball. No other player out on the field is so exposed and vulnerable, so close to the batter (the catcher excepted), or so obviously in his line of fire.[14] Whan a pitcher delivers a ball and follows through on his motion, he is probably no more than fifty feet from the batter and extended in awkward fashion, in poor position to protect himself. The ball hit his way can be a weak bouncer easily snared or a slow roller readily caught, but it also can be a sharply hit ground ball or a vicious line drive that arrives within a split second. It is these that are most feared, that are a clear menace to the pitcher. If he's lucky, he'll get his glove into position and knock it down or somehow catch it. More likely his reaction will come too late and he'll be struck by the ball — just about anywhere. Then it's a matter of assessing the damage — anything from a bad bruise to a shattered bone.[15] Undoubtedly, pitchers hit more batters than batters hit pitchers, but out there on the mound every pitcher knows that intentionally or otherwise he is a target at all times.

Baseball is deceptive. Leisurely, cordial, often it is — but always lurking there is a fear and danger uncomfortably close to the surface.[16]

THIRTEEN

As Time Goes By

To MANY, baseball is fundamentally flawed. The game, they insist, is too slow, drags on too long and offers too little sustained action to break the monotony. It's much like watching paint dry and requires rare patience and persistence, they note, to sit through an entire contest. Games start on time, but after that it's entirely open-ended; the clock, as everyone knows, is reduced to an irrelevancy.

Not only is the game too long, it is getting longer. Three-hour contests are now common and four- or five-hour marathons not at all that unusual.[1] The crisp, rapidly moving game most admired by baseball purists occurs but rarely. Games begin in broad daylight, continue through dusk and into the night. Night games drag on through the darkness into the early hours of the next day. Fans come to the ballpark late and often are tempted to leave early. In an age of impatience, limited attention spans, where time is carefully packaged, and where boredom always threatens, baseball is decidedly anachronistic.

Fans of baseball appear to have no problem with the length of games.[2] In fact, many account it as a principal reason for its charm. This feature of baseball Stephen Jay Gould regards "as a blessing and an oasis."[3] In a hurried world where too many march in lockstep, continually pressured by time dictated by the clock, baseball stands out for its defiance, its rejection of time limits—its relaxed pace and long stretches of inactivity a rebuke to the accelerated tempo of modern society. All this has been noted many times and requires no elaboration. What does invite attention is the manner in which time is consumed in baseball and how that affects the game.

Baseball is certainly no miser when it comes to spending time (though umpires sometimes appear stingy in their attempts, never quite successful, to move games along). Despite this generosity, time is not in any real sense wasted in baseball. Players on both sides must, of course, move out to their positions in the field and return to the dugout thirty-four to thirty-six times in each nine-inning contest. Players and fielders alike are permitted to warm up each inning. (No other sport allows such continuous on-field preparations during the course of a game—a fact obviously related to the game's slow pace and disconnected segments of action.) There are few limits to player-initiated time-outs. "Time" is nearly always granted. Consultations among members of the team on the field are virtually unrestricted. Boston catcher Bob Melvin can go out to the mound to calm Frank Viola almost as often as he wishes. Gregg Jefferies can remind Rheal Cormier that he'll be playing off the bag in the event the pitcher was of a mind to throw over there to keep the runner close. Chuck Knoblauch can tell Scott Leius who will be covering second base in the event of a steal. Ron Gant, uncertain of the sign, can head down toward Jimy Williams, the Braves' third-base coach, to see if the hit and run is still on. Then, of course, the man on the mound may need reassurance or a reminder about faltering mechanics or a warning about becoming too preoccupied with the runner at first. Style and pace differ, but ordinarily, pitching coaches stroll casually out to the mound to begin their consultations. Managers usually walk even more slowly and deliberately, giving themselves time to think through their decisions and to allow a relief pitcher additional minutes to warm up in the bullpen.[4] Unless it is absolutely necessary, players and managers prefer to stroll rather than dash about.

Changing pitchers proceeds at its own deliberate pace. A discussion may first ensue on the mound, usually between the manager, pitcher, and catcher, to determine the proper course of action. The manager may indeed be on a legitimate fact-finding mission, or it may just be a bogus encounter giving the appearance of a serious discussion to disguise a delay so as to allow a relief pitcher additional warm-up time before entering the game. Once it was that most relief pitchers arrived by car or jeep, were ceremoniously deposited on or about the mound, and were thereby spared a long stroll in from the bullpen. Today, it is judged no hardship if the reliever walks to the mound under his own power. Some, like Steve Bedrosian and Frank DiPino, in their apparent eagerness to take charge, come jogging in at a rapid clip, and after performing some grooming and housekeeping chores on the mound, promptly begin their eight warmup tosses. Others, apparently unmindful that relievers are often likened to firemen, amble in, stopping here to exchange a few words with outfielders and infielders before taking up their chores and toeing the rubber. Should he be replacing an injured pitcher, he will be granted all the time he needs to warm up. Compare that to a quarterback replacing an injured signal caller. In he goes, off to get his lumps immediately. At least in hockey a new goalie is given some time to ward off a few practice slapshots sent whizzing in his direction. What may now follow is further discussion involving the manager, catcher, the infielders, and the new pitcher. Consider that more than one pitcher often enters the game in a single half-inning, and it becomes clear why pitching changes deserve to be ranked among the leading consumers of time.

While pitching changes always slow the pace, the time of each at-bat varies considerably. Notorious first-ball hitters like Matt Williams may remain for just several seconds before putting the ball into play, while skilled, selective batsmen pitched most carefully will spend considerably more time at home plate. Against them, pitchers will be in no hurry, and will need to think over their approach, often only after consulting their catchers. Indeed, the delay may be quite deliberate, designed to unsettle hitters. Rick Sutcliffe operates in this fashion, as does Mike Eichorn and Nolan Ryan. Ryan, Tony Gwynn believes, realizes that the more time batters spend thinking about his fastball, the more effective it will be. "Nolan knows he throws 95 and the batter knows he throws 95. Nolan is going to take his sweet time and nobody is going to say anything about it because he's Nolan Ryan."[5] "Sweet time" slows the pace down considerably.

Foul balls contribute substantially to the march of time. Consider a pitch hit high and deep to left field, the batter on his way to first while the third-base umpire dashes out to left field for a better view. Foul ball! The pitcher, shaken but relieved, strides off the mound to regain his composure, then carefully and deliberately rubs up a new ball tossed out to him. The batter, meanwhile, slowly retreats back to the plate, shaking his head, heading off in search of the bat he had just tossed away. All this takes time, in abundant amounts. Foul balls invariably lead to others. The next pitch is met by a late swing that sends the ball bouncing swiftly just wide of first base but foul. Slamming against the field box rail, it caroms out into short right field, where it happens, no one is stationed. Someone must retrieve it—a ball girl, the second baseman, the right fielder—and once done, every-one waits until he or she has returned to normal position. The next few pitches, clearly out of the strike zone, pitches designed to lure the batter into a wild and futile swing, go sailing by. Now we're deep in the count, a few minutes having elapsed. Assume that after all this the batter makes solid contact and sends the pitch far over the fence in left field—a home run, a hitter's supreme triumph. His reward is to go on an uninterrupted, unhurried tour of the bases. Most players undertake this enviable task in workmanlike fashion, not too slowly so as to offend the pitcher, and not so quickly as to suggest there is anything about which to be ashamed. However done, it does hold up further play, especially as the pitcher will usually take this oppor-tunity to stride off the mound, collect his thoughts, settle down, and prepare to bear down on the next batter.

In baseball, play tends to be discontinuous. There is no flow as there tends to be, for example, in hockey or basketball, where the ac-tion can swirl about without stoppage.[6] In this sense, baseball resembles footfall, where a play may consume ten or fifteen seconds, then come to a complete halt as the pile of bodies untangles and players return to their respective huddles and later gather at the line of scrimmage. Baseball, too, proceeds in this intermittent fashion—brief spurts of action followed by a series of preparations for the next play.[7] A base-hit grounder into left field may take less than ten seconds before the play concludes and the ball is returned to the infield. Far more time is consumed in between plays. At this point the infielder probably will call time and walk the ball back to the pitcher's mound, where he will likely exchange a few words and mention the possibilities of a sacrifice bunt or an attempt to steal. The pitcher will now wait for the first baseman to position himself on the bag, and may even toss the ball over there a few times before turning to concentrate on the new batter now digging in at the plate.

Actually the number of "normal" spontaneous slowdowns in a game are probably beyond reckoning. They include, in no particular order, pitchers calling for a new set of signs, fans running out onto the field, coaches rushing out to remind a pitcher how best to approach a par-ticular batter, beach balls or paper planes alighting on the playing surface, cats intent upon strolling about the field, airplanes taking off (New York City), debris tossed out by fans, bench-clearing brawls, umpires deciding to brush off home plate, balls getting loose from the bullpen, the sun breaking through, prompting fielders to head into the dugout for sunglasses, equipment failures such as a broken webbing in a glove or a shattered bat, or mud in the cleats, and so on. Then, of course, there is an injury or an occasion when players are shaken up. Two outfielders collide chasing down a fly ball, both lying out there dazed while the trainer and manager race to the scene to assess the damage. A runner comes up limping after sliding into third base, and then gingerly starts walking about to test his legs. A batter, hit by a pitched ball, writhes in pain and tries to walk it off as the trainer rushes out to spray freeze the area and provide some relief. There's no pressure or rush to resume play. Delays are tolerated usually long enough for the player in question to recover and stay in the game. Much is at stake. Should he be removed for medical attention he can't, as in other sports, return. So fans, thus treated to the sight of the recovery process from beginning to end, look on as athletes battle the pain, determine whether they're still intact and attempt to convince themselves and those around them that they are not disabled and can remain in the game. There's no need to fake injuries in baseball as there is, for example, in football. (Closest in intent are claims by a batter that he's been hit by a pitch. He may clutch his arm, wince, and begin trotting down to first unless the ruse is uncovered and the "injury" rejected.) Injury time-outs can be critical in basketball and football with the game hanging in the balance and the clock running down. Baseball's timelessness eliminates the need for this sort of deception.[8]

No one enjoys rain delays. Rainouts disrupt schedules, diminish revenues, complicate pennant races, and are generally disagreeable — yet they add an element of unpredictability, excitement, even flimflammery to the game. It's a struggle for pitchers, especially once they've warmed up and then cooled down, while awaiting developments. (That makes what Cincinnati pitcher Tom Browning achieved in 1988 quite remarkable. Against the Dodgers at Riverfront Stadium, Browning waited until 10:05 P.M. for the rain to end and the game to resume.

Once it did, he settled in and tossed a no-hitter.) Rain delays can prove tiresome and frustrating, and watching the tarpaulin being rolled out and in can be altogether tedious.

Rain delays take their toll on all players, but pitchers especially, who after a lengthy stoppage are likely to find their arms stiffening up. Managers are understandably reluctant to risk sending them back out to the mound after a prolonged interruption. New plans and line-ups must be devised. As it is, baseball consumes a lot of time; add rain delays, and it becomes altogether gluttonous. Not to be overlooked is the deliberate stalling introduced in the hope that a rain delay and ultimate rainout will ward off defeat. A team behind in a game not yet official will employ a variety of strategies, most altogether transparent, to consume time and allow the rain clouds an opportunity to produce unplayable conditions. (Baseball is the only sport where games can be decided without their going the complete distance.) They will include anything from repeated trips to the mound, tying and untying shoelaces, to frequent use of the pine-tar rag. Any complete listing here would be tedious and unduly time consuming.

Elapsed time is not simply a void between plays or the absence of developments. In baseball, it is a valuable asset subject to deliberate expansion and contraction as situations change. Note this striking contradiction. Almost all agree a player performs more effectively when the game proceeds in rapid fashion. Pitchers stay in the groove, fielders remain alert. But the stubborn reality is that most contests are prolonged, as we have just discussed, and for several reasons not yet mentioned. It is almost unalterably true in baseball that when the going gets tough, the tough come virtually to a standstill. In tight, tense, crucial situations the pace of the game slows dramatically. Too much is at stake to rush, too many wheels are in motion to accelerate the pace. The time between pitches slows to an excruciating yet spine-tingling crawl. The pitcher retreats off the mound, perhaps calls for a new ball, then reviews what he plans to do. With runners on he must concentrate on keeping them close, throwing over often. There may be successive tosses to first before the ball is even fired home. (On one occasion with Wally Backman on first, Rick Sutcliffe tossed over there eleven times. On the twelfth throw he picked Backman off.) Pitchers and catchers will likely confer on the mound, to review options and decide on strategy. Infielders will gather there, as well, to establish positioning and coverage. Even when all is in readiness the pitcher will continue to peer in at the batter who, in turn, may glare back at the man on the mound.[9] Staring contests of uncommon intensity are usually designed to unnerve an opponent. Dave Winfield, by all accounts, ranks high in this regard. According to Jesse Barfield, "Winfield stares right through a pitcher. Sometimes pitchers don't want to admit it, but that can intimidate them." Bud Black believes Don Baylor was a close second to Winfield for staring and intimidating. "His whole demeanor is intimidating. He stands over the plate like he owns it and doesn't smile."[10] Pitchers do their share of staring as well. Dave Stewart's "death stare" has attracted notice while Nolan Ryan gets the nod as one of the game's more discomforting starers, according to pitching coach Ray Miller. "Usually if a young guy hits the ball hard off Nolan, the kid will get the stare when he's in the on-deck circle for his next at-bat. Nolan will step off the rubber, rub up the ball, and stare directly at the kid. The kid starts thinking, 'What's he going to do to me?'"[11]

The batter for his part will, in addition to staring and glaring, employ delaying tactics to break the rhythm of a pitcher, in hopes of gaining some slight advantage over his adversary. He'll spend time setting himself at the plate, then break his stance and step out of the batter's box. Dissatisfied with his grip on the bat, he'll retreat back in the direction of the dugout in search of a pine-tar rag. He'll peer down for a lengthy look at his third-base coach, making sure he has the sign. If uncertain, he'll leave the batter's box and head over toward third base for a face-to-face meeting. Finally the pitch arrives. Let's assume now he grounds it sharply wide of third—foul ball! Still, at the crack of the bat he was off and running. When he stops, he's already just short of first base. Everything must now be reset. The ball has to be returned, thrown in to the umpire, examined, and probably tossed out of the game. A new one is put in play which the pitcher needs first to rub up. The runner on first, who had probably already rounded second, turns heel and retreats to first as the batter heads back to home. The entire sequence, with all attendant delays, may well be repeated several times during the course of a single at bat.

Critical situations will also bring forth pinch hitters and pinch runners. Relief pitchers will also be dispatched to do battle (often a procession of them as managers attempt to capitalize on lefty-lefty and righty-righty matchups to gain an edge). Stalling techniques, some notably imaginative, will be employed so that a pitcher may gain time for a few more warmup tosses in the bullpen. Rick Rhoden recalls one such incident with Tommy Lasorda orchestrating the scene. "One time when I was with the Dodgers, Tommy Lasorda went out to the mound for a pitching change. He had two relievers warming up, but the one he wanted to bring in wasn't ready yet. Since it was Lasorda's second trip to the mound in the inning, he had to make a move. So he stalled for time. He waited for the umpire to come out to the mound. The ump said, 'Who do you want to bring in?' Lasorda then asked him, 'Who would you bring in?' The ump said it wasn't his decision and Lasorda kept saying, 'Well, what should I do?' The ump demanded that Lasorda make up his mind and they began arguing. By the time they finished, the reliever was ready. The ump asked again, 'Who do you want?' Lasorda asked him, "Who would you bring in?' Finally, the ump said, 'The righthander.' And Lasorda said, 'Then bring in the lefthander.'"[12] Here is a game within a game, an unabashed transparent effort to gain time. Contrast this with the frenzy surrounding the climax of a tight game in basketball, football, or hockey. Teams constantly practice two-minute drills to prepare themselves for the waning hectic moments of a game. Plays must be devised to stop the clock—every moment is precious. And when the number of time-outs allowed is exhausted, a mood of desperation sets in. Baseball can ignore such contingency planning, need not rush for the panic button; baseball is timeless.[13]

FOURTEEN

Close Encounters

BASEBALL is the only major American sport in which teams regularly play each other for several consecutive games. It is a game of leisurely visits, not one-night stands. Rarely are there single games or even a pair. Three, four, sometimes even five games in a row are common. The schedule consists of a succession of such series with teams arriving in a city, checking into their regular hotel, and remaining there for several days. Though scarcely a revelation, this matter does illuminate certain previously unexamined aspects of the game.

A series reminds us that baseball is not an all-or-nothing confrontation; it's a competition best understood over the longer haul. Winning the first game of a series is most welcome, but it's not enough. The challenge resumes the very next day, much the same as it does for each contest over the course of a lengthy season. A series diminishes the significance of a single game, underscores the importance of consistency. Losses are better absorbed (buoyed by the hope of rebounding the next day) and complacency avoided because in short order, a team must once again prove itself. A series reminds us that baseball is not a hit-and-run engagement but a lengthy campaign in which, before a winner is determined, many prolonged struggles will be fought.

A series requires planning and preparation. Scouting reports on the opposition are compiled, presented, and reviewed by each team. Injuries are noted and attention directed toward players who are especially "hot." Strategies to neutralize this threat must be devised. Meanwhile, individual players recall past records against the upcoming opposition, and wonder whether these patterns will continue true to form.

In a series, pitching rotations are a key ingredient in the matchup. Indeed, if classified as a "crucial" series, each manager has already manipulated his pitching order well in advance so as to have his most effective starters properly rested and ready. Ideally the "ace" of each staff will take to the mound in game one, pitting strength against strength. It is at such times that a Clemens faces a Stewart, a Doc Gooden contends against Zane Smith, and a Randy Johnson is opposed by Jack McDowell. Also inserted into the lineups are players who have in the past, for whatever reason, performed well against this particular opponent. Thus a series places a premium on planning and rewards teams amply staffed and flexible enough to juggle their pitching staffs and reposition players in a deliberate effort to tilt the balance in their favor.

Over the course of a series, teams come to know each other well. Beyond the pregame socializing around the batting cage, the games themselves, with their ever-changing flow of situations, require that players perform under a variety of circumstances. In due course, the full range of each team's talents and limitations will be displayed. Its personality and its character will surface, its strengths and weaknesses will likely be revealed. There may even be time enough to decipher the other team's signs. According to former coach Joe Nossek, "Say you've been watching a team the first two games of a series and it hasn't tried anything in the way of stealing or hit and run and then you suddenly pick up a whole new series of signs, you just assume the runner's going and you call a pitchout."[1] In short, everything will be noticed and recorded, and most certainly recalled when next these two teams meet.

A series is much like a drama in three or four acts, each part related in some way to what came before and that which follows. A certain momentum, for example, in evidence early on can carry through over the entire series. If a reliever like Rick Aguilera, Dennis Eckersley, or Duane Ward performs effectively he may very well appear in all three games. Should a team employ its running game and enjoy success, it's likely to maintain that pace in all the remaining games. Hostility, too, may carry over. Should an incident like a hit batter occur under suspicious circumstances, the anger and hard feelings will probably persist over the entire series. An umpire thought to have made an improper call or two can expect to be challenged repeatedly, resulting in short fuses among the entire umpiring crew. A series, then, develops its own unique mood and rhythm, and creates a full-length drama rich in detail and intricately scripted.

Series magnify opportunities and heighten risks. The opportunities are obvious if the two teams are both division contenders. The instant they appear, schedules are scanned to determine when "critical" series are to be played. In close pennant races a Boston-Toronto, a San Francisco–Atlanta, a Texas-Chicago, or a Pittsburgh-Cardinals series anytime in September can prove decisive. Fans and players alike anxiously await the head-on collision between those probable contenders. It represents the celebrated showdown that epitomizes the classic pennant race much beloved in baseball circles. (In 1991, the American League faced considerable criticism for having failed to schedule a late-season confrontation between Boston and Toronto, likely front runners. When the schedule keeps divisional contenders apart at season's end, expect considerable grumbling and dissatisfaction at the absence of such face-to-face showdowns.) No need for scoreboard watching here or waiting for another team to upend this rival. This is the long-awaited opportunity to take charge, to leapfrog over the opposition, to reach the point where "magic numbers" define the situation.

A series can at any time assume even greater significance when the possibility develops for a "sweep." With the first game won, speculation mounts as to whether the opposition can be overcome on successive days. No other sport offers the possibility of delivering such a sharp series of setbacks in the regular schedule (and offering fans the opportunity to display their brooms at the ballparks). There is nothing more uplifting than capturing three, or sometimes four, games in a row from an opponent. "Four-game sweeps," sports writer Murray Chass properly notes, "can be devastating to the losing teams and exhilarating to the winning teams."[2] Momentum is instantly established, confidence soars. Losing all games, on the other hand, is a serious matter remedied only by getting out of town and hoping the team will rebound in the next series.

We would be remiss to overlook another type of series, this one altogether unique to baseball (though becoming increasingl rare), representing a series within a series—the doubleheader. (Given their intense physical demands, doubleheaders in football, basketball, or hockey are practically inconceivable.) What is in store is a heavy dose of baseball, adding up to perhaps six or seven hours of playing time (rivaled only by the five-setter in tennis). For fans, it is a baseball bonanza; for the players, an endurance contest, a marathon much like the season itself. It starts in daylight and may conclude at night under the lights, with the players close to the point of exhaustion. Most everyone is involved in a doubleheader. It's unusual, for example, for the same catcher to be behind the plate in both games. Although both count equally, the first game becomes the focus of attention and is often contested most fiercely. A team that wins is in a position for a sweep; to lose poses the severe threat of a double loss. In game one, moreover, players are fresh, so also the fans. Game two presents problems of motivation and certainly of energy, especially for fans who begin to file out in the latter innings after daylight has given way to darkness.

As with extra innings, doubleheaders accentuate the positive and underscore the negative. With eight or nine times at bat in the course of two games, a slumping hitter will see his average plummet, while a streaking batter may produce four or five hits for his day's work. It's the same with a team. While the majority of doubleheaders end in splits, those that don't can produce a notable boost or a demoralizing jolt. A classic instance occurred in the National League's Eastern Division a few years back. The Mets were in first place almost from the start, but had not, despite a superb pitching staff, been able to put substantial distance between themselves and the rest of the league. This failure to deliver the knockout punch plus the absence of consistent hitting kept the door open for challengers. Pittsburgh's young team hung in gamely, and late in July, Montreal, a team to be reckoned with, began its run for the top. A winning streak cut the Mets' lead to six-and-a-half and brought the Expos, confidence soaring, into New York to begin a four-game weekend series. Montreal took the first two games; a sweep seemed a distinct possibility. The Mets appeared vulnerable. It all hinged on a concluding Sunday doubleheader. Montreal took the lead in game one, but the Mets rallied and gained a 4-3 victory. It was much the same story in game two, an early lead for Montreal, a final victory for the Mets, and a sweep of the doubleheader. Thus, the Montreal challenge had been met and repelled. Stung by this setback, the Expos headed into a tailspin and a sustained slump. The Mets, on the other hand, their complacency shaken by the Expos' challenge, reawakened, and were never seriously threatened for the rest of the race. Recalling that doubleheader in August, both Mets and Expos agreed it was the turning point of the 1988 season.

FIFTEEN

Talking a Good Game

I T IS A CRUCIAL GAME as the Dodgers drive for the pennant in late September of 1991. They are trailing the Giants 2-1 in the eighth inning when plate umpire Eric Gregg suddenly begins shouting in the direction of the Dodger bench, apparently in response to a growing chorus of criticism originating there. This brings Los Angeles manager, Tommy Lasorda, bounding out of the dugout in the direction of Gregg. What follows is a torrent of words, Lasorda's mouth engaged in perpetual motion less than a foot away from Gregg's face. Gregg, meanwhile, responds with his own non-stop verbal barrage, the two men talking furiously, seemingly oblivious to what the other is saying, a comic opera in two parts.[1]

This classic scene is familiar to anyone who's paid the least attention to the game. Separated by little more than their opposing views, the two scream at each other, as if performing in an ancient ritual of aggression. One might marvel at the ability of each to produce an endless stream of words and withstand the adversary's withering verbal assault, except that the encounter has become stylized and lost much that might once have been viewed as menacing. In no other sport are players and managers permitted to engage in such demonstrative and embittered backtalk, to challenge so vocally the usually irrevocable decisions of officials (even the most bitter exchange remains a model of restraint, because only rarely does violence intrude).[2] But that's because talk is so much a part of the game. Baseball encourages talk, often celebrates it, and is, on the whole, unabashedly verbal. Baseball is, as writer Wilfred Sheed reminds us, "preeminently the talking man's game."[3]

In baseball, there is ample time for talk. Managers and coaches generally direct less by dictation than by discussion. Tales about the game circulate in never-ending profusion and most everyone around the sport is expected to be a storyteller. And even when there's no talk, mouths nevertheless remain constantly in motion. What other sport features so many players so busy chewing gum, sunflower seeds, or tobacco, then gleefully spitting out the remains in all directions? In baseball, the oral tradition lives on.

The talking begins well before game time. The scene on the field resembles a friendly picnic, folks strolling about, chatting, conversing, teasing, everyone relaxed and cordial.[4] Former pitcher Don Drysdale likens it to "a class reunion every day of the week." Off on the side, reporters are conducting interviews with whatever players they can manage to corral and coax into responding to their questions.[5] Radio and TV announcers preparing for the game question some of the players to develop stories and background information that will be retold to listening audiences later on. Players hanging around the batting cage rib each other playfully as each takes his practice swings. In the outfield, players chat amiably, breaking off every so often to chase a long fly ball. Back near the infield, opposing managers exchange pleasantries while players from the two teams mingle and oldtime friends catch up on news. In no other sport do pregame preparations proceed in such a leisurely fashion and permit players from both sides to mingle so freely, involve so many oppportunities to converse. Some former players resent this pregame camaraderie. Don Drysdale suggests that the fraternity among ballplayers should not extend onto the field. "When I played you not only didn't talk to opposing players, you hated them when you played." One time major-league outfielder Jim Piersall agrees. "I hate it when I see guys all chummy on the field before a game. It may mean a pitcher won't knock a player down during a game if he's a friend. It's not fair to the owners or the fans." Still this pattern is well-established and seems likely to continue.[6]

Opposing players will continue to talk to each other even with the game in progress.[7] When runners reach base and await the resumption of play it's not unusual to see them talking to a fielder positioned nearby. They might on the same occasion strike up a conversation with the umpire patrolling in the area. Ryne Sandberg observes that "I talk to umpires and other players, especially if they get on second base or I get on base. That's a fun part of the game for me."[8] These conversations are generally cordial and innocent. Because baseball limits physical contact among the players, tensions and intensity levels do not ordinarily build to levels found in football, basketball, and hockey.

As a result, polite conversation does not seem inappropriate among players who the next instant will not be battering one another.[9] In addition, runners, especially those on first and third, have someone else they can talk to—their coaches positioned a few feet away. In no other sport are coaches actually located on the field of play, able to provide instructions, relay signals, or just simply talk to players. It's not unusual to see a runner call for time out and stroll off with his coach, the latter reminding him of the situation at hand. (Why it is necessary that coaches be so close at hand is not altogether clear. Is it to assist the offense in some modest way or simply a method of providing runners with someone to talk to?)

The most conspicuous conversations between opposing players occur at home plate when exceptionally gregarious catchers habitually greet each batsman. Catchers can be friendly and chatty, but such gestures often are intentional and insidious, designed principally to distract batters and break their concentration at the plate. Many can recall such incidents. Doc Gooden tells of the reception he ofttimes received from former catcher Jody Davis. "Seems anytime I'm up Jody tells me, 'You're getting pretty good, huh?'; he'll get me talking about anything—my hitting, my pitching, food. Before I know it, I'm out. Davis plays with my head, too. Couple of times he'd say, 'Fast ball coming, Doc?' and there it was just like he said. So one time I tell him, 'Make it outside curve this time, Jody,' and it was right there. I couldn't believe it. I took strike three." Rick Manning notes that pitch calling by catchers is not uncommon and can be effective. "You don't know what to think," he observes, "whether he's telling the truth or not . . . personally I try to ignore it." Catcher Darren Daulton relates a similar instance: "We were facing a hitter who was wearing us out, so I started telling him what was coming. It messed with his mind and we got him out."[10]

Dave Winfield agrees that "some catchers try to mess up your mind. Guys like Mike Heath and Carleton Fisk talk a lot. I used to have to tell Heath to shut up. I don't want to hear any of that. Fisk is always talking to batters, crying about his aches and pains or his bad swing. Catchers like that are just looking for ways to get me out because they know I'll do some damage." Mike LaValliere, for one, doesn't deny his intention is to throw batters off with his talk. "If there's a batter who is wearing us out, I'll talk to him about his family, the weather, anything but baseball. Most batters don't like that—and I know they don't like that—especially good hitters like Glenn Davis and Jack Clark. I try to say something to them every time they get up just to break their concentration."[11]

Catchers may also converse with umpires, although their primary goal remains that of distracting hitters. Rick Manning once complained about catchers carrying on a "conversation with the umps while the pitcher is in his windup. One time it got so bad that I turned around and said, 'Hey, if you guys want to talk, then wait until after the game and go out to dinner. Just let me hit in peace.'"[12] Catchers will, of course, take issue with umpires, even complain on occasion in the hope, not of having the call reversed, but of paving the way for more favorable attention in the future. A fine line must be observed here. Catchers can complain, but not if, in the process, it appears that they are directly challenging the umpires. It is, for example, certainly ill-advised to turn toward the umpire to object to a call.[13] Holding the mitt frozen in place with the ball inside is also considered bad form. The message of such maneuvers—that the umpire erred—is far too obvious. Cocking the arm in preparation for a throw down to third—the standard ritual following the strikeout, isn't likely to be viewed favorably by an umpire who had just called a ball on a two-and-two count. What catchers are "allowed" to do is look straight ahead and speak their mind—enumerate the umpire's derelictions in such a way as to avoid notice by the fans. Gary Carter, according to some, generally did so on a regular basis. Wallace Johnson notes that, "Carter will whine at every pitch that's called a ball and he does it so often that the ump will finally call that same pitch a strike. The umps respect Carter, so if he whines about a pitch, then the ump thinks it must be a strike. I've seen it happen many times." Carleton Fisk's no less vocal behind the plate. According to Bobby Meacham, when Fisk "complains he makes the ump aware that his pitcher needs a certain pitch to be effective, and if it's close, he wants to get that pitch." Kelly Gruber recalls taking a pitch inside, then hearing complaints from Fisk. "It would be a foot outside and Fisk would say, 'That's close, let's go, make the call. That's too close for this guy to take.'"[14] An important part of the catcher's job, it's now clear, begins once he's caught the ball.

Players out on the field have plenty to talk about and generally do. Fielders in pursuit of popups and fly balls ordinarily will call out to those around them that they are preparing to make the play. Infield chatter intended to keep everyone alert and encourage their teammate on the mound has long been a staple of the game. So, too, are conferences. In no other sport do players gather on the field of play so often for pep rallies and strategy sessions. Infielders will collect to discuss positioning, pick-off plays, and ways to deter base stealers. Pitchers and catchers meet with regularity somewhere around the mound area, usually to talk about pitch sequences and opposing batters. The catcher may have called the meeting to calm down a pitcher who's been hit hard, to discuss sudden streaks of wildness, or resolve differences of opinion about which pitches to throw. Sometimes it's the pitching coach who convenes the get-together to consider mechanics or pitch selection, or attempt to buoy the sagging spirits of the pitcher, or simply stall for time.[15]

High-level conferences on the mound have long been a fixture of the game, and usually attract a crowd — the pitcher, all the infielders, the catcher, and eventually the manager. Fans are forever speculating on the content of these summit sessions. No doubt most of them are rather trivial or completely predictable, still most fans would give anything to eavesdrop and discover the "inside" story. It will, of course, vary with the situation, but is likely to include defensive alignments, reminders of past pitching sequences, along with the usual encouraging words and occasionally contradictory advice.[16] Inevitably these conferences consume too much time — at least in the view of the umpires who almost always are seen plunging into the circle of players and requesting that the talking end and play resume. There's no official limit on the number of conferences that can be held (records are not kept on how many actually take place) but abuses are rare, the players themselves realizing that even with talk there comes a point of diminishing returns.

In no other sport are managers and coaches granted as much latitude to argue and dispute official decisions as they are in baseball.

Nowhere else are they allowed to storm onto the field and vent their displeasure while delaying the game indefinitely. Indeed, disputation and rhubarbs have been incorporated into the very fabric of the game, have been orchestrated and choreographed in ways altogether familiar and expected. Some of the interchanges go unnoticed by spectators, as when players or managers from within the confines of the dugout begin venting their displeasure over calls by a particular umpire. If the baiting and banter continue, he will generally stop play and glare into the dugout. If this fails to silence his critics, he will likely "call time," stride over to the dugout, point his finger at the offending player(s) and issue a stern warning against any additional commentary. The more serious situation involves a disputed call on the field with the argument initially taken up by the "wronged" player, who is then usually restrained by his coaches and teammates, who fear his unbridled emotion and anger could lead to ejection from the game. As he is removed, the argument is taken up by his manager, who has arrived on the scene. At one time, umpires preferred to back off at this point, to turn heel in an attempt to defuse the situation. Recently, observers have detected heightened aggressiveness among umpires, an inclination to stand toe-to-toe with the managers and players. Lively exchanges and angry gestures have become commonplace, spirited discussions escalating rapidly toward explosive levels, followed by an apparent thaw and return to reason, but flaring up again, then culminating in a final eruption (concluding either with the ejection of the manager or a defiant parting of the two). Such angry talk and menacing gestures appear to be baseball's way of discharging hostility that in other sports can be expressed more readily in direct physical contact during the course of the game.[17]

Baseball fans are not by reputation reticent spectators. It has long been considered a tradition of baseball for fans to communicate directly with players out on the field. In pregame practice sessions, it is not uncommon for fans in the stands to chat with players parading about the field. During the game it is expected that they will shout encouragement to particular players, urging them on, calling upon them to deliver. This is more apparent in baseball than in most other team sports because here players, for example pitchers and hitters, perform more often as individuals, and their success and failure is easily noted and judged. More distinctive is the verbal abuse of players by fans, baiting them in all manner of ways, attempting somehow to bridge the gap between players and spectators and affect the flow of events on the field. Major-league ballplayers ordinarily ignore such communication, viewing that as part of their professional burden. In recent years, levels of tolerance and capacity for restraint have receded, and in a number of celebrated instances, players have directly responded or physically challenged their tormentors. It may be just talk, but increasingly, baseball players have not been disposed to "take" such abuse.

There is a more benign side to fan talk. Sports call-in shows are heavily weighted all year round with fans eager to discuss baseball. Few areas escape scrutiny. The game's no longer the same, the impact of skyrocketing salaries, criticisms of managerial strategy, players who are "dogging it" or clearly in decline—the topics appear inexhaustible. Such discussions can be heard all year round, before, during, and after the season. No other sport has produced a "hot stove league," or granted fans an open license to discuss the game in the post-season months. In baseball, talk is cheap, plentiful, and persistent.

There's also talk aplenty in the announcers' booth. No other sport can be described as accurately or as pleasurably as baseball. While it is difficult to picture the action on a football field or basketball court or hockey rink on the basis of a radio description, baseball's simple organization, structured patterns and individual roles permit the listener to "see" more readily and to experience the slow, leisurely rhythm of the game. In no other sport will radio announcers repeatedly stop talking and allow silence to reign (the background crowd noise being the only assurance the station has not gone off the air). In what other sport are announcers so closely identified with the game as celebrities in their own right? Red Barber, Mel Allen, Phil Rizzuto, Jack Buck, Harry Carey, Ernie Harwell, Vin Scully, and Tim McCarver have, over the years, attracted as much attention and fan loyalty as many of the players themselves. For many fans, memories of the game relate not so much to their having witnessed baseball's dramatic moments but to having listened to the unforgettable descriptions of these events from these and other announcers. Wilfred Steed recalls "those days [when] every barber shop had a radio, every butcher shop—the whole block was a symphony of baseball." In 1992, a company in Connecticut offered fans the choice of over fifteen hundred audio cassettes of actual play-by-play accounts of games from 1936 to 1991. It is no surprise, then, that baseball alone, among the sports, selects its most celebrated announcers for inclusion into its Hall of Fame (or that in April of 1993, the Smithsonian Institution presented a nine-part series entitled "Voices of the Game: Legendary Baseball Broadcasters").

No other sport in the United States commands so large a radio audience. For many fans, listening to the game on the radio at the beach, in the car, in the back yard, or most anyplace has its own singular satisfactions, often almost as rewarding as being there.[18] Some part of that relates to the talk of announcers that ranges beyond the action itself to include all manner of relevant and irrelevant observations. No other sport is so devoted to tradition, so heavily populated with characters, so productive of stories, tales, and legends, so adept at telling and retelling them. It is, Ernie Harwell reminds us, "a storytelling kind of game."[19] No one, even those remotely connected to the game, is without his lively tales of oddball doings, heroic deeds, and warm reminiscences of events on and off the field, in and out of season, both from yesteryear and yesterday. These are all familiar to the veteran announcers who, not unlike premodern bards, delight in passing them on, elaborating and embellishing no doubt, but in that way preparing the way for these tales to enter baseball's vigorous and varied oral tradition.

SIXTEEN
A Taste for Drama

ALL SPORTS APPEAL on a variety of levels by emphasizing physical skill and competitive challenges, while featuring star performers and charismatic players. All capture audiences by intensifying experiences, encouraging team loyalty, stimulating hope, and ultimately providing a final resolution, that is, producing winners and losers. Indeed, all achieve dramatic fulfillment, with some, at their best, offering intense emotional involvement and catharsis. But no other sport has learned to manipulate and elevate its dramatic potential more than baseball. Certainly, it can be the most languid and tedious of sports, devoid of action, decidedly dull.[1] With its slow pace, routine plays, and the tendency toward domination by pitchers, it can try the patience of even its most loyal fans. On the other hand, it has an incomparable knack for elevating anxiety, for creating dramatic situations, slowly milking them in ways almost shameless and then discharging most suddenly all the accumulated tensions until it's time for the process to repeat itself.

In every other sport, the drama often depends heavily upon the relentless passage of time, the sure knowledge that unless decisive action is taken, the clock will have run down and the period or game declared over. That accounts for all the feverish activity in the waning moments of a contest, the measured use of precious time-outs to devise strategy for one final effort. Intensity levels soar, the excitement reaches a fevered pitch. Football players on the bench rise to their feet and inch toward the sidelines shouting encouragement, fists clenched, urging their teammates on. Basketball players leap from their courtside seats, pour out onto the court to greet and slap the backsides of team members heading to the bench for a time out. Coaches huddle together in earnest and rapid discussion while diagrams are produced to illustrate the play deemed appropriate to the situation. The last minute or two of such a contest moves the clock to the center of attention, its numbers nearly as vital as those posted on the scoreboard.

In baseball, the drama is performed mostly in slow motion with complete disdain for the clock. As tension mounts, the pace slows to a crawl as if to rebuke the frenzied rhythms of the other clock-driven sports, seemingly weighed down by complexities demanding thoughtful unhurried reflection. Baseball's rituals on such occasions become a model of deliberate deceleration, a studied languor that has the exquisite effect of calling attention to every component of, and heightening the meaning of, this minutely scripted end-game.

It all begins in the later innings of a close, usually low-scoring game (where a run is likely to prove decisive). At this point, both teams become keenly attentive, sensitive to any indication that the tide may shift ever so slightly. A lead-off batter getting on base is certain to draw attention, produce a state of active alert, and elevate tensions throughout the ballpark. In the dugout, the casual conversations and distractions cease and attention turns to the field of play. The managers and coaches assume worried looks and draw closer to each other. This may be the occasion to stick another wad of tobacco into the mouth or replenish the supply of sunflower seeds. A quick nod by the manager sends the pitching coach telephoning the bullpen. In short order, relief pitchers and bullpen catchers begin their soft tosses, such warm-ups a clear signal of potential problems that may be ahead (and, no doubt sending a mixed message to the pitcher presently in the game, (1) that there will be relief if he falters, and (2) that the manager is not entirely confident he can contain the opposition).

Should the pitcher now fall behind to the next batter, it will prompt a buzzing in the stands, a clear indication of mounting concern. The manager may set out on the first of several visits to the water cooler, or use the occasion to expectorate more rapidly, sure signs that he senses trouble brewing and attention shifting to him. A signal to his catcher sends the latter out to the mound to confer with his pitcher, the first of several meetings likely to be convened as the crucial inning unfolds. The gathering appears productive, the pitcher shaking his head approvingly, the catcher striding back confidently to his position behind the plate.

Ball three. The pitcher, clearly upset with developments, wanders off the mound and begins rubbing up a new ball with decidedly more vigor than he's previously displayed. It's the first baseman, now, who decides a meeting and some words of encouragement are in order.

The wisdom of baseball holds that delay produces dividends, that consuming more time between plays is sound strategy. The first baseman also arrives to inform the pitcher that he will either (1) hold the runner on or (2) play off the base.

A strike brings the count to 3 and 1, a welcome reprieve, the reward perhaps for the recently concluded pep talks. The batter, sensing the pitcher may have righted himself, steps out of the batter's box to review the situation. With the count in his favor, the hitter turns excavator, digging in at the plate, signalling his readiness to swing at the next pitch. Largely unnoticed, the time between pitches has now increased measurably. No one, it appears, is in a hurry. The pitcher looks in for the sign, seemingly frozen in that pose and place atop the mound. That, in turn, unsettles the batter, who asks for time and uses it to step out of the box and unleash several powerful swings. Once more he returns; again he digs in. The pitch arrives, the batter swings, but succeeds only in dribbling the ball into the dirt off to the side where it is quickly retrieved by the catcher and thrown back to the pitcher. This minor byplay does not go unnoticed. The hitter requests that the ball be looked over. It fails inspection and is tossed out of the game by the umpire, who promptly tosses a new ball to the pitcher. He shifts it about repeatedly in his hands, getting the feel of it, sensitive to every seam and curvature.

A 3 and 2 count produces one of baseball's many mini-dramas as all await the upcoming "payoff pitch." But a delay here should not be unexpected. The pitcher may at this point decide to pay close attention to the runner on first, glancing in his direction, then throwing over to keep him on or close to the bag. A secondary encounter has thus begun, one that creates its own interest, and for the moment reduces the mounting pressure. (Indeed, pitchers will often toss over to first several times, not expecting to trap the runner off base, but to break the tension and allow him time to consider his next pitch.)

The 3 and 2 pitch is hit solidly, the ball ascending in a steep trajectory, traveling high above the field. But the pitch was hit an instant too soon, and the ball's path is perilously close to the foul line. The crack of the bat has brought everyone in the stadium to their feet, the crowd and the players alike straining to follow the flight of the ball. It descends well beyond the field into the outfield stands but clearly foul. Officially, it's as if nothing happened, but the reality is quite different. Electricity has filled the ballpark; its energy lingers, a spark waiting to be reignited. The batter meanwhile has flexed his muscles, demonstrated his power, sent an unmistakable message. The pitcher is at once shaken but relieved to have escaped disaster by the narrowest of margins. Still and all the tremors can be felt. It's no surprise that the next pitch sails high and wide.

Two men on, no one out, is by all measure a threatening situation; time, all agree, for the manager to make an appearance out on the mound. Will he remove the pitcher or allow him to attempt to work his way out of difficulty? Is the reliever sufficiently warm, ready to enter the game? Is the earnest discussion out on the mound at all serious, or merely a diversion—a way of stalling for time? So whereas nothing appears to be happening, in reality several developments are underway, as excitement mounts across the stadium. Off in the on-deck circle a pinch hitter is observed to be limbering up most demonstrably. The home-plate umpire now decides it's time to adjourn the meeting on the mound. But as he approaches the circle of players, the manager suddenly signals for a new pitcher. That move brings the game to an abrupt halt. Music now floods the stadium, its cheerful mood usually at complete variance with the serious situation prevailing out on the field. Still it is proper to relax, at least for the next few moments. The runner on first will probably strike up a conversation with the first baseman while the umpires themselves gather for a chat. In one dugout the manager surveys his lineup card and consults relevant records and statistics while on the mound his counterpart reviews the situation with his reliever newly arrived from the bullpen. Meanwhile, amongst the crowd speculation mounts about likely developments. The new pitcher, meanwhile, proceeds to deliver his allotted eight pitches from the mound, attracting some attention from those anxious to see the kind of "stuff" he might have.

At this point, the next tactical move is announced, a pinch hitter sent in for the scheduled batter, and a runner dispatched to second, a speedier man likely to score from there on a hit. For the moment, he becomes the center of attention. The pitcher on the mound eyes him intently while the second baseman begins edging toward the base in an effort to keep the runner close. Suddenly the pitcher pivots quickly, wheels, and fires the ball towards second. A slide, a cloud of dust, a tag . . . safe, the runner is safe. The pitcher then begins his windup but once more steps off the rubber, but this time only to fake a throw to second. The feint is sufficient, however, to send the runner diving headlong back into the bag. Meanwhile, the pinch hitter stands impatiently at the plate, having witnessed much action, but as yet not seen a single pitch. In no other sport is there so much by-play incident to the main focus of the action, each sideshow, however, contributing on its own toward the dramatic denouement. This may, of course, be the turning point of the game; the margin for error has narrowed considerably.

The new pitcher peering in for the sign appears uncertain, and signals for the catcher to send them out again. Still, the communication is imperfect, so time is called, and the two meet to talk it over. Minutes have now elapsed; still, the reliever has yet to throw a pitch. So much has gone on although nothing has happened! One measure of baseball's uniqueness is that the preliminaries invariably consume far more time than the play itself, and are often dramatically more compelling.

Finally, the pitch is thrown. The batter makes contact, sending a sharp ground ball to the shortstop, who snares it, tosses it to the second baseman, who promptly relays it over to first. One pitch, two outs — double play. In that brief moment all has been resolved, the tension long in the making is dissipated almost instantaneously. All the strategizing, all the maneuvers have resulted in that instant in a severe setback to the offense, a swift triumph for the team out on the field. Sure enough, the next batter is retired, the attempted rally squelched. But in the course of these events there was baseball at its agonizingly deliberate best, milking the moment, proceeding in its own unhurried manner, elevating ordinary movements into great adventure and riveting drama. And this was only the seventh inning. There is every reason to expect a repeat performance before game's end.

PART THREE
Points of View

We are by now prepared to appreciate other complications
associated with the game. Accordingly, we should note that
baseball at times seems to defy rational expectations and to
involve situations not readily explainable. On the other hand,
it has been rationalized to excess by the introduction of numbers and statistics in reckless profusion. Swollen box scores
and arcane statistical studies threaten to obscure, even diminish the game itself. Fans also have made a decided, if
uneven, impact. It is uniquely in baseball where they feel so
specially empowered, uncommonly knowledgeable about the
game, and so insistently vocal about how it should be played.
Players generally welcome the support of fans, but these same
ardent supporters too often prove fickle and feisty, and when
that happens, the game turns complicated. We discover, furthermore, that baseball isn't only about hitting, pitching, and
fielding, it's about arguing. No one in and around the game
shrinks from disputation, or lacks the ability to hold his
own in such encounters. And so arguments grow heated,
players are ejected, and fans ever more insistent upon their
points of view. Thus, it may appear as a quiet
and orderly game, but only if one ignores
the debates that often rage
around it.

SEVENTEEN
Mysteries of the Game

CALL IT CHANCE. Surely that's what it is. But what is one to make of the strange sense that events occur for which explanations are not readily apparent. It's this sense of mystery that explains why baseball commands respect from all those who play it. What it allows you to do, it can instantly withdraw; success is readily offset by failures, expectations by disappointments. "The game," says Orel Hershiser, "can humble you in a hurry." Some raw elemental force appears to govern play, mocking the pretensions of mere humans. Indeed maybe it is, as Kirk Gibson considers it, "the Beast."[1]

A gust of wind will suddenly spring up to carry a ball, ordinarily catchable, well out of reach. A high pop fly to the infield will begin its descent, three fielders waiting underneath, any one of them quite capable of making the catch. But each looks toward the other, crowd noise drowns out sound, and the ball lands safely no more than twenty feet from home plate. The ball dribbled to the right side suddenly develops "eyes" and squeezes past two infielders in hot pursuit. Another chopped into the dirt near home plate bounds high into the air, the third baseman camped under it waiting helplessly for it to descend while the batter crosses first base. A ball hit directly at the shortstop, an easy out, suddenly dives under his waiting glove and out into short left field. Follow this ball on another occasion as it again bounces toward the shortstop. This time it takes an erratic hop, hits him in the throat, and falls safely. This was, of course, the crucial play of the 1960 World Series when the Pirates beat the Yanks, the downfall of the New Yorkers, traceable to this bizarre play in which shortstop Tony Kubek was struck by this "sure double-play ball." What forces are at work here? What causes the gusts to blow, sows confusion amongst the outfielders and arranges it so that the bouncing ball will find its way through the infield or strike that hidden pebble that alters its course? You may think you know, but don't be so sure.

The following mysterious event occurs repeatedly, defying the laws of probability and suggesting the operation of forces less well understood. Andy Van Slyke dashes to the wall in left center field, leaps high, and pulls the ball back just before it is to disappear for a home run. Ozzie Smith races deep in the hole, and in one motion, scoops up the ball, leaps into the air, twists his body, and delivers a looping throw to first that just nips the runner. Nothing unusual here — exceptional fielders do such things. But now add the strange fact that gives one pause. When plays such as these and others like it are made, that very next half-inning the player who's just performed so brilliantly leads off and is showcased. Why should that be? Who knew a spectacular catch was in the offing? Who arranged that the fielder then be scheduled to hit first when his team came up to bat?

Baseball offers a mysterious mix of heroics and heartbreaks often involving the same person in the course of a single contest. What of the batter who has knocked the stuffing out of the ball, all game. Still, his team needs him once again as it trails in the ninth inning. Sure enough there he is at the plate with a chance to achieve glorious personal achievement and team victory. Expectations are high, given his performance up to that point. This time, however, he's not equal to the occasion. The team loses, and though his totals for the game are impressive, the spotlight falls on his final failure at bat. But baseball or those higher powers that appear so much involved also believe in redemption. It will hold out the possibility to a player who has failed early on to redeem himself by so arranging circumstances that he again faces a crucial situation and has it within his power to be reborn, this time a hero. Kirk Gibson in a game some years ago against the Phillies came to bat in the third inning with the bases loaded and struck out. But then in the very next inning, there he was up again, once more with the bases loaded. This time he doubled. "I didn't do my job the first time and I felt terrible about it. But baseball being the beast it is, put me back up there in that spot."[2]

Consider the American League Championship Series in 1986, when Dave Henderson entered the game for the Red Sox and proceeded to have a ball pop out of his glove and over the fence for an Angel homerun. But then in the ninth inning, Henderson redeemed himself with a homerun to tie the score, then won it in the eleventh with a sacrifice fly — from "goat" to "gamer" with a brief interval in between. Thus, a baseball game provides a compelling stage and a bright spotlight, then assigns a variety of demanding roles to test the full range of performance skills and emotional capacities. Joe Garagiola understood this well. "Baseball gives you every chance to be great. Then it puts every pressure on you to prove that you haven't got what it takes. It never takes away the chance, and it never eases up on the pressure."[3]

Streaks are the greatest mystery of them all, whether a batting slump or a prolonged hitting spree, a string of victories or an unbroken succession of defeats. Streaks take on a life of their own and follow a preordained path, seemingly resistant to all supplications and direct intervention. In the grip of a streak, one is simply carried along in its path, helpless to affect the outcome or its duration. Tony Gwynn, reflecting on one of his rare slumps, noted that, "I didn't have a clue as to what I was doing. But as quick as it went, it came back." Chuck Conners, not quite as fortunate, realized he was a victim of higher forces. Tommy Lasorda recalled an incident involving Conners when the latter was, many years ago, playing in the International League and mired in an extended slump. "The first time up, he hit a line drive right to Russ Derry. The next time, he hit one right at Steve Bilko. The third time, a liner right to Lew Ortiz. That made him o-for-20. Halfway to first base, he fell to his knees, looked up to the sky and yelled, 'Come on down and fight me like a man.'"[4]

Winning streaks and batting sprees are to be enjoyed, and though explanations may be offered, most are content to let the good times roll, and to hope that tomorrow merely brings a continuation of the unexpected good fortune of today. Slumps, on the other hand, rivet the attention, produce agonizing quests for explanations, frantic efforts to reverse the flow of circumstance. Advice pours in. Experiments, however bizarre, are considered, but in the end it is agreed, the fever must simply be allowed to take its course. These highs and lows are ever a part of the game, but they come and go without warning or explanation, mysterious elements, eerie intruders into the realm of reason and responsibility.

EIGHTEEN
Statistically Significant

THAT "the boys of summer," who cavort in the lush grass playing their simple sport before adoring fans, are enveloped by a complex web of numbers seems strangely paradoxical. How odd that a game rooted in innocent pastoralism relies so heavily upon columns of numbers, and all manner of statistical data. Yet everyone who knows baseball understands this long and intimate association. To be a fan is also to be a student of the numbers that have always been a central focus of the game. Youngsters otherwise indifferent to math become exceptionally facile at calculating batting averages, ever eager to explain other prominent arithmetic indices of the sport.[1] When it is a matter of box scores and of numerical arrangements, their reading comprehension soars. Minds ordinarily forgetful turn remarkably retentive when recalling the statistics of the game. And much there is to remember. Every player in every contest generates a bundle of statistics that, once processed, will be deposited into a vast repository that both defines and enriches the game.

Baseball came of age early in the twentieth century at a time when "time and motion" studies and worker evaluations were introduced in the name of greater efficiency. Was it not reasonable, then, to subject players to comparable performance tests, especially when numbers abounded which could be put to such use? Baseball was played out in the open with players arranged territorially and held accountable for discrete tasks which could be observed and measured. And so scribes recorded their deeds in numerical fashion, books stored these figures, and followers accepted them as important, indeed almost as substitutes for the game itself. "I don't think baseball could survive without all the statistical appurtenances," one observer suggests. "As long as they got the box scores, some people," he adds, "could do without the games." It is preeminently, says George Will, "a game marinated in numbers."[2]

What amounted to a cottage enterprise in the early years has, in recent times, become a growth industry. Thanks to the incredible processing powers of computers vast quantities of numbers can be introduced into the mix and unending permutations produced. The flood gates have opened, and powerful interests have summoned forth the numbers and accelerated the flow. Across the broad landscape of baseball—fans, managers, players, agents, arbitrators, announcers, reporters, writers, and statisticians are all awash in numbers, attempting in their own ways to reap the benefits from this rich harvest. It has been, most would agree, something of a mixed blessing with obvious benefits offset by occasional excesses, keen insights diluted by mindless clutter. Nevertheless, the phenomenon has reached a point where preliminary assessments would be useful both to delineate the current situation and identify likely trends.

Each game produces multitudes of statistics relating to individual performance and team totals. Every play, nearly every move is recorded, then registered, within a host of related categories deemed important for describing the action and accounting for the outcome. Refinements are forever appearing, along with "new" improved compilations designed to provide for a more complete and accurate explanation.[3] The simplest play produces numerical ripples up and down baseball's bustling statistical assembly line. Consider a situation when, in the eighth inning of a game, left-handed batter (A) facing right-handed pitcher (B) flies out to center field stranding two base runners. Here, then, are some of the affected categories involving just the hitter:

(1) The hitter's batting average will drop starting with his overall average, plus a separate one based upon his performance against right-handed pitchers (and another based exclusively on his success with this particular pitcher).

(2) In addition, if it is a night game, that particular average will suffer.

(3) As will a separate calculation based on the fact that the game was played on artificial turf.

(4) Furthermore, assuming the game to have taken place, for example, in Cleveland's Municipal Stadium, the batter's average in that location will be affected.

(5) So will a separate batting average compiled for his performances in road games.

(6) The fly ball out will also appear as an entry in the player's ledger reflecting his ground ball-to-fly ball ratio.

(7) It will also be recorded in the category that indicates the directional ratios of his batted balls to the outfield (right, center, and left).

(8) Because there were runners on, the fly ball will impact adversely on the batter's average with men on base.

(9) Because the play occurred within the last three innings of a tie game, the player's average in late-inning pressure situations (LIPS) will suffer.

Thus, the ramifications of this simple event are legion, even without considering the recorded changes in those categories related to the pitcher, the outfielder, and the two teams. Is it any wonder, then, that each game produces a plethora of numbers, every season a veritable avalanche. Consider the fact that the modern game of baseball has been played since the turn of the century, then recognize how immense is the storehouse of accumulated numbers. But because necessity serves as the mother of invention, along came the computer, the only device (excepting those young baseball wizards that every neighborhood once seemed to spawn) capable of containing, sorting through, and categorizing statistical strata of all those seasons past. The result is that each game is enveloped by a larger statistical environment that affects the content and our overall perceptions of the game in significant ways. It is time then to consider, if only in a preliminary way, how this wave of statistics is affecting the game.

In a languishing economy, the production of baseball statistics nevertheless ranks as a growth industry. The evidence leads to no other conclusion. Publishers rush to put out statistical books and yearly updates promise more penetrating analyses and unique statistical wrinkles. All discover a broad market for their products. Statistical services flourish amidst the rotisserie-league phenomenon furnishing participants with an endless stream of numbers to support their player selections and inform their simulated play. Sports magazines and newspapers such as the *National* (until its demise in June of 1991), the *Sporting News,* and *USA Today's Baseball Weekly* generate impressive amounts of baseball numbers to accompany the accounts of games and their feature stories. The daily newspapers, especially those in major-league cities, have kept pace, offering richly detailed box scores of all games plus charts and tables to illustrate various statistical data and track record-setting performances and comparative statistics.

Radio and television announcers of the game are all prepared to offer statistical backdrops to their play-by-play accounts. Radar gun technicians are poised to transmit data on pitch velocities, while statisticians stand by in the broadcast booth to research certain of the more obscure situations, as well as to update existing numbers with new data produced by the game in progress. If additional backup sources are required for more elusive research materials, there are agencies like the Elias Sports Bureau prepared to supply it. Production managers create statistical capsules which are then flashed on the television screen to enlighten viewers and substantiate statements offered by those covering the game. Throughout the year, baseball researchers, many of whom are members of the Society for American Baseball Research (SABR), diligently comb through the records of the game and publish their findings, while millions of baseball card collectors pore over their holdings, which contain, among other things, a range of statistical information printed on the backs of those sacred icons of the game.

This flow of baseball statistics has left its mark. An entirely new universe of statistical categories has been added to the traditional compilations, producing a veritable explosion of information. Numbers are now available, among other things, on a ballpark-by-ballpark basis, for day and night performances, for outcomes on grass as opposed to artificial turf, for balls hit on the ground as opposed to those sent skyward, for hitting right-handed or left-handed, batting while leading off an inning, hitting in late-inning pressure situations, and hitting with runners on and with the bases empty. Pitching effectiveness has been calculated for the first inning of games, at night, on grass, against particular hitters, and so on. New categories are forever being suggested and evaluated. With numbers of all sorts so plentiful, an abhorrence of statistical vacuums may be observed, an uneasiness when assertions are unaccompanied by statistical verification. The new reality of baseball demands continuous numerical validation.

The new statistical imperative demands constant refinement of numbers, and a ceaseless search for new categories that will be more specific, more revealing, and more predictive of future performance. Every true fan knows that pitchers' won and lost records are deceptive and that ERAs are better indicators of effectiveness. They also understand that such numbers are best supplemented by figures that reveal hits-to-innings ratios and batting averages of opposing teams against a particular pitcher. Fans have learned to appreciate the limitation of batting averages when evaluating the true contribution of individual hitters. They have been taught to examine numbers that reflect the ability to advance runners, to get on base leading off an inning, to drive in runners with two strikes or with two outs, or with the game tied in the late innings. Clearly a new age of statistical sophistication and analysis has dawned.

It's been a mixed blessing. To some critics, it represents an unfortunate deluge. Amidst the flood of numbers, too many are poorly digested and lack perspective and breadth. Moreover, the rush to produce new statistical categories threatens to trivialize the game and offer us little more than "calculated meaninglessness." Not long ago former baseball commissioner Fay Vincent displayed some impatience with this phenomenon. "I saw a statistic on TV recently—steals after the pitcher had thrown to first base. I wonder how that would improve my enjoyment of the game. I wonder how much is enough." Others decry the "clutter and confusion," and question the tendency to highlight so-called "records" or "streaks," some of which are little more than statistical quirks of which the players themselves are unaware or consider insignificant.[4] It's unlikely, for example, that Chicago White Sox pitcher Jack MacDowell was cognizant of the fact that in 1990 he led the American League in throws over to first base (209).

The surge in statistics has spotlighted player performance to an unprecedented degree and in a manner supremely judgmental. What other employees are subjected to such intense scrutiny of their day-to-day performances, or face withering criticisms for very specific kinds of failures or inadequacies? Few workers (and most certainly their unions) would tolerate public notice that they failed too often in the clutch, fade in the latter months of the season, perform in dismal fashion in certain ballparks, or inexplicably, against certain teams. Of course, the news is never just one-sided, and "good" statistics inevitably can be unearthed. And we are, after all, considering athletes who perform for the public and have reached the highest level of their craft, who are richly rewarded for their efforts even when the results are not satisfactory. Still the practice of having one's special skills called into question, being defined by unflattering statistics and judged in the cold light of impersonal numbers is a burden all players must bear.

Still and all, it's been a seller's market in baseball for some time now. All major-league players have benefited from the bounty that has flowed so generously from team owners. And if statistics have been used to underscore flawed performances, they have also become the most tangible basis for player remuneration. If the "numbers" are there, the dollars will follow in a manner singularly precise and predictable. There's little mystery to the process; players recognize that if they put up the "numbers," those figures will translate into equivalent dollars. Such correlations have in fact been subjected to economic analysis. The most recent study, undertaken at the University of Pennsylvania, succeeded in predicting baseball salaries one year in advance based upon the previous year's performance, achieving a level of accuracy, it said, that approached 94 percent. Holding other variables constant, it revealed that for hitters, every home run was worth $9,000 in next year's salary, and every extra run created (runs scored plus runs batted in minus home runs) was valued at $6,000. Pitchers earned $38,000 for each victory, $16,000 a save, $3,000 for each inning pitched, and $12,000 for each one-tenth of a point shaved off their ERA. Pittsburgh's Bobby Bonilla, negotiating for a multi-million-dollar contract in 1991, understood well that his "numbers" could speak for him. "The back of the bubble gum card ain't lyin'," he observed. "It's there in black and white. They know what they're going to get in me."[5]

The revolution in baseball statistics for many has been a welcome development stimulating new interest in certain of the finer points of the game and answering questions hitherto elusive, teaching "you something new all the time." The numbers will be produced to end speculation about performance differentials by players in night and day games. Uncertain about the impact of grass as opposed to artificial turf, some answers can be offered. (Extra base hits increase on artificial surfaces but overall batting averages are largely unaffected.) Baseball wisdom warns darkly about the dire effects of walking the leadoff hitter. But are the consequences any more severe than if he gets on base any other way? No. What about "one-run" games, considered a most sensitive indicator of team success? Close analysis reveals that such tight games are more likely to be won by the poorer team (i.e., the team with the weaker record) than games in which the margin of victory is far more substantial. A moment's thought might produce the answer, but a statistical chart will reveal instantly which fielder practically never catches a foul ball (the center fielder). Statistical studies suggest how often the "law of averages" comes into play in baseball. A team that wins a disproportionate share of one-run games one season will likely level off noticeably in the following year. A pitcher who yields an abundance of hits but still manages to compile an impressive ERA generally will see his ERA climb markedly in the following season. MVP and Cy Young Award winners in one year ordinarily compile records that are far less impressive the following season. Baseball arguments have long fueled fan interest. Thanks to the statistical record, much of the shouting and speculation now must accommodate to the dispassionate determination of numbers.[6]

The wisdom of baseball, the recommended strategies of the game have, it is maintained, been bound up in "The Book." No written document, "The Book" represents the accumulated lore of the game, the tactical traditions that have stood the test of time. But can they, one wonders, withstand the new challenge of statistics? Tested by time, can these truisms be substantiated by the numbers? Keeping the lead-off runner off base stands as a hoary maxim of the game. According to "The Book," those runners were quite likely to score. Do the statistics bear out this urgent warning? Indeed, when the leadoff runner reaches base a team is three times more likely to score than if he makes out. It had also been proclaimed that scoring first put a team at a considerable advantage. And so it is when the numbers are analyzed, for two of every three games are won by the team that first takes the lead. "The Book" was concerned but unclear on the issue of outcomes when pitchers and batters faced each other for the first time. Who held the advantage? The pitcher had little knowledge of the batter's strengths, whether he was a first-ball hitter, a low-ball hitter, or one anxious to hit to the opposite field. The batter had little sense of the pitcher's motion, his release point or the break on his curve or the rise on his fastball. What then did the record reveal? Advantage pitcher.

A broadly based study of confrontations revealed that batting averages of initial encounters were lower than in subsequent contests when the same players faced each other. "The Book" may be amiss when it suggests that "pull" hitters played accordingly by the opposition could increase their batting average by going to the opposite field. The numbers do not offer support here. They reveal that such players hit with greater success when they pull the ball rather than direct it the "other way." It is also apparently off the mark when it proclaimed that the taller the pitcher, the more awkward his motion and the greater the likelihood runners would steal successfully off him. The evidence, however, does not support this long-standing assumption.[7] Accordingly "The Book" is now rapidly evolving, reassessing its wisdom, common assumptions yielding to numerical analysis.

Managers who played the game by "The Book" once were generally immune from criticism. It was when they chose to deviate from its prescriptions that they placed themselves at risk. Many relying upon exceptional memories would justify the maneuver by recalling a similar move in the past that had proved effective. But memories, even of baseball managers, were selective and possibly faulty. The advent of statistical compilations has added substantially to their tactical repertoire and, better still, provided them with ready-made "explanations" for their decisions. In 1987 Milwaukee manager Tom Trebelhorn, hoping to keep Detroit's runner on third from scoring, positioned six men in the infield when Pat Sheridan stepped to the plate. It seemed to make sense because statistics revealed that in twenty-four at bats against his club, Sheridan had hit seventeen ground balls. So with the infield rendered "leakproof," Trebelhorn watched as his pitcher delivered a high ball which Sheridan promptly lifted to the outfield to score the run! Former Minnesota Twin Greg Gagne, a fair hitter under normal circumstances, becomes a dismal failure in clutch situations of two outs and runners on base (career average .195). These numbers did not escape his manager, Tom Kelly, who in 1990 removed Gagne (thirty-one times) for a pinch hitter in such situations, more often than any other Twins batter. When former Mets' manager Bud Harrelson was criticized in a 1991 game against San Diego for using pinch hitter Tom Herr over Hubie Brooks, who had batted .282 over his last fifty games, Harrelson offered statistical justification. "I'd rather have Herr than him," noting that Herr was 3 for 5 off San Diego pitcher Greg Haris while Brooks was 1 for 10.[8] Because statistics revealed that right-handed batter Kevin Seitzer hits the ball quite often to the opposite field, opposing managers have reason to position their right fields accordingly. Knowing that Chris James over his career against Nolan Ryan has but one hit in twenty at bats would certainly have encouraged the Texas manager to let Ryan pitch to James in a crucial late-inning situation. The same would be true with pitcher Mike Scott, who faced Andy Van Slyke thirty-seven times in his career and retired him on every occasion except one. The statistics on one-time slugger Steve Balboni revealed that through his first 907 games in the major leagues, he had never been credited with a successful sacrifice bunt. Knowing about such numbers likely kept infielders from playing in too close over the years. All these numbers provide no guarantees, but they do remove some of the guesswork and permit managers short on hunches to turn to history. It has also served to justify the patience of managers, enabled them to stand up to critics who question their consistent use of certain players who are not producing. Invariably they will respond by pointing to career statistics of those players, suggesting that the numbers don't lie and that "normalcy" will return shortly. That certainly was the explanation of Mets batting coach Mike Cubbage when asked to explain why certain slumping hitters remained on the lineup. "We're going on the players' track records more than hope. Their bios tell us they're going to hit."[9] Few managers or coaches today will direct a game without referring to charts and numbers as they look on from the dugout, relying increasingly on statistical tables to supplement instinct and savvy.

Numbers have served to reinforce the essential ties between baseball present and baseball past. Indeed the past offers a broad expanse of territory, often untracked terrain for the numbers people to explore and explain. Did the legends of the game produce the kinds of numbers to justify their elevated status? The famed Chicago Cubs trio of Tinker, Evers, and Chance, for example, long-celebrated for their finesse in the infield, emerge after close inspection of fielding statistics to be competent, but hardly superior, glove men.[10] Former president George Bush, first baseman for Yale in the late forties, was reputed to have been a mediocre hitter. New evidence, however, derived from box scores taken from the *New Haven Register, The New York Times, The Washington Post,* and the *Yale Daily News* revealed that he was decidedly less than that (a .224 average and one home run in seventy-six games).[11]

The dialogue between past and present is never so lively as when records are at stake. "We need," Roger Angell wisely observes, "constant statistical reassurance that the latest wonder on the field . . . equals or exceeds anything from the past before we can accord it a full measure of awe and delight."[12] When Pete Rose became a legitimate contender for the consecutive hitting-streak record set by Joe DiMaggio, interest quickened in that record-setting season of 1941. So it did again in 1991, the fiftieth anniversary of that seemingly unassailable hitting record. In baseball, record holders are often players from the distant past, so it is back there that one must go for information and numbers. This is most evident in relation to the Hall of Fame, baseball's proud pantheon of heroes. Each year as new candidates are considered, there is the inevitable debate over whether the aspirants deserve admission. No more telling question could be asked than whether they have the "numbers" comparable to those already in the hall who played the same position years ago. How satisfying for today's veteran players to learn that they have compiled Hall of Fame stats and may one day gain their "just" reward.

That the numbers have added a new and often illuminating dimension to the game is undeniable. Meanwhile, the process of refinement continues, spurred on in part by a rising tide of criticism. No one questions that trivialization and excess have arrived along with the numbers, or that there is a problem with arcane and insignificant records,[13] bloated box scores and statistical compilations that defy simple analysis. Certainly there are those statistical conservatives who sympathize with sports announcer Jack Buck, who views the "old reliable statistics" as "still the best." There is also the suggestion that written accounts of games rely too heavily upon statistics, and at times fail to convey the emotions and the feel of the contest.[14] More substantial is the charge that because numbers largely determine financial rewards, the game has been adversely affected, even distorted by that fact. In truth, rewards are based almost entirely on offensive statistics. What this does is downplay defensive achievements and encourages players to reorient their game so as to enhance offensive production. Rather than sacrifice, they will swing away. Rather than wait out a walk, they will offer at any delivery. They will risk stealing a base even when the situation suggests greater caution. More destructive is the fact that they will resist managerial direction and subordinate team play to personal accomplishment. It's been generally accepted that toward the end of the season with a team clearly out of contention, an individual player could neglect team play and work to bolster his own record. This "playing for the contract," considered acceptable for brief stretches of time, now threatens to extend over entire seasons. This is especially true of players about to become free agents or who are contemplating arbitration. According to Tony Gwynn, "The emphasis for a lot of players isn't on being the best player you can be, it's on being the best player you can be on the year your contract is up and getting the most that you can get." Whitey Herzog, reflecting upon his departure from the St. Louis Cardinals in 1990, noted that four members of his team were heading for arbitration. Because the rewards would be based strictly on numbers, Herzog felt powerless. "I couldn't ask them to sacrifice for the team."[15]

Numbers are bloodless and impersonal; they produce abstractions rather than delineate real people. Players unable to produce impressive statistics may nevertheless serve as the mainstays of their team. Baseball people speak of the "intangibles," of contributions players make that do not appear in the box scores, of numbers that do not reflect "true value." Tom Boswell reflecting upon the play of Kirk Gibson and Orel Hershiser noted that for such players intensity counts more than numbers. "For once in a baseball discussion we'll be forced to say, 'Forget statistics.' You don't measure these men that way. They played to win at all costs."[16] Behind these comments is the fear numbers are narrowing the sense of possibility, stripping away the drama and mystery of the game, and imprisoning players in a web of facts and figures that snuffs out their individuality. It was baseball announcer Gary Thorne who best captured this uneasy sense of closure and confinement. "Thank goodness they [the numbers] don't always hold up or there'd be no reason to play the game."[17] Baseball is not, if Thorne is correct, on the threshold of statistical predestination—a most comforting albeit tentative conclusion.

NINETEEN

Fans: A Special Connection

WHATEVER THE GAME, fans of that sport feel a special connection, and might even admit to a love affair. Nowhere is this truer than in baseball. Indeed, a strong case can be made that baseball fans maintain a uniquely intimate relationship unmatched in any other sport. "There's something special about the game of baseball," Andy Van Slyke notes, "that links the fans with the players like no other game."[1] This closeness is well-documented, so too, a cluster of plausible explanations. Most convincing, perhaps, is the length of the relationship, measured always by years, often in decades. Most every male child has played the game, or at the very least worn a glove and tossed a ball, and probably even tried to hit one on occasion. Chances are, he did so at one point with his father, that act long-memorialized as among the most noteworthy and celebrated rituals of father-son relationships (along with attending baseball games together).[2] In all likelihood the youngster collected baseball cards, idolized particular players, and memorized the statistical histories of countless others.[3] Surely growing up with baseball in this manner left a positive impression, indeed probably paved the way for an intimate and enduring relationship to develop, nourished over time by nostalgic reveries of youth (and reinforced in later years by rotisserie leagues and "fantasy" weeks at major-league training camps).

Baseball's a year-round sport; always it's open season. Played for eight consecutive months, it's then discussed, dissected, and debated the rest of the year. Day in and day out, even as spring turns to summer, and summer to fall, it remains an inevitable fact of life. The often-antic stories of fans somehow cut off from the game on particular occasions and attempting to discover the score could fill volumes. Most compelling are those endless tales of fans abroad requiring the daily baseball scores as if to validate their identity as Americans. Baseball stands committed to the long haul.

To be a baseball fan is to be a perpetual cheerleader, judge, critic, and sage all in one. "Everybody talks about baseball," writer George

Vecsey remarks, and then "everybody tries to do something about it."[4] Passivity has no place here. Nowhere but in baseball are so many convinced of their superior acumen, of their ability, of their right to question what they've observed. They watch games, keep score, cite statistics, and are quick to second-guess tactics, most notably those that have fallen short. They regard managers as no better than their recent records, always candidates for replacement when their teams falter. When that happens they will boo the "skipper" at the ballpark, voice their anger to call-in show hosts, and spread the word among their associates. In short order, such grass-roots sentiments mushroom into a general sports community consensus. Whether ownership bows to these "demands" is another matter, but the pressure will produce some form of response. For baseball fans, loyalty translates into empowerment, justifying a voice in team affairs.[5]

When team deficiencies surface as inevitably they do, fans are quick to offer remedies. There are new lineups to suggest, new tactics to propose and trades to be made. And thanks to the proliferation of sports call-in radio shows, their ideas, and their calls to action, will be discussed and circulate throughout the sports community. Talk-show hosts encourage such efforts and are themselves quick to add their voice and views to the ongoing debate. The fact that the athletes themselves appear on these shows and respond in some manner to questions put to them tends to legitimize the entire process and lend substance to the idea that more than idle chatter is being exchanged.

Baseball fans, quick to judge managers, feel an obligation to be more constructive when players are involved.[6] Fan mail, ever a constant in sports, is especially notable in baseball, but with a difference. Here fans assume a higher level of responsibility, are convinced they have something to contribute, that their suggestions can make a difference. This is especially evident when hitters go into a slump. The longer it persists, the greater volume of fan mail that is likely to arrive. Some of it will include charms and good luck pieces intended to break the spell. Many more letters will contain close analysis of the hitter's batting problems, suggesting new stances, swings, and attitudes. Indeed, some hitters mired in prolonged slumps and having exhausted conventional remedies, admit at times that they do take a peek at fan letters, looking for something that might unlock the mystery. Dusty Baker speaks of the time "some guy off the streets called me and told me I'm pulling off the ball and to leave those high pitches alone."[7] Pitchers, too, are open to suggestion. Lee Smith recalls how a youngster brought him victory over the Tigers. "When I was warming up this kid yelled at me to stay within myself. I kept thinking about this when I was out there. I followed his advice." When some years back pitcher Tom Candiotti was mired in a slump, he appealed to fans for good luck charms. The response was immediate. Dolls, rabbits' feet, and a chocolate-covered baseball were among the more conventional items he received.

In no other sport are fans (in recent years at least) offered the opportunity to vote on most of the players who appear in the mid-season All-Star Game. In short, they control the composition of the two all-star teams in what is one of the premier events of the sport. Objections are frequently raised about the process, with fans voting as often as they please (and generally backing hometown favorites), but defenders counter by citing the unique relationship baseball has with its fans and the value of voting in bringing them even closer to the game.

The truest measure of the special relationship between fans and baseball may be seen in the attachment most have for the ballparks themselves. No other sport lavishes so much attention and love on the fields and structures on which the game is played. Fans speak with reverence about such places as Fenway Park, Yankee Stadium, and Wrigley Field, and with admiration about Dodger Stadium, Toronto's Skydome and Kansas City's Royals Stadium.[8] The Smithsonian Institution conducts tours of the major-league ballparks, and fans off on trips frequently place a high priority upon attending games in various ballparks.[9] Several recently published volumes have offered photographic essays of the stadiums, and another has detailed every imaginable feature of each one, including quality of frankfurters, sight lines, lavatories, and so on. A New York newspaper featured a lengthy piece describing the dugouts at all of the ballparks. It would be hard to name any football stadiums, hockey rinks, or basketball arenas that are accorded such attention or occupy such an exalted position in the sport. Though prices have risen, baseball tickets remain, compared to other sports, a bargain. Families can attend, likewise lower-middle and working-class fans. (In some ballparks inexpensive bleacher tickets remain where, symbolically at least, the common man is represented.)[10]

At the ballpark the fan enjoys unusual latitude and is given an enlarged role unlike that accorded him elsewhere. Fans of course, include the wives of the ballplayers. In no other team sport do the players' wives attend games together with such regularity or find themselves in the TV camera's eye repeatedly during a game. (Inevitably a wife's range of reaction as her husband faces a crucial situation out on the field will be covered in considerable detail.) It's not by chance. "The fans own the game," according to Fay Vincent, former baseball commissioner. "We have to give fans," he declares "a very wide level of tolerance."[11] Where else do signs and banners proliferate in such fashion, offering support, keeping track of strikeouts, speaking out, poking fun in unusually forceful ways?

Baseball fans badger managers and players more than in any other sport. Late in the 1991 season, Mets manager Bud Harrelson admitted he let his pitching coach head to the mound to remove a pitcher so that he (Harrelson) could avoid the trip and the hearty boos certain to accompany it. The next year Bobby Bonilla early in the season took to wearing earplugs to drown out the boos from the stadium fans responding to his prolonged batting slump. For a time former Toronto shortstop Manny Lee could certainly empathize with Harrelson and Bonilla. "They [the fans] hate me. I hear people say bad things about me all the time. If I make a mistake they yell at me." Sustained fan anger can take its toll, as Ed Whitson discovered when he pitched for the Yankees. "There wasn't a day that went by where I didn't fear for my life or the safety of my family. Every day I went out the door I wondered what would happen to me. . . . I felt like I was carrying a bullseye on my back waiting for someone to take that first shot." Whitson's tale of woe was not much different than Mike Stanley's encounters with hometown fans while with the Red Sox. "It starts before the game," he tells us. "I'm down in the bullpen warmin' up, they're yellin' at me. They're booin'. This one guy was screamin' at me. Screamin'. You guys wouldn't believe what I hear in the bullpen sometimes." He then continues: "You know my kids don't come to the ballpark anymore. They used to. They used to come all the time. A kid should see his dad play ball, right? But when this booing started, and the stuff, the insults, that was the end of it. I don't want my kids to hear the stuff I listen to."

Fortunately fans, even critical ones, are not everywhere the same, according to Jack Clark. It was, he said, easier to be booed by the San Diego fans than elsewhere. "Being booed in New York or St. Louis is not like getting it down here. The fans here just go 'boo, Dude!'" The wisest course, Roger Clemens counsels, is to ignore it. "We all complain about the fans sometimes," says Clemens, "but it's best not to do so publicly," a truth players ignore at their peril. Certainly that was true of Pete Incaviglia when he remarked that, "When you get out there . . . some stupid jerk who is half-drunk boos you, it hurts." Naturally, the booing continued. A more somber Incaviglia then reflected that "these are the times you have to get through if you're going to make it. The same people that are booing me will be cheering me. It's a tough thing to accept but you have to keep going and doing your job."[12]

Fans boo because they care, because they are so emotionally identified with their favorite teams that losses leave them depressed, sometimes in despair. "No one bleeds," says sports columnist Jim Murray, "like a baseball fan whose team is in a long slump." Baseball fans deal in disappointment," he says. "[They] jeer so they won't sob." And their sobbing can turn to bitterness and anger. After Pittsburgh's Stan Belinda yielded the winning hit in the National League Championship Series in 1992, "I had a lot of hate mail," he recalled. While players don't relish losing, they are able to take defeat in stride.[13]

For fans to speak their minds is a presumed right conferred upon all those having paid the price of admission. "They pay their money, and they're entitled to boo," says Eric Davis. "Professional" fans, such as Bob Northrup, considered by some as the worst heckler in the American League, revels in the role. "This is a democracy," says Northrup, who often can be found at the Oakland Coliseum. "Where else can you come out and get some millionaires agitated. . . ." Outfielders will be singled out by those sitting in nearby stands. When Brian Jordan played his first game at Candlestick Park in 1992 he was treated rudely by some outfield fans. "They were on me," he admitted. "Even the ladies were talking trash."[14] Players occupying the bullpen area can expect to hear comments directed their way. Dugouts provide some measure of protection, though players heading in or out of them are vulnerable. Players generally learn to accept all this as part of the game, but not all remain models of restraint and will on occasion lash out at their tormentors.[15] Umpires, on the other hand, can in no way respond to taunting by fans. This, despite the fact that no other sport virtually sanctions aggression towards these officials. Nowhere else can one impute blindness or shout, "kill the umpire" with impunity.[16] Amazingly, fans located a good distance away feel justified in berating umpires, standing right alongside batters, for "missing" calls. On the other hand, they will breathe collective sighs of relief most audibly when, with their team at bat, close pitches are called balls.

Players do on occasion get a chance to retaliate. Wally Backman, for example, turned a hose on a fan near the dugout after a game in 1988 at Atlanta's overheated Fulton County Stadium. "He'd been getting on us all series. I thought he'd be mad but I think I did him a favor." Furthermore, fan hostility can cause some players to lift performance levels. Dave Stewart in the 1988 World Series turned the catcalls of Boston fans into added incentive when he took to the mound. Stewart recalled how "a bunch of fans down by the bullpen started heckling badly and it made me mad. So I took it out on the mound with me. The fans motivated me and I'd like to thank them." Keith Hernandez, when he played for the Mets, often felt the same way. "I've loved playing on the road," he said, "where there are the opposing crowds booing. You want to send them home unhappy." When Eric Fox of Oakland hit a three-run homer to beat the Twins during the 1992 season there was no mistaking Fox's elation. "It's a special feeling to silence forty-three thousand people, people calling you a bum, saying you stink. It's all part of the game. My job is to silence them."[17]

For years sports fans have watched indoor hockey and basketball arenas turn into ear-shattering, mind-numbing cauldrons of sound, the crowds cheering on their favorites and attempting to unnerve the opposition. That is a decisive part of the home-team advantage. It's most evident when a visiting quarterback will retreat from under the center and appeal to the referees to call time. His signals can't be heard. On the foul line a player will hear the deafening roar and may decide to back away momentarily to wait for the din to subside. The same form of crowd control happens in baseball, fans rising to their feet and shouting loudly as the opposing pitcher, facing a 3-2 count in a clutch situation, prepares to throw the payoff pitch. Finding the plate amidst all that noise is no simple matter. The most notable recent examples of the crowd factor came in the 1987 World Series when the air in the Metro Stadium in Minneapolis stirred to the vigorous waving of "homer hankies" amplifying the already boisterous sounds and cheers of the fans and boosting the Twins past the shell-shocked Cardinals. And as if to prove they had not lost their touch, these same fans cheered their Twins on to victory again in 1991, Minnesota capturing all four games at the Metrodome.[18]

Baseball is rarely in a hurry. Accordingly, spectators need not always be paying attention; other activities may intrude. Fans seem to feel exceptionally comfortable and playful out at the ballpark. Where else will thousands of spectators join together by rising to their feet in proper sequence to produce a human wave rippling across the stadium? There will be frequent launchings of paper airplanes, many destined for the playing surface, or in the case of some Dodger fans of 1989, a chicken will be let loose onto the field. They will toss beach balls around the stands, batting them skyward, directing them from one section of seats to another. If it happens to drift out onto the field—a not infrequent occurrence—play will stop until it is retrieved.[19] Far more serious are those disruptions caused when fans themselves dash out onto the field in an attempt to "meet" some of the ballplayers or simply to call attention to themselves (or to a portion of their anatomy, as was the case of the fan who in 1991 ran onto the field at Toronto and bared his backside). It happens with sufficient regularity to be considered an almost normal aspect of the game. On April 17, 1992, during a Montreal home game at Olympic Stadium, no less than six fans headed out onto the field. Where else do fans feel comfortable enough to attempt to interfere with play in such a manner? Though they are almost always ejected from the ballpark, trespassers are generally applauded by fans for their daring and for the diversion provided.[20]

For many fans, especially younger ones, the game is no more important than their earnest efforts to latch on to a baseball that's been hit out of play. Many will bring gloves, nets, and other apparatus to

173

the ballpark to aid in their quest, and will occasionally display incredible bravery (or is it foolhardiness?), and risk injury attempting to catch baseballs rocketed their way. As each ball heads toward the seats, all rise and attempt to judge where it will land and to position themselves to compete for this most prized possession (and if a fine catch is made, that fan can expect appreciative cheers from the crowd). There are few more memorable experiences than leaving the stadium ball in hand. Baseball's generosity here represents a wise investment,[21] cleverly cultivating fans who will never forget that the game always provides the unique opportunity for a special bonus. Certain drawbacks are present, however.[22] In their eagerness to acquire a souvenir, fans may interfere with play itself.[23] It's generally acknowledged that a player in pursuit of a foul pop-up near the stands will compete for the ball with spectators eager to catch it themselves. If the home team's on the field, they may exercise restraint and "permit" him to make the catch and retire the batter, but just as often they'll ignore the benefits to their team and attempt to take possession themselves. Such interference will also occur on foul balls close enough to the outfield stands for fans to reach out and touch them. And it's beyond dispute that such actions can prove decisive — a runner who might easily have made it to third base on his hit had a fan not touched the ball; a batter who would have been held to a single had a fan not made contact with the ball — these are not inconsequential happenings.[24] This, too, "changes" the game and makes baseball unique for incorporating some portion of fan behavior into its rules and outcomes.

The arrival of the seventh inning brings us to one of the enduring rituals of the sport. Just before the home team prepares to bat in the second half of the inning, fans are invited to rise and together enjoy the "seventh-inning stretch." Most usually do; otherwise their loyalty might come under suspicion. In many stadiums there is also the occasion for a chorus or two of the most popular song ever associated with a particular sport. Is there a fan who does not know the lyrics to "Take Me Out to the Ball Game," and who is not willing, whatever his or her vocal abilities, to sing the song together with thousands of others? This communal act reaffirms fan commitment to the sport much as the singing of "We Shall Overcome" signified support for civil rights in the 1960s.

Throughout the game, fans follow events on the field, but are concerned as well with developments elsewhere around the major leagues. While rooting for "your" team it is just as important to follow how division rivals are faring, as well as the races in the other leagues. All this is easily accomplished thanks to the installation of massive scoreboards at each ballpark which list all scheduled games and update scores, usually inning by inning. Thus it is possible to follow many games simultaneously and to delight when rivals are trailing and, when ahead, hope for a rally by their opponents. It is quite common at all baseball games to hear cheers go up when new and "promising" scores are posted. In no other sport is there so systematic an effort made to provide such an updating to keep the larger picture in view. It is yet one more indication of baseball's superior wisdom, and of its long-term success in drawing fans to the ballpark and to the game.

TWENTY
Anticipation

They watch the ballgame as if it were a hockey game. They wait for something to happen and then they cheer. There is no sense of anticipation.

— Ken Singleton

Baseball isn't scoring, it's the threat of scoring. You have to take something to the Game. It's contemplation and reflection, a moment of action, anticipation, aftertaste.

— Steve Jacobson

IN LAMENTING the lack of sophistication on the part of Montreal fans, Singleton, a former major-leaguer, offers insight into one of the most intriguing and subtle elements of the game of the game of baseball. Knowledgeable fans, Singleton implies, ought to be aware of developments before they happen in a game. He faults Montreal fans, for example, for not "rumbling when the 3-4-5 hitters are coming to the plate." Such comments remind us of those subtle undercurrents operating during a game whose every shift can provide an edge to one team or another. It is no doubt what Oakland A's general manager Sandy Alderson had in mind when he remarked that "the beauty of the game" was that it was "all nuances and anticipation" or when Tom Boswell observed that the exceptional ballplayer had to be "a student of expectations." Baseball announcer Norm Hitzges agrees, viewing baseball as fundamentally "a game of leverages, a game of tiny advantages." "That's what the game is all about," according to Hal McRae. "You are fighting for an edge." Players and managers alike must be aware of and exploit such opportunities. Fans, too, must be attentive; otherwise they miss out on one of the most entertaining and compelling dimensions of the game.[1]

In major-league contests there are no sure things, no obvious pushovers. "The beauty of the game of baseball," Dave Duncan of the Oakland A's observes, "is that you can get beat on any given day no matter how good you are."[2] The stronger team will be favored but not by very much (especially when facing a skillful pitcher). One may anticipate a particular outcome, but in baseball, the perils of prognostication are well understood. The only indication may come when, with the game underway, slight advantages appear, when subtle edges and "little things" suggest which way the tide may be turning.

Even before the first pitch is thrown the search for advantage begins. In all sports, baseball not excepted, the edge belongs to the home team. Research by the baseball commissioner's office reveals, for example, that through the entire decade of the eighties not one team managed to compile a winning record playing on the road. The reasons for this are many and generally well understood. They include fan support, familiarity with peculiar conditions of the field, and teams specifically tailored to a ballpark. (A case in point was the St. Louis Cardinals of the eighties, a group of lean, slap-hitting jackrabbits able to exploit the artificial surface, hot temperatures and spacious dimensions of Busch Stadium.) It may also have something to do with which team is better rested. During a "home stand" many team members actually live at home, are reunited, however briefly, with families and friends, and presumably ingest a number of satisfying home-cooked meals. The opposition, on the other hand, flies into a town (often in the early hours of the morning after a night game), stays cooped up in a local hotel, sleeps fitfully, eats irregularly, perhaps takes in some diverting local color before being herded onto a bus for a trip out to the stadium.[3] Amidst all these distractions and inconveniences, the wonder is that visiting teams do as well as they do.[4]

Other advance elements may enter into preliminary assessments. Streaks are a most prominent feature of baseball, everywhere discussed and analyzed at length.[5] Teams about to face each other are always aware of how the other has been performing of late. Most players will read up on such matters or inquire of reporters. If not, the team's advance scouts will provide this information, on the opposition in general as well as on individual players. Streaks, most players believe, are a rather mysterious phenomenon, generally beyond the control of mere mortals. A team on a "roll" may be formidable indeed, perhaps unstoppable for the moment. On the other hand, a streak produces a compensatory reaction, a desire on the part of the opposing team to end the "run," to restore normal patterns. It may therefore produce in them exceptional exertion and positive results. Of course, a team in a severe slump can also be dangerous. At some point a slump must end; teams always rebound. The opposition hopes for recovery, but only after the slumping team departs.

Much of this pregame speculation, the substance of local sports columns and fan discussions, tends to be inconclusive. Not only are the elements intangible or beyond measure, but many of the factors work to neutralize each other. Early in the 1991 season the New York Mets traveled to Philadelphia to begin a three-game series with the Phillies. The Mets were last in the National League in team hitting and were leading the league in the number of runners left on base (105 in thirteen games). With six of the team's eight regulars hitting .206 or lower, could one project a continuation of this offensive futility or predict that the team, long "overdue," would snap out of it? The picture for the Phillies was even cloudier and much bleaker than the Mets' outlook. Philadelphia already occupied last place in the Eastern Division, featured the worst record in the National League, and had a manager, Nick Leyva, who, according to the media, was about to be fired. Would this galvanize the Phillies? Would they rally around their beleaguered manager and defeat the Mets? But what of reports that team members were disenchanted with Leyva, upset with his public criticisms of particular players. Would the team conspire to go through the motions, a signal to management of its desire to have Leyva removed? If these circumstances provided one team or another with an edge, it was not apparent.

Certain elements and tendencies can be weighed prior to game time. Whether it is a day or a night contest does make a difference. Players vary considerably in their ability to perform by day or at night. In 1990, Rob Deer batted .234 in night and .152 in day games. For Cecil Fielder, a similar pattern prevailed. At night he was a formidable .301 and by day a vulnerable .213. From 1986 to 1990, Dave Parker batted for a higher average in night games while Dante Bichette, over a similar period, batted .261 at night and only .194 in day games. More hitters perform at a higher level during the daytime, a pattern one presumes is related to their ability to see the ball more easily at such times. In 1990, Candy Maldonado hit .343 by day and slumped to a very mediocre .245 at night. Darnell Coles provided an even more dramatic example, hitting .309 in the daylight and .175 at night. Over a period of years, hitters like Craig Biggio, Dan Pasqua, Mike Devereaux, Mike Fitzgerald, Jim Eisenreich, and Randy Ready were notably more proficient hitting in daylight than under the lights.

Similar patterns persist among pitchers for reasons as yet insufficiently explored. The records of men like Bob Forsch, Mike Boddicker, Jimmy Key, Jeff Robinson, Eric King, Terry Leach, Brett Saberhagen, Mike Witt, Dave Stieb, and Mike Scott have been notably more impressive when they've pitched night games. On the other hand Doug Drabek, Chris Bosio, Bert Blyleven, Jose Bautista, Scott Bankhead, and Bob Welch have kept batters at bay more consistently during day games. As for games that begin in daylight and end in darkness—baseball's statisticians have yet to reckon with this phenomenon.[6]

When searching for an edge, it pays to look at history. As has been noted previously, pitchers have, over time, established patterns which, understood or not, tend to persist and affect any particular calculation of advantage. Some, like John Smiley and Frank Viola, are unusually effective early in the season, while Jim Acker, Mark Gubicza, Tom Browning, Eric King, and Rob Murphy, among others, have usually saved their finest outings for the latter half of the schedule. Knowing that Dave LaPoint customarily had fared poorly in June, and that Tom Candiotti has over the years been outstanding in August is information that must be filed and factored in. That Jimmy Key and Rick Aguilera often dominated in September could not be ignored in the last weeks of a tight pennant race.

There are in the major leagues eighteen fields of grass and ten ballparks where they play on artificial surface. It makes a difference to pitchers, among others. Terry Leach, for example, had at one point compiled an outstanding 16-3 record on artificial surfaces, whereas on grass he was a mediocre 15-17. Opponents have batted an average of fifty-one points higher against Rob Murphy on grass than when he's worked on green carpets. Similar tendencies have been shown by Roger Clemens, Todd Burns, Eric Show, and Bob Welch. On the other hand, Jack McDowell and Brett Saberhagen have been more formidable on grass than elsewhere.

Starting pitchers generally throw more effectively in their home ballparks. The records of such pitchers as Sid Fernandez, Paul Gibson, Kirk McCaskill, Tom Bolton, Walt Terrell, and Ted Higuera bear this out. Still, this general pattern often did not apply to Jimmy Key, John Dopson, Scott Bankhead, Bobby Witt, and Roger Clemens who kept hitters in check more consistently when playing on the road. One must also not ignore the strange but enduring hold certain pitchers have over particular teams. Whether these are statistical quirks or represent real yet elusive powers of selective dominance cannot be determined. When these pitchers stride to the mound they immediately affect the balance of power. Entering the 1991 season, David Cone had never lost to the Pirates. Jim Deshaies had consistently beaten the Dodgers, Eric Show had devastated the Braves, and Jack Morris was more than a match for the Indians. On the other hand, certain pitchers time and again have faltered against specific opponents. Rick Mahler has enjoyed little or no success against the Mets, the Oakland A's have repeatedly thwarted Roger Clemens; Nolan Ryan suffered defeat after defeat at the hands of the Orioles, and Mark Knudsen had never beaten the Twins. Each game represents a fresh start, there is no score at the beginning, but the memories of performances past are not readily dismissed and operate to tilt the balance.

Recall that our discussion concerns the matter of anticipation and seeks to identify those factors that cause shifts in the patterns of probability. At the very outset, one of the teams may have an advantage if it is facing a pitcher chronically incapable of getting off to a strong start. Indeed, there are many who time and again experience difficulty pitching effectively in the opening inning. Included in this category are such superb talents as Nolan Ryan, David Cone,[7] Bert Blyleven, along with John Smiley, Bryn Smith, Charlie Hough, Randy Johnson, Matt Young, Frank Tanana, and Bud Black. For them to escape unscathed in the first inning represents a notable, albeit partial, triumph. Maneuvering past these shoals, these same pitchers often find clear sailing and become more dominant as the game progresses. In such cases, the pressure is on the opposition to score early or face the prospect of an uphill struggle in the later stages of the game.

Taking advantage of a "slow starter" and scoring a run in the first inning translates into a distinct advantage. Approximately two out of three games are won by the team that strikes first. Strong confirmation of this trend can be found. In 1990, for example, figures of surprising consistency were compiled both in the American (68 percent) and National Leagues (66 percent). What is not clear is why this should be so. When teams average between five and six runs a game, the first run should not be all that formidable an obstacle. One-run deficits should not cause a team to depart from its customary offensive tactics. Perhaps the answer lies more with the psychological edge a lead brings to pitchers. Baseball wisdom has it that given a lead, certain pitchers become noticeably stingy, dogged competitors determined not to relinquish it. [8]

Thus far we've ranged over a variety of general circumstances that create advantages or expose vulnerability. During the game, the knowledgeable and observant fan understands that there are a multitude of "little things" that can produce a small advantage, a slight edge, so as to tilt the balance. Most are savvy enough to understand that baseball is more often than not about failure and that glimmers of hope are all too often extinguished. Still and all, opportunity may be calling.

With every batter there is great significance in the very first pitch he sees. First strikes, pitching coach Ray Miller believes, are "90 percent of the game. If you throw strike one, you've got five possible pitches left to throw for two strikes." [9] Roger Craig is in perfect agreement. "The most important pitch in baseball," he insists, "is strike one. If you're hitting .350 and I get a strike on you, now you become a .250 hitter." [10] What is at issue here is, of course, "the count," registering the score of that highly competitive encounter between pitcher and batter that is at the very heart of the game. [11] Both are in balance as the confrontation begins, but with each pitch shifts occur, the edge often moving back and forth. Hitters up 1-0, 2-0, 2-1, and 3-1 understand they're ahead in the count. The pitcher, reluctant to "lose" them and issue a walk, will likely throw the ball over the plate. The time is ripe for the batter to make solid contact, to drive the ball. At such favorable counts, fans begin buzzing, hopeful the hitter can capitalize on the situation. Alternately if the pitcher "works" the count his way, 0-1, 0-2, 1-2, he is clearly in command. [12] A hitter must now become defensive, guard the plate, even swing at questionable pitches. He is for that reason most vulnerable, and often will lunge at pitches distant from the strike zone. In 1992, once hitters had two strikes, they could only manage an overall batting average of .187. "Get ahead with strikes, get them out with balls," is Tim McCarver's apt epigram describing a pitcher's triumphant strategy.

All fans are familiar with the advantages enjoyed by a right-handed pitcher over a righty batter and a southpaw over a left-handed hitter. Less publicized is the edge batters enjoy if they succeed in fouling off a succession of pitches. In this battle of wills, it is the batter who gains increasing confidence with every pitch he sees, with every one he manages to spoil. At the same time, a pitcher's frustration level mounts and he may, as a result, "groove" a pitch and suffer the unfortunate consequences. With an aggressive runner on base, some advantage, albeit limited, may go to the hitter. Edging off first base, feigning a burst towards second, the runner will draw repeated looks and throws from the pitcher. He has without doubt become a distraction, complicated the pitcher's job, made it more difficult for him to concentrate on the batter. Furthermore, a left-handed hitter will gain additional benefits from the fact that the first baseman, obliged to stay on or close to the base, must leave a large and tempting gap between first and second bases. (With the runner threatening to steal, the batter also can expect a lot of fastballs.) Offsetting these benefits is the fact that the hitter, with a swift runner on first, will be expected to take a few pitches so as to allow the runner the opportunity to steal second. Thus, before he can swing, he may fall behind in the count. Furthermore, the hitter may find it hard to concentrate with the runner bobbing up and down, rushing back and forth, and with the pitcher repeatedly breaking stride and firing over to first base. Such distractions may put him at a disadvantage. While the overall situation favors the hitter, the edge can shift back and forth quickly.

Tim McCarver, among others, delights in proclaiming that baseball is preeminently a game of "firsts"—first pitch, first strike, first out, first run. We have not, however, as yet commented on the significance of getting the first or leadoff runner on base. To do so represents a threat of the highest order. The statistical evidence is impressive. A team is three times more likely to score if its leadoff man (via either a walk or a hit) reaches base than if the first batter is retired. Over half (54 percent) the time the first hitter reaches base, the team scores. Small wonder that interest builds across the ballpark when this happens. With a runner on and none out, the advantage shifts to the offense. It can employ a variety of stratagems (bunt, hit and run, steal, and so on), thereby forcing the defense to guess at what might be next, to deploy fielders somewhat out of position, even put them in motion, which usually reduces their effectiveness. On the other hand, the defense takes great comfort in recording that first out, while batters now face added pressure to mount a threat.[13]

The batting order itself represents various levels of potential and triggers a range of expectations. The prospect of seeing one's seventh, eighth, and ninth batters coming to the plate does little to quicken the pulse. On the other hand, there is a stir when the top of the order is due up. Ordinarily the first six batters in the lineup offer the greatest potential for offensive production, but even among this group more specific roles are assigned. The leadoff man is expected to be the catalyst, the most versatile hitter in the lineup, capable of resorting to almost any stratagem to get on base. A speedster, a switch hitter, a bunter, a slap hitter, a patient hitter able to work out a walk — a leadoff man is expected to qualify in many, if not all, these categories. With him on base the prospect of a score becomes very real. The number-two man is expected to contribute to building a run by advancing the runner into scoring position in any number of ways. The first two batters have in baseball parlance "set the table." The batters who follow ("the meat of the order") (3-6) must "clean up," that is, drive the runners home. Since they are the weakest hitters, whatever the last three men (the "bottom of the order") contribute is a bonus, an unexpected dividend. In baseball, therefore, hopes rise or fall according to who is coming to the plate. There are few sights more encouraging than seeing runners on and the most capable hitters about to bat. But have those same men on base with the "tail end" of the order due up and dark thoughts of wasted opportunity are inescapable.[14]

Assuming the game has entered the late innings and remains close, additional developments may be anticipated. If a pitcher has escaped unscathed from a number of difficult situations, he may still pay a price. Having expended considerable energy and applied maximum concentration to the task, he may fall short and succumb to the next threat.[15] A pitcher may also be victimized with his team at bat if he's forced to sit through an unusually lengthy half-inning. His body may stiffen during this interval, and because his rhythm has been interrupted he may be unable to regain his previous form.[16] Moreover, recent years have seen the rise to prominence of the "pitch count," a calculation of the number of balls thrown by a single pitcher in the game. Such counts are carefully monitored, with managers loathe to permit hurlers to exceed certain predetermined levels. This suggests the possibility some pitchers may weaken in the latter stages of the game as their pitch count mounts. So if, in the early innings, a pitcher has been obliged to throw many balls, it may take a toll rendering him vulnerable as the game progresses.[17]

It is in the latter stages of a close game, according to baseball wisdom, that a baseball manager earns his money. He will be expected to make a number of moves to replace players (especially in the National League where pitchers hit and therefore represent a drag on the offense) and devise other tactics that can turn the tide. One can anticipate a number of these maneuvers and judge their likely impact. A pitcher who has been notably effective may nevertheless be removed for a pinch hitter if a scoring opportunity presents itself. (This may actually be welcomed by the opposition, especially if the pinch hitter fails and the new pitcher is not nearly as mystifying as his predecessor.)[18] If a manager has handled his pinch hitters well, the best of them will still be available for duty late in the game. The goal now is to bring hitters in who match up well against particular pitchers. Almost always there will be a lefty against a right-handed pitcher (and vice versa), or it may rest on a hunch, a feeling, or a page out of the charts which show certain batters hitting unusually well against particular pitchers. Against Zane Smith, the Braves would likely send up Terry Pendleton, who at one point was 26 for 53 against the left-hander. Tom Glavine on the mound might be a signal to send up Robby Thompson, who through 1992 had batted an immodest .441 (15 for 34) against Glavine.

Late in the game is also the occasion for making defensive replacements and inserting speedsters as pinch runners. It is a time when a slight edge may make the whole difference, when a swift runner, a strong-armed outfielder, a pitcher who throws ground balls, or a batter who always makes contact can mean victory. If a manager is wise or lucky enough to have or to have placed the right people in the proper places, winning will be his reward. And those who watched the various strategies unfold and wondered what it might take to succeed may come away with an even greater appreciation and understanding of these subtle ingredients that often provide an edge and result in victory.

TWENTY-ONE
Looking Ahead

BASEBALL, ALL AGREE, is open and visually accessible, with most plays clearly defined and unfolding in full view of spectators. The game proceeds in a deliberate, even leisurely, manner allowing an interval for analysis and more than a few anxious moments. One feature of the game, however, is at variance with the pattern, involving, as it does, instant drama and its immediate resolution. Under consideration here is a type of imaging that attempts to project the outcome of an action sequence while it is yet in progress. Such moments of concentration, anticipation, and uncertainty are well known beyond baseball. Pedestrians watching an automobile skid along an icy surface, toward an unyielding barrier project forward to a collision even as they attempt to will the vehicle to a stop. Countless spine-tingling dramas have exploited hide-and-seek sequences with potential victims trying to elude discovery while being stalked by a lethal aggressor. Anxiety levels mount as audiences look ahead and calculate the likelihood of discovery.

Sports other than baseball incorporate this "fast-forward" phenomenon. Observe a three-point shot attempt in basketball. The ball ascends into the air, arcing gracefully as it heads toward the basket. This provides the opportunity for instant visual reckoning. Does the basketball have the proper trajectory and distance to pass through the hoop? A suddenly elevated noise level reflects the excitement and expectation of those already projecting a basket. A similar phenomenon may be observed in football, occurring when the quarterback lofts a long pass downfield intended for a receiver speeding goalward along the sidelines. Will the flight path of the pass and the runner intersect— that is what spectators strain to determine and "see" as the play unfolds. Among the observers is the quarterback and all the players who have just collided along the line of scrimmage. Suddenly they disengage, turn, and anxiously watch the conclusion of the play a considerable distance away. Much the same occurs on a long field-goal attempt; the clash of opposing linemen, the liftoff and flight of the football heading toward distant crossbars. Eyes fix on the ball, then the goalpost, then the ball. Is it on target? Is it high enough? Is it about to hook? Does it have the distance? Is it fading? There is, strangely enough, time for all these questions. Even within the rapid-fire action setting of ice hockey such an abrupt suspension of time and space can develop. It occurs when the opposing goalie has been removed, and an empty net beckons. Suddenly, a shot is propelled across nearly the entire length of the rink toward the unattended goal. As it glides across the expanse of ice, eyes turn and minds calculate whether or not it is on target, a harmless miss or a goal—even as the puck is en route.[1]

With the phenomenon now understood, let us consider its presence within baseball. More than other sports, baseball is, in this connection, uncommonly generous, offering players and spectators many and varied occasions to observe this unusual conjunction of perception, prediction, and pseudo-participation. No doubt the enjoyment of the game derives, in part, from this largely unacknowledged fact.[2] Oddly enough, one notable instance occurs only on television. That is because coverage here offers a view of the game altogether unique. With cameras installed deep in center field, viewers are placed behind the pitcher and can observe close up as his ball heads plateward. No one in the ballpark has a comparable view. What TV viewers see is where and how the ball is proceeding. It's possible, therefore, to "call" the pitch with the ball in flight. So, on a 3 and 2 count watching the pitched ball streak toward a point out of the strike zone ignites a spark of hope if, for example, one's team is in desperate need of a base runner. But the play isn't over. The batter may nevertheless misjudge its location, be determined to swing, or the pitch may, at the last moment, dip through the strike zone. Early promise has given way to disappointment, all in less than a second.

To play the outfield in the major leagues, one needs projection skills of the highest order. The instant after the ball has been propelled aloft by the batter, the outfielder must get a fix on its flight pattern and project a landing area, which hopefully he can reach in time to make the catch. It is a remarkable skill usually performed flawlessly, despite the extended territorial responsibility of outfielders. Often a base runner must be equally adept at this kind of depth perception

187

and projection if he wishes to take full advantage of a base hit. What he must do, even as the ball is still in flight over the infield, is to project where it will come down, and decide instantly whether or not it can be caught. This is an exceptional talent, especially since the runner is himself in motion and concerned with other matters as well. Most of the time they prove to be accurate forecasters, sometimes just barely so, as the ball hits the ground within a few feet of an oncoming fielder.

Few calculations need be quite as precise as those made by a runner leading off first with the intent to steal. He must determine just how quickly the pitcher is able to rifle the ball over to first and judge how far off the base he can stray and still return safely. Few contests are as keen as are those conducted by pitchers and aggressive runners. Our unique perspective develops when the pitcher whirls and throws to first just as the runner turns, and in full flight retreats toward the bag. The umpire watches this convergence of ball and runner. The throw is quick and seems likely to arrive ahead of the runner, a pick-off in the offing. The crowd leaps to its feet, anticipating the out call. But the play's conclusion betrays the projection as the first baseman's sweep tag misses the runner, who dives back safely in a cloud of dust.

In a related play, the runner on first bolts in an attempt to steal second just as the pitcher releases the ball toward the plate. What follows ranks among the more exciting action sequences in the game. The catcher snags the ball, leaps to his feet, cocks his arm, and rifles the ball toward second, toward which the runner is sprinting. The issue is in doubt; the runner is almost at second, but the ball is traveling rapidly. At this point, the mind's eye foresees a tie. So it is, except that the runner slides beyond the bag and is tagged out.

A series of throws and a runner in full stride are the central elements in this next scenario, one of the most aesthetically satisfying action sequences in baseball. Here, the runner is attempting to score from first base on a distant hit to the outfield. When the ball finally is recovered, the base runner is halfway toward third. The outcome is at hand. The shortstop, having positioned himself to receive the throw from the centerfielder, is now prepared to relay it toward the plate. Meanwhile the runner is in the process of passing third base and is heading home. The eye catches the ball sailing over the infield and spots the base runner several strides from the plate. The ball flies fast and true; the runner labors, unable to generate a final burst of speed. Before it occurs, the result is in. As "predicted," the catcher is waiting with the ball, the runner beaten by two perfectly executed throws. In the 1992 National League Championship Series the winning run in the seventh game scored in much this way, with the Braves Sid Bream running hard to beat Barry Bonds' throw to the plate. With the ball in flight and Bream heading home, *New York Times* reporter Joe Sexton noted that, in that instant, "everyone now [became] an amateur physicist, tracking speeds and arcs."[3]

A bunt down the third-base line can produce, for the moment, one of the most distressingly inconclusive situations in the game. The vigil begins once the third baseman chooses not to field the ball, hoping instead that it will roll into foul territory. Attention focuses on the ball as it hops erratically toward third, alternately flirting with and backing away from the foul line. Closely watched though it is, predicting its final destination is difficult, so completely is it at the mercy of the subtle contours and occasional pebbles along its path. Still, one notices that ball speed is diminishing rapidly; it will soon be at rest, fair or foul.

Nowhere are sightings more common and suspenseful than when batters make contact and propel the ball on a long journey that will end beyond the playing field. Home run distance is not in doubt, but what is not clear is whether or not it will remain in fair territory. Attempts to extrapolate from the ball's current position are useful but not conclusive. What knowledgeable fan can ignore the fact that many balls hook while in midair and veer away from their initial flight paths? (There are some who may even believe that "body English" applied by the batter standing at home plate may alter the direction of the ball. Who can forget or doubt the utility of the heroic effort of Carleton Fisk of Boston, who in the ninth inning of the sixth World Series game against Cincinnati in 1975, twisted and pulled his body, seeming to urge the ball he hit to stay fair as it landed for a game-winning home run?) A well-hit drive straddling the foul line has all the fans in the ballpark rising to their feet, straining to observe the flight of the ball and, in the intervening second or two, depending upon their loyalties, projecting a fair or foul ball.[4]

Many other visual dramas could be discussed — Baltimore chops, Texas leaguers, infielders leaping high to snare line drives, and so on, but no further substantiation is necessary. More than any other sport, baseball has succeeded in generating a remarkable number of plays, that in a special sense, can be previewed by the spectators. Such recurring moments of scintillating suspense, when the outcome hangs in the balance, contribute in a way not fully recognized to the abiding popularity of the sport.[5]

TWENTY-TWO
Argument as Art Form

ARGUMENTS can be a most compelling form of interaction with the potential for marvelously exciting encounters. An exchange of conflicting points of view represents an intellectual exercise of the highest order, as ideas forcefully expressed are dispatched into battle, buttressed by the courage of conviction, and reinforced by a display of carefully marshalled facts. Upon encountering resistance and weighty defenses, first one side, then the other, must rethink its position, and assess its strengths, while exploiting the weaknesses of the opposition. Original thinking, illuminating evidence, penetrating questions—all come into play during the confrontation. Alas, in the real world such creative conflicts are rare. Most encounters deteriorate rapidly, are reduced to shapeless melees, overwhelmed by a barrage of clichés, arid debating points, and emotional appeals that defy facts and deny the opposition's credibility.

Is creative argumentation then a lost art, surviving only in the rarified hothouse environment of high school and college debating teams? If polite society has proscribed discussions of religion and politics (and probably race, sex, money, and illness as well), is there any room, any suitable subject left for serious debate? Fortunately, there is. Sports. At least among men, heated discussions about sports are perfectly acceptable, even admirable contests. They offer a welcome outlet for aggressive instincts otherwise threatening and disruptive. They provide opportunities for creative display, an arena for cerebral sparring otherwise suppressed by bureaucratic obfuscation, anti-intellectualism and other mind-numbing institutional restraints. And they serve as a vehicle for pointed, yet prolonged, exchanges with established references and shared vocabulary that cement relationships among otherwise isolated and socially inhibited males. Tens of millions of folks know their sports, have declared loyalties to specific teams, and feel some sense of commitment to defend their choices and convert others to their way of thinking. That arguments will flare up, and that worthy adversaries will lock horns, is then no surprise.

Sports arguments, even when partially frivolous or clouded over by an excess of beer or cocktails, contain an interior logic and forcefulness not always evident in other supposedly more serious debates ongoing in the society. Each side recognizes the need to be well-informed, attentive to nuance and false assumptions. Evidence must be presented, contrary facts explained, and authoritative texts such as record books, consulted. Both sides can be expected to be well-armed with facts and supporting statistics.[1] Arguments are often subtle and sophisticated, not unmindful of historical contingencies (before and after the shot clock appeared in basketball), shifting criteria (strikeouts were once deemed morally reprehensible), and the physical evolution of the athletes themselves (the consequence of weight training and developments in diet). There is little expectation of concession speeches or easy triumphs, rather the sense that the argument once joined will continue, that positions staked out will be developed over time with debating points scored here and there. Sports may well be one of the few remaining arenas in which to engage in non-ideological, serious, structured verbal encounters where there is mutual respect and tolerance, where the dialogue is passionate, pointed, and yet thoroughly enjoyable.

Debates are ongoing in most every sport, but nowhere do they appear as rich or as varied as in baseball. The game, by American standards, is ancient—well over a century old. Traditions abound, memories are full, the records bulge with information to be sorted and assimilated. In few other areas are past and present both joined in joyful celebration and locked in ongoing competition. Nowhere else does the past step forward so confidently to challenge the present, to provide such stunning benchmarks of performance, and raise questions about presumed progress. Baseball, moreover, is a game that appears accessible to its followers whether savvy or unsophisticated, and operates with a vocabulary largely familiar to all.[2] "Expert" opinions are not hard to come by. The game, moreover, is performed out "in the open." No tangle of bodies or complex team patterns operate to obscure the essential plays. "No game in the world," Paul Gallico once observed, "is as tidy and dramatically neat as baseball, with cause and effect, crime and punishment, motive and results so clearly defined."

That debate flourishes in baseball should be no surprise when one considers how well the game lends itself to talk. "The greatest conversation piece in America" was how historian Bruce Catton characterized baseball. With the game played at a pace ever so slow and deliberate, there is time for discussion, whether in the dugout, the grandstands, the den bench, or bar. "One of the chief duties of a fan," Robert Benchley once wrote, "is to engage in arguments with the man behind him." No other sport provides announcers with so much time or latitude to discuss developments and debate their merits, play by play. In no other sport do reporters spend so much time with players over so long a period. Faced with the challenge of producing newspaper and magazine copy and compelling sound bites day after day for months on end, is it any wonder reporters stir the pot and spark debates? In no other sport do they feel as empowered to raise questions and to ignite controversy.

True believer that he is, the baseball fan nevertheless, must on occasion, contend with those who are indifferent, or even hostile. Despite its standing as the national pastime, or perhaps because of it, a vocal minority exists who fearlessly call baseball before the bar of judgment, and declare it altogether unimpressive as a sport, undeserving of the adulation lavished upon it. It is, they contend, tiresome, ("Six minutes of action crammed into two and a half hours," according to one writer), dramatically deficient, and requiring performance skills not of the highest athletic order. Faced with such a challenge, some fans, mindful of baseball's broad popularity and indifferent to the value of converts, refuse to engage such doubters, but dismiss them as misguided, quite possibly misanthropic, assuredly unpatriotic. Most, however, will recognize that such dissenting views are not altogether bizarre, that baseball loyalists are obliged to defend their choice, and display patience with those whose background, temperament, or imagination has somehow limited their level of appreciation. The devoted fan also understands that baseball is accessible only at the most rudimentary level, that the richer rewards are reserved for those aware of the inner game. Surely it is, as Kenneth Turan observes, "a contemplative sport that delights in its nuances, not a brazen game eager to sell its thrills cheaply [but] an understated affair that must be courted if it is to be loved."[3] So the devoted fan is likely to respond to the snide remarks of skeptics, not in anger, but with compassion and a strong desire to share generously in the game's delights.

Overwhelmingly, baseball arguments involve not the skeptics, but the faithful, who are themselves divided over a variety of issues. As noted earlier, baseball's ties to the past are singularly strong, but that, in itself, creates a tension and an ongoing debate between past and present. The canonization of baseball past cannot help but generate controversy. Elevate baseball to landmark status, consider it as a symbol of an older, simpler, presumably more secure, confident society ("an island of surety in a changing world," as Bill Veeck once remarked), and the die is cast. Baseball then becomes not just a game, but a symbol, a yardstick with which to measure and evaluate the contemporary scene. In the "good old days, we are reminded, lofty and uncompromising standards were maintained. Baseball players displayed more intensity and loyalty, were impervious to pain, unmindful of self, astute students of the game, and even more colorful. They played smart, they played hurt, they played hard, they played without complaint, even for pennies. The message is clear: today's athletes don't measure up in this regard. There are the occasional throwbacks, of course, the intense, scrappy, nonconforming types, the likes of Lenny Dykstra, Wally Backman, John Kruk, and Kirby Puckett, but these are exceptions clearly out of step with their contemporaries. Listen in on such debate, and invariably it will produce an argument about whether today's players can measure up out on the field. Surely they are better trained, more thoroughly conditioned and equipped, with gloves that can envelop impressive amounts of space, but why can't they bunt as adroitly as once they did, and why are those base-running skills so obviously deficient, and starting pitchers so eager to depart from the game? Why can't pitchers hold runners on, or catchers throw them out with any degree of consistency? Hitters appear as menacing as ever, but why do they now complain so bitterly at pitches that brush them back, or strike out with such complacence and unparalleled regularity? To all these questions there are, if not final answers, credible explanations, but there is no end to the debate. Ever elusive and inconclusive are comparisons between past and present, obscured by faulty memories, altered circumstances, emotional predispositions, and weighted down by unspoken assumptions.[4]

Competitive athletes always produce winners and losers, outstanding performers and performances, record-setting and record-breaking occasions. Stars emerge, winning teams are hailed, new and higher levels of accomplishment attained, all of which give rise to endless debates, to a relentless quest to define, identify, and relish the ultimate performance, the never-to-be-forgotten moment, the once-in-a-lifetime contest. The search for the superlative, a quintessentially human endeavor, is a special feature of athletics, where winners are identifiable, accomplishments closely measured, and where virtually all activities are subject to intense scrutiny. Nowhere is this more evident than in baseball where the cast of characters is huge, the traditions rich, and the fans ever eager to advocate for their favorites. Wasn't Babe Ruth the greatest player of them all? Who can dispute the fact that the 1927 Yankees were the most formidable team ever assembled? No one, absolutely no one, will compile a pitching record comparable to Cy Young. The victory of the New York Giants in the 1951 National League pennant race must stand as the greatest late-season comeback in history. No one will ever surpass the remarkable record of Lou Gehrig's consecutive game streak. There's no denying that what Joe DiMaggio accomplished in 1941—batting safely in fifty-six consecutive games—is the single most formidable hitting achievement in all of baseball history. As for the most dramatic moment in baseball history—what's to compare with Bobby Thomson's ninth-inning homerun in the 1951 playoffs? There will be strong support for all these assertions, but the naysayers will be ever numerous, insisting always that their choices must be given respectful attention. And they will come prepared with artful explanations, astute analyses, and calculated statistics to support their particular causes. Circumstances must be more clearly scrutinized, the level of competition evaluated, ballpark conditions assessed, the state of the game then explored, and the role of the press understood, before one is able to reach reasonable conclusions.

Who would you want on your team, a Rickey Henderson or a Kirby Puckett, a Willie Mays or a Duke Snider, a Jackie Robinson or a Ryne Sandberg, a Nolan Ryan or a Whitey Ford? Has anyone ever played shortstop more expertly than Ozzie Smith, been a better third baseman than Mike Schmidt, or a more accomplished catcher than Johnny Bench? We here enter upon slippery terrain colored by childhood memory, legendary tales, hometown loyalties, the variable engines of publicity, and a vast array of statistical information susceptible to different interpretations. Fans must, in these instances, rise to the top of their analytical skills to win their arguments. They will patiently explain how an otherwise almost flawless fielding record obscures the fact that the player under discussion too often failed to get to the ball or settled for the safe play. A batter's .343 season average, at first glance, is impressive, but observe an anemic RBI total and a notable failure to deliver in crucial late inning situations. Doc Gooden's record in 1990 shouldn't be dismissed, but bear in mind the Mets scored more runs for him than they did for any other pitcher on the staff—indeed more than any team supported any other pitcher in the National League.[5] No doubt Jack Clark could once deliver the long ball in crucial late-inning situations, but he struck out with disturbing frequency and was not much of a catalyst in the clubhouse. Who is to be preferred, a team-oriented spark plug with average skills, or a self-absorbed player with considerably more talent but only occasional performance? Do you select the workhorse pitcher who will be credited with two hundred plus innings each year, or the occasionally brilliant southpaw who seems little inclined to go beyond five innings at each outing? The speedster or the slugger, the brilliant relief pitcher or the reliable starter, the sensational rookie or the reliable veteran, the clutch hitter or the flawless fielder—such choices are not easy, and were not meant to be. Instead, they serve as a starting point for spirited and heated debate among fans who will be tested to the limit as they go to bat for their favorites.

The matter of relative evaluation is not just an irresistible topic for ongoing debate; it can become a serious issue requiring crucial decision making when a matter of a trade is proposed. No other subject, excepting that of actual game performance and outcome, so captures the attention of fans as trades. Listen to any sports talk show, and expect to hear deals of every imaginable sort and of startling complexity being proposed by fans as quick remedies to existing deficiencies, or as a means of bolstering their teams as a pennant race heats up. Many are mindless journeys into the implausible and unreal, fantasy adventures that reveal only the depth of fan loyalty and their urgent need to contribute to their team's success. But amidst some of the surreal swapping are sensible suggestions—deals that could be done. Proposing "real life" trades is a delicate and demanding enterprise open to serious differences of opinion and subject to sharp debate. Is the player past his prime? Was last year's performance indicative of his talent or a "career year" unlikely to recur? How wise is it to pay top dollar for an injury-prone player one year before he becomes eligible for free agency? How will team chemistry be affected by acquiring a player known for his occasional moodiness? Is the organization sacrificing too much by including two top prospects in Triple A to make the deal? Clearly, strong differences of opinion will surface once the trade winds blow and rumors of impending deals circulate. And then, after the deal is done, there is the inevitable second-guessing, the rush to judgment as to which side benefitted the most. Few question the fact that Cincinnati's trading of Lee May and Tommy Helms for Houston's Joe Morgan was a pivotal move in fashioning the "Big Red Machine" in the 1970s. It is generally accepted that the Mets after trading Calvin Schiraldi and others to Boston for a number of players, including Bobby Ojeda in 1985, set the stage for the pennant and World Series victory the following year. But what of so many others, where high hopes soon faded, where expected contributions never materialized?

Baseball fans are prone to argue and debate whenever the occasion presents itself. The most likely situation, however, is when they're at the ballpark or at home watching a game in the company of other devotees. The game's slow, deliberate pace, the frequent intervals between plays, and the multitude of tactical options available offer exceptional opportunities for speculation, argumentation, and self-assured second-guessing. Only the most exhaustive of lists could encompass the range of issues likely to be on the agenda. With the pitcher indisputably wild, should the batter wait out the walk or swing, on the likely assumption a fat pitch will be next? Should the right-handed hitter try to pull the ball, which is no doubt his strength, or attempt to advance the runner from first by making sure he directs the ball to the right side? Is it worth "wasting" a pitch on an 0-2 count with a runner on third, and running the risk of a wild pitch or passed ball? Are the runners, bouncing off the bases with every pitch, disrupting the pitcher as much as they are unsettling the batter? Do you throw on through to second base when you suspect the speedy runner on third will attempt to dash home on a double steal? Is the pitcher running out of gas? Should he be removed or should one wait until he gets into trouble? A fly ball is vital. Who should be the pinch hitter? In almost every late inning of the game there are choices to be made, different tactics to consider. How many fans can avoid arguments when those around them dispute their wisdom and offer unsolicited judgments about what needs to be done? What fan sits comfortably, silently, and lets a manager pull the strings without offering him advice, without taking issue when his suggestions are not "accepted"?

Repeated failure, a string of losses, a disappointing season brings with it a growing restiveness among the team's fans. And soon enough, debate begins, initiated most commonly by the local media and the beat reporters. To what degree is the manager responsible for the team's sub-par performance? Has he lost the confidence of the team and its owners? Must he go? Fans relish such situations and the opportunity to participate in this great public debate. Surely this is a critical juncture for the team? No doubt fan sentiment will be taken into account before there's a final decision? Debate rages, sides are taken, arguments presented. Can he be held accountable for the injuries that plagued the team during the season? But did he not lose the confidence of his players, especially the younger ones, whom he seemed unable to motivate? His bullpen-by-committee tactic seems suspect. He should have instead developed a reliable "setup" man and "closer." He relied too heavily on the long ball and the big inning, and didn't get the team running as it should. But he's always been a winning manager. The team requires stability, not a managerial revolving door. But it needs to be shaken up; there is entirely too much complacency. Back and forth goes the debate; the manager's fate hanging in the balance. All of this is sadly familiar to men like Bucky Dent, Davey Johnson, Jimy Williams, John McNamara, Larry Bowa, Pat Corrales, Nick Leyva, Don Zimmer, Buck Rodgers, Doug Rader, Doc Edwards, Joe Morgan, Bud Harrelson, Frank Robinson, Jim Lefebvre, and many others, all of whom in recent years have stood by as the storm swirled about them. In the end, these managers were swept away by the rising tide of negative sentiment.[6]

Observers often lament the fact that far too many Americans relate to sports as spectators, that their presumed distance and passivity is evidence of a disturbing failure of energy and involvement. The foregoing discussion suggests the limits of such a view. Baseball fans may be sitting in the grandstands or watching on TV, but they are very much in the game, energetically arguing, competing like their heroes out on the field, struggling valiantly to win.

TWENTY-THREE

Innocence as Salvation (Spring, 1993)

FOLLOWERS OF THE GAME still look for it, celebrate it, re-gard it as a source of reassurance. So long as baseball remains mindful of this tradition, they say, so long as there is exuber-ance and joy on the field, all is not lost. Fortunately, such innocence endures; evidence is not lacking.

It may appear in spring training. The pre-season training activities of no other sport attract as much attention or elicit as much enthusi-asm. What else would explain the fact that two seasoned veterans, Doc Gooden and Bret Saberhagen, whose jobs were in every way secure for the 1993 season, were still unable to sleep the night before pitchers were due to report to the Mets' Florida training camp? And this was only February! Each awakened by 5:30 A.M., and Saberhagen even ad-mitted sheepishly that he beat the clubhouse attendant to work. Not long afterwards, Mets rookie Mike Draper fell for one of the oldest of baseball pranks and ended up being doused by an assortment of vile liquids poured all over his body by gleefully triumphant team-mates. Perhaps unwittingly, Mets manager Jeff Torborg sounded a fa-miliar note when he discussed his pre-season tinkering with the Mets' batting order. "I don't have an overwhelming basis in statistics for do-ing it this way," he admitted, "I just have a strong feeling in my bones."[1] That "strong feeling" certainly must have cheered many a traditionalist.

It seemed like old times when excitement and overflow crowds gathered to watch the Florida Marlins and Colorado Rockies launch their maiden seasons as major-league franchises. When fans at Mile High Stadium roared in appreciation of a successful sacrifice bunt by the home team during a game in the middle of April, one could take heart in how well these new "unsophisticated" fans had already come to appreciate the "fundamentals." Across baseball there was admira-tion for teams like the Cleveland Indians—with young ballplayers and modest payrolls, they nevertheless performed with zest; there was also a grudging respect for the Pirates, where talented rookies had broken into the Pittsburgh lineup to replace veteran stars who had flown away to snatch lucrative contracts elsewhere. Baseball welcomed a bumper crop of promising rookies; the *Sporting News* called it a "Season of Hope," in reference to the young players.[2] All the same time, however, fans celebrated the aging but spry cadre of veterans—Nolan Ryan, Charlie Hough, Dave Winfield, Kirk Gibson, George Brett, Andre Dawson, Fernando Valenzuela, and Carlton Fisk, whose very names evoked past glories and baseball at its best. This likewise brought to mind those stalwarts of the game who had, over the years, remained steadfastly loyal to their teams and so had come to symbolize a welcome stability and commitment. While vast numbers had wandered city to city, from team to team, Robin Yount, Don Mattingly, Doc Gooden, Roger Clemens, Kirby Puckett, Cal Ripkin and others had put down roots, remained true to one town and one team, rejecting the merry-go-round of baseball.

Innocence, tradition and stability, alas, was not the only story (indeed had never been, as we have seen), the sole theme, or the defining characteristic of the game. Innovation, complexity, materialism, shifting standards, and cynicism had ever proceeded hand in hand, had always complemented the more publicized and sentimentalized elements of baseball. And so it is today. Expect, we are told, a new round of playoffs to be introduced to determine entry into the World Series. Observe as recommendations flow in from any number of sources to hasten baseball's leisurely pace, that is, to shorten the game. Accept the fact that interest in Rotisserie baseball continues to soar while statistical services to satisfy the new breed of baseball fans flourish. Is Rotisserie baseball a boon to the sport, or will its focus on individual players (detached from existing teams) undermine traditional loyalties? Meanwhile baseball shows abound, and baseball cards and assorted memorabilia continue to attract legions of collectors and investors. Is there any time left or interest in watching a ballgame or in heading out to the ballpark? Can the game compete with all this clutter and commercialism? Has its principal function become one of supporting and justifying all this extraneous activity and profiteering? Indeed have the sentimentalists become the problem? Andy MacPhail, Minnesota Twins general manager, seemed to imply so when commenting on the type of baseball commissioner best suited to replace the deposed Fay Vincent. "We need," he said, "someone who understands the long-term problems of the game rather than someone who has just fallen in love with baseball who can wax poetically on it."[3]

The continued tension within baseball between simplicity and complexity, between innocence and innovation, would not be in the least worrisome had not the argument been joined lately by those who have declared the game to be deeply troubled, plagued by a plethora of problems that threaten to undermine its credibility, cast doubt on its continued popularity, indeed endanger its standing as the national pastime. These critics (more in sorrow than in anger) have focused on those elements of complexity to demonstrate that the game has somehow lost its moorings and its innocence. They have, moreover, added an additional layer of "problems" that, they suggest, could signal the "downsizing" of baseball in the public's estimation. Charges of racism continue to echo through major-league baseball even while Cincinnati's Marge Schott sits out her suspension. Despite long-standing criticisms and promises to correct imbalances, few teams have made significant changes in their off-field hiring practices. Instead, baseball's magnates remain ever inept at cultivating good will, their bickering, power plays, and overt hostility to the players suggesting how ill equipped they are to tackle the pressing problems. And these problems, it is said, can only intensify as the economics of the sport shift ominously. Large market teams threaten to swamp those operating in smaller economic arenas, while rising ticket prices and food costs threaten to limit family outings to the ballparks. Television contracts soon to expire will put an end, most everyone predicts, to the flush times that fueled baseball's reckless spending. How then will teams be able to meet the demands of players and their agents who insist upon guaranteed long-term contracts and levels of compensation that are, by all reckoning, monumental? And hanging over the entire scene threatening, some would suggest, the very edifices of the game, is the possibility Congress might at some time see fit to remove baseball's long-standing anti-trust exemption.

Somehow opinion makers and shapers have decided, almost in unison, that the correct view to take of baseball at the moment is gloomy. So the ever-present sportswriter John Feinstein publishes *Play Ball: The Life and Troubled Times of Major League Baseball*, while a related theme is pursued in yet another book, *Coming Apart at the*

Seams.[4] *Time* magazine suggests 1993 will mark "The Last Great Season," while the Public Broadcasting System distributes to member stations a documentary entitled "The Trouble with Baseball." Predictably, all offer a multi-count indictment, including a list of on-field deficiencies along with numerous delinquencies attributable to team owners and management. The talent, we hear, is increasingly diluted; pitching staffs are distressingly thin (with too few traditional fastballers at work in the majors); the players, though rewarded to excess, are grumpy; and the games are unacceptably lengthy. Others cite a "badly managed industry" led by narrow-minded owners pursuing baseball's equivalent of voodoo economics, devising all manner of expansion and realignment schemes, all the while unable to act in concert in the best interests of the game. No one is yet predicting baseball will go the way of IBM, *Life* magazine, or the American steel industry, but neither is there any assurance that next time the Japanese will purchase not a team but a league.

Is there an answer? Across many parts of the world the answer being offered to rapid modernization and commercialization and to complex changes has been a return to basics. Fundamentalism. So it is in baseball, with many urging a return to a past where it is presumed team loyalty, unspoiled, hard-nosed ballplayers, grass, day games, and cozy stadiums of human scale and interest combined to create the "good old days." But even those advocates probably understand that such longings cannot be satisfied and that such sentimentalism may even hinder sensible approaches to current problems. To one thoughtful writer "the past is quickly becoming an encumbrance," while "a rearguard approach to reinstating baseball's glory days" has become "untenable."[5] Actually the answer commonly given from fans and followers alike does involve a return to "basics," to common sense, to the game itself. "Come on folks," writes Dave Kindred of the *Sporting News.* "This is silly. All this moaning. All this doomsaying by the media. It's plain silly. You'd think baseball is on its deathbed." Another observer suggests that all the sound and fury will hardly shake the foundations of baseball. "Its perfect symmetry shall endure, its sounds and smells won't perish, and all the beasts in the world can't ruin the beauty of a green diamond."[6] What so many seem to be saying is that the remedy is to be sought in the game itself—in the multiplicity of skills it requires, in its leisurely pace that encourages involvement, conversation and analysis, in the exquisite drama it orchestrates so expertly. The answers will be found in a marvelously executed double play, in a majestic game-winning home run, in a pitcher extricating himself from a bases-loaded-no-out situation, in a pick off, a suicide squeeze, in a no-hitter in the eighth inning. "The game," explains Tim McCarver, "has its own way of expunging the toxins." "Forget the despairing of the game and all those extraneous things," adds sportswriter Roger Kahn. "People love the game. The magnificence of the sport—that's what saves it." "The game itself is stable, the game is solid, the game is good," says Jim Leyland. "Always has been and always will be."[7]

The 1993 baseball season saw record attendance figures and exciting pennant races in all four divisions. It was, according to one sportswriter, "one of baseball's greatest" seasons. Despite the predictions of experts, the gloom had lifted. A sport, supposedly ailing, suddenly seemed remarkably robust, once more full of life. And the innocence remained. The season ended dramatically when Joe Carter's ninth-inning home run made the Toronto Blue Jays world champions once more. As the ball settled into the outfield stands, Carter clapped his hands repeatedly and jumped for joy. In an instant, he was a little boy once more, his face beaming, his arms whirling about in triumph. As he rounded the bases, his teammates dashed onto the field and threw themselves atop one another, a joyous, exuberant ritual of elation and innocence. "I feel like a kid again," Carter declared, adding, "Well, baseball's a kid's game." And so it is, and so it must remain.

Notes

Introduction

1. *New York Review of Books,* Oct. 5, 1992, p. 42; Wilfred Sheed, *Baseball and Lesser Sports* (New York: Harper Collins, 1991), p. 7.
2. *Sporting News,* May 11, 1992.

1. Passion for the Past

1. *New York Times Magazine,* Mar. 8, 1992, p. 43. It is incontestably the oldest of the major American team sports with researchers busily at work documenting its early nineteenth-century origins. "No sport," George Will observes, "matches baseball's passion for its past." "Baseball," sports writer Rick Lawes adds, "is defined by its past." "For every step into the future," says writer Richard Firstman, "there is a cry for the past." George Will, *Men at Work,* (New York: Macmillan, 1992), p. 294; *Baseball Weekly,* Apr. 12–18, 1991; *Newsday,* June 11, 1989.

2. For a contrary view expressed in the early days of the sport, consider Mark Twain on the meaning of baseball. In an 1889 speech he referred to the game as "the very symbol, the outward and visible expression of the drives, and push and rush and struggle of the raging, tearing, booming nineteenth century." For many, baseball's ills mirror the malaise within contemporary society: inflated salaries, lackadaisical players, the retreat from fundamentals, the frequency with which players strike out, and so on. All are cited to demonstrate just how pervasive is the spiral of decline in America. *Newsday,* Apr. 7, 1991; Will, *Men at Work,* p. 296; *Newsday,* Oct. 19, 1990.

3. *New York Times Magazine,* Sept. 4, 1988, p. 3; Wilfred Sheed, *Baseball and Lesser Sports* (New York: Harper Collins, 1991), p. 11; Ralph Schoenstein, *Diamonds for Lori and Me,* (New York: Beach Tree Books, 1988), p. 11.

4. One company (there are others), Ebbets Field Flannels of Seattle, Washington, "purveyors of historic baseball apparel," capitalizes on this interest and offers fans "authentic reproductions of wool jerseys, jackets, caps and sweaters from the Minor, Negro and Federal leagues 1900–1965." SportsChannel in New York City features throughout the fall and winter months telecasts of the greatest games in baseball history. In December of 1991, WKNR-AM in

Cleveland rebroadcast the 1948 World Series, an upbeat holiday treat for Cleveland fans, for 1948 marked the last time the Indians had won the World Series.

5. What better example than to see fans across the nation donning replicas of uniforms from the early days of baseball and reenacting the game with the rules that were once in force. In 1992, Montreal's Delino DeShields wore his socks high, tucked under his pants just below the knees, a reminder of the old Negro leagues. "Never mind how it looked," he declared. "A sense of history is always in style." *Sporting News,* April 13, 1992.

    Baseball also maintains its past connection in a manner quite concrete. It leads all other sports in bringing former players into the managerial and coaching ranks. For example, during the 1991 season, nineteen of twenty-six managers, or 73 percent, were once major-leaguers.

6. Past stars are also offered special recognition by their own teams when their numbers are "retired" and then displayed at the ballpark. Baseball was the first sport to retire numbers, thereby creating, in miniature, a local version of the game's Hall of Fame.

7. Baseball Weekly, Apr. 12–18, 1991; Jack Lessenberry, "A Game for All America," *Michigan Alumnus,* Mar.-Apr., 1992, p. 22. *New York Times,* Oct. 10, 1992.

8. So vast a field is baseball's past, and for some so alluring that research ventures of all kinds find willing practitioners. Baseball historian Herman Kraffenhaft, for example, undertook to investigate the frequency of ultimate sudden-death home runs which he defined as "multiple-run, extra-inning, come-from-behind, game-ending home runs." Near the end of 1991 he had, after poring over mountains of baseball records, concluded that ninety-three such home runs had occurred since 1901. *Sporting News,* Aug. 26, 1991, p. 4.

9. Roger Angell, "Homeric Tales," *The New Yorker* 67 (May 27, 1991), p. 80.

10. When in 1991, Devon White struck out four times against Roger Clemens, announcer Gary Thorne, without a moment's hesitation, informed viewers that the strikeout record for a player in a game was six, and that occurred first seventy-eight years ago in 1913—an acute sense of historical awareness.

11. That Mickey Mantle is today somewhat bemused (albeit delighted) over the fact that he can earn more money over a weekend of autograph sessions (upwards of sixty thousand dollars) than he made in his early years of playing baseball is not surprising. *Forbes Magazine* reported that in the 1991–92 off-season, Nolan Ryan signed ninety thousand baseballs, photos, and posters at twenty dollars for each signature. Fans are quite aware that a booming

market exists for all manner of baseball artifacts. On May 9, 1992, Montreal rookie Archi Cianfracco hit his first major-league home run. When he attempted to retrieve the ball, he encountered resistance. The fan who caught it, aware of its potential value, would not surrender the ball unless he received something of value in return—in this instance, an autographed bat. In the end a deal was struck. Earlier in the season, Eric Karros of the Los Angeles Dodgers also hit his first major league home run in his first at bat of the season. The fan who caught it refused to surrender the prize, held it for ransom demanding that it be exchanged for two baseballs autographed by Karros and Dodger star Darryl Strawberry. His demands were met by Karros. *Sporting News*, April 20, 1992. *Baseball Weekly*, April 22–28, 1992.

12. *Newsday*, July 14, 1991. Accordingly, many newspapers across the United States during the season feature a column that recalls "this day in baseball" and highlights memorable events and personalities from the past. In 1991, New York City newspapers daily recounted the performance of Joe DiMaggio during his memorable fifty-six–game hitting streak in 1941. They also followed the New York Giants and recounted the miracle finish of 1951, culminating in Bobby Thomson's "shot heard 'round the world" to defeat the Dodgers in the third game of the playoffs.

13. See Lawrence Ritter's *Lost Ballparks: Fond Remembrances of Baseball's Legendary Fields* (New York: Viking, 1992) for a nostalgic look at 22 classic ballparks; also see Philip Lowry's *Green Cathedrals* (Reading, Mass.: Addison-Wesley, 1992) for a review of 271 major- and Negro-league ballparks. Baltimore's Camden Yards does represent a ray of hope for the future, as do plans for the Indians' new home.

14. A word of caution here, for George Will reminds us that "it is an old baseball tradition, complaining about the character and quality of contemporary players." "These modern ballplayers care about nothing but money. They don't care about their teams, or their city or their fans. In my day they were different." These are the words of a former player speaking in 1868!

More troubling is the fact that many of today's younger players admit to little knowledge of the old-time heroes and legends of baseball, and represent, for that reason, a threat to the kind of continuity and commitment to the past that for so long has characterized the game. "Players don't want to hear about the old days," says San Francisco manager Roger Craig. Younger players, according to sports writer Peter Gammons, "don't have as much respect for the game." *USA Today*, July 6, 1991; Roger Craig, interview on ESPN, July 21, 1991.

15. *Sporting News*, Aug. 12, 1991.

16. *USA Today,* July 10, 1991.

17. For a typical rejoinder, listen to Len Dykstra. "I don't want to get on the old-timers. I mean I get a kick out of listening to them tell stories. But they could never do what they did then now. The pitching is better. The defense is better—way better. It used to be if the count was 2 and 0, you got cheese. They didn't have forkballs or sliders. They left their starters in the game for the duration. Now they bring in a $2 million relief pitcher to get you out with gas." And then there is Cubs general manager Charley Frey to remind us that "a lot of older guys would like to have us believe everybody used to be a hustler, used to be a team man, to play hard and play smart. That's just not so. We had our share of lazy, dumb careless players back then too." *Sporting News,* June 13, 1990; *Ibid.,* Sept. 3, 1990.

18. One exercise traditionalists delight in is that which attempts to project the salaries past stars would have made in today's inflated-salary world. Implicit here is the notion of lost opportunity and the assumption that with less money in the game, baseball then was, in some sense, more innocent and purer. One recent study by two economists at the University of Dayton evaluated 250 former stars, and among other conclusions revealed that Lou Gehrig would be drawing an annual salary of $7.83 million, Babe Ruth $7.49 million, Walter Johnson $7.51 million, and Mickey Mantle $4.83 million—in short, that they would be worth more than most of the contemporary ballplayers. The *New York Times,* April 7, 1991, reported a revealing conversation several reporters had with Willie Mays.

    "If you were playing now," [someone] asked, "how much money do you think you'd be making?"

    "I never think about that," Mays said. "Doesn't do me any good to think about that."

    "Maybe $6 million a year," somebody suggested.

    "Only $6 million!" Mays said, his voice rising. "If a pitcher can make $5 million just starting every fifth day. I'm playing 154 games and I'm only getting $6 million!"

    "I thought you didn't think about it," somebody said.

    "Since you brought it up," Willie Mays said, "Let's talk about it."

    "In today's market his contract negotiations would start at $10 million." *USA Today,* July 10, 1991.

2. True to Life

1. Thomas Boswell, *Why Time Begins on Opening Day,* (Garden City, N.Y.: Doubleday, 1984), p. 61.

2. Observe the rookie pitcher making his major-league debut nearly incapacitated by the jitters during that first day on the job, an experience almost everyone has endured. Is the hitter increasingly exasperated awaiting a pitcher's next delivery much different from a shopper grown impatient with the lack of service? What of the pitching coach out on the mound attempting to reassure and assist a struggling pitcher much as a classroom teacher seeks to explain a lesson to a puzzled student? Many such obvious connections exist but our discussion will consider broader parallels.

3. And as the "heavyset" Chicago Cub Hector Villanueva wryly noted, when he hit home runs, invariably he would be described as strong, whereas striking out led writers to see him as "fat"! *Chicago Tribune,* Sept. 8, 1988; *Sporting News,* May 25, 1992.

4. And true to life, baseball players seem at least as prone to freak accidents as the rest of us—maybe even more susceptible. It would seem so from the following very partial accident record gleaned from the last several years:

Player	Injury	Circumstances
Reuben Sierra	sprained ankle	helping daughter onto an escalator
Chuck Finley	sprained ankle	walking to a restaurant for lunch
Cecil Fielder	sprained ankle	slipped getting out of bed
Mike Heath	cut finger	slammed medical case on finger after striking out
Kevin Elster	back	getting up from watching television
Kevin Brown	bruised hip	slipped in hallway at Baltimore's Memorial Stadium
Glenallen Hill	cut feet and elbow	sleepwalking fall
John Smiley	broken finger	slammed taxi door on hand
Dwight Gooden	sprained ankle	teammate Mackey Sasser moved chair on top of foot
Nolan Ryan	sore thumb	slammed by taxi door
John Franco	tender hamstring	slipped on ice
Jim Essian	broken toe	walking in dark hotel room
Carney Lansford	knee injury	snowmobile accident
Bob Ojeda	severed finger	hedge clipper accident
Kent Hrbek	fractured bone in foot	chasing clubhouse attendant through locker room
Jody Reed	pulled groin muscle	stepped on water sprinkler

Kevin Wickander	fractured bone in arm	caught spikes in concrete at Anaheim Stadium
Jimmy Key	broken ankle	jumped off collapsing ladder
Tony Gwynn	broken finger	caught it in car door
Jesse Barfield	broken finger	fell in sauna at home.

5. *New York Times,* Mar. 25, 1990. Baseball players are just your average guys except that a disproportionate number are left-handed. Whereas approximately 10 percent of the general population are lefties, baseball boasts a much higher percentage of left-handed ballplayers. And, whereas lefties encounter discrimination out in the general society, in baseball, where they enjoy distinct advantages, they are valued highly and come at a premium, especially left-handed pitchers. In 1991, over 30 percent of major-league pitchers were southpaws!

6. Boswell, *Why Time Begins,* p. 298.

7. One might even go so far as to call this the "winter league" as teams are judged and then ranked by fans and sports writers alike based on whether they have strengthened or weakened themselves subsequent to the shuffling and reshuffling among squads that has occurred. ("People can't keep up with who's on what team anymore," says George Brett.) *Baseball Weekly,* Apr. 8–14, 1992.

8. Newsday, June 26, 1991.

9. New York Times, Aug. 15, 1988.

10. "Baseball's a routine game," says Tim McCarver, and he's right. In a given day, most people go through the same motions they've performed countless times before. Predictable patterns allow for few surprises. A baseball game can be much the same, most plays requiring an easy, almost automatic repetition of tried-and-true maneuvers. Often the game will hinge on the outcome of the one or two nonroutine, unique situations that arise. Comment on CBS television broadcast, Oct. 2, 1991.

11. Roger Angell, *Late Innings,* (New York: Ballantine, 1988), p. 331.

12. The presence of a dominating pitcher is but the most obvious situation of helplessness present within the game. A batter who has just hit a pop fly into foul territory stands helplessly at the plate awaiting the play's inevitable conclusion. He can do absolutely nothing other than watch as he is retired. A player caught in a rundown is literally a condemned man with little hope of reprieve. He may scramble around for a time, but his fate is essentially sealed. A runner picked off base is largely helpless and will, in all likelihood,

be tagged out. An infielder can do nothing but wait as a "Baltimore Chop" takes flight over the field and the batter scampers to first safely. An outfielder watches helplessly, may indeed not even move as a ball sails over the fence well beyond reach, or he can only catch the ball but is positioned too deep to challenge the runner who has tagged up at third and headed home. A hitter eager to take his turn at bat in a critical situation can do nothing if the pitcher decides on an intentional walk. With the ball still in the outfield, a catcher stands by home plate, hands by his sides, unable to respond as the opposing runner dashes toward the plate. Like the rest of us, baseball players sometimes encounter situations in which they become essentially bystanders, uninvolved and powerless.

13. *Sporting News,* Nov. 6, 1989.

14. Angell, "Homeric Tales," *The New Yorker* 67 (May 27, 1991), p. 22. Some ballplayers are even frustrated in their sleep. Mike Schmidt when he was playing, for example, reported on two recurring dreams. In one, though he was in uniform, he was unable to get into the game. In the other, he couldn't find his shoes. "I couldn't get on the field. There was always something I couldn't find. It's a lot like life." *Newsday,* May 27, 1990. Failure also comes into play when considering the odds against an individual advancing out of the minors to the major leagues. Despite the received wisdom about mobility in America and rags-to-riches success stories, in truth, the overwhelming number of minor-league ballplayers are destined to labor for years on end, like most folks, in unrelieved obscurity, waiting in vain for the big break.

15. Quoted in Will, *Men at Work,* p. 75.

16. One is often unaware of the number of obstructions on or above a baseball field. On opening day in 1988, Darryl Strawberry hit an extension of the roof at Montreal. The next year Dave Valle hit a ball at the King Dome that was headed for the left centerfield stands when it hit a speaker suspended from the ceiling, 132 feet above the field. (Of course, the all time bizarre in-flight incident occurred on April 12, 1987, at Shea Stadium when a flyball by Dion James hit and killed a dove, then fell in front of Kevin McReynolds for a double.) On the field itself, rolled up tarpaulins occasionally obstruct fielders chasing down balls in foul territory, as do pitchers' mounds in the bullpens, some located just off the foul lines. Then there are railings that jut out and photographer areas that cut off portions of the field of play. And of course there's the ivy-covered wall at Wrigley Field—but who would dare question this national treasure? In a 1991 game between Detroit and Texas, the Rangers' Julio Franco hit a ground ball toward short where Alan Trammell prepared

to make the play. But perched in front of Trammell were four pigeons who flew up as the ball approached, causing the shortstop to misplay the ball. Playing the field does have its surprises.

17. Consider them "designer fields" when baseball unabashedly allows teams to refashion stadiums to suit themselves. In baseball's version of affirmative action, teams deliberately alter playing dimensions to favor their own and reflect their particular strengths and weaknesses. If, for example, they've acquired two left-handed long-ball hitters, the right-field fence may be shortened to increase home run totals. If, on the other hand, their pitching staff yields an excess of home runs, they may choose to move the walls back, thus reducing home run production. Considerable effort goes into making ballparks user-friendly for home teams.

18. Here's shortstop Dale Sveum on field conditions at Milwaukee's County Stadium some years ago. "Everybody knows it's the worst field in baseball. I can understand the infield dirt being bumpy, but it's pretty bad when you can drive down the street and see lawns that are in better shape than our outfield." Before Terry Pendleton and Sid Bream would agree to play for Atlanta in 1991, the Braves had to assure them that the condition of the playing field at Fulton County Stadium would be improved. *Los Angeles Times,* May 8, 1988; *Baseball Weekly,* Apr. 12–18, 1991. Much talk lately has concerned the need for renewed commitment to equal opportunity by the United States, commonly expressed by the image of a level playing field. Curiously, while every other sport features such a surface, baseball violates this basic principle. Ballfields might, at first glance, appear level but they are not. Most dramatically, the pitcher is permitted to operate from an elevated position on the field. Up there atop the mound he enjoys a distinct advantage (including those occasions when balls heading through the box hit the mound and become playable by one of the infielders). Infields vary. Most are crowned and dip as one nears the foul lines, making it likely that a bunt hit toward the line will go foul. A few present slight depressions near the lines (Oakland, for example) so that bunts are inclined to stay fair. Then there is the line separating the infield dirt from the outfield grass or artificial surface, a raised border area that can affect the progress and direction of a ball. One could, of course, spend considerable time detailing the height variations of the grass found around the major leagues and discuss how teams tailor the turf to suit their strengths and neutralize weaknesses. (No one ever accuses football teams of tampering with gridiron grass.) Finally, there are the bases, which rise above the playing surface and create unique opportunities and hazards. Routine ground balls, sure outs, suddenly collide with the base and

careen crazily past a waiting fielder for a hit. A ball just out of reach hits the bag, then bounces up easily, and a certain hit becomes an out. So once more, baseball parallels life. Dispensing with a level field, it reminds us, yet again, that rarely is life fair, and that only some "get the bounce."

19. Home teams have won 53 percent of all World Series games. On average, teams win 55 percent of their games at home. Still, the Red Sox before they won on June 26, 1990, had lost to Toronto fifteen times in a row at Fenway Park. And in the 1991 American and National League playoffs, won by Minnesota and Atlanta, the home team won but three of twelve games. In the World Series, Minnesota extended its streak of consecutive World Series games lost on the road to fourteen, but by winning all four at home, captured the series.

20. "The first game I ever played in that had all four seasons." That was Glenn Wilson's response to a game that saw rain change to snow, and then before it was over, the clouds gave way to bright sunshine. *Sporting News,* Apr. 24, 1989.

21. *Washington Post,* Aug. 9, 1988; ibid., May 29, 1988. *Los Angeles Times,* Apr. 10, 1988.

22. In recent years, the easiest places to hit home runs have been in San Diego and Detroit. Busch Stadium, St. Louis, has had the fewest.

23. *Boston Globe,* Sept. 22, 1988. *USA Today,* July 12, 1988.

24. *Washington Post,* May 24, 1988.

25. *Newsday,* June 3, 1990; Bruce Nash and Allan Zullo, *Baseball Confidential* (New York: Pocket Books, 1988), p. 67.

26. Ibid., p. 27.

27. *The Boston Globe,* Aug. 5, 1988.

3. Country Boys and Green Pastures

1. Entering a ballpark and gazing out upon the expanse of green produces for many fans a moment of ecstasy, of magic. Andy Strasberg, now in the front office of the San Diego Padres, recalls the time his father took him to the Polo Grounds in New York. "In the middle of Harlem was this immense cathedral," he writes, "and inside was all this green, green grass. Incredible."

2. While reporting from war-torn Lebanon, David Lamb, the author of a book on minor-league baseball, dreamed of the ultimate escape. "Maybe I'll find some little ballpark in Montana, and just sit there in the sunshine for a sum-

mer." When finally he did get to tour the minor-league *parks* (italics mine) he discovered that many "were little gems, nestled in wooded hollows and the shadows of grain silos." *USA Today,* May 30, 1991.

Kevin Costner, who starred in the baseball movies *Field of Dreams* and *Bull Durham,* recently narrated a promotional spot for ESPN's coverage of the College World Series. The theme is unmistakable. "At some time in our life, we all wish we could return to a time when life was simpler, when all we wore was the wonderful mantle of childlike innocence, when springtime and life itself seemed eternal. Here in Omaha, they play a game that transcends time and generations, that allows every adult a chance to realize their youth again." *Newsday,* May 29, 1991.

What could have been more appropriate than the large soybean field in Minnesota, a striking design plowed into it in support of the Twins in the 1991 World Series? *Newsday,* Oct. 27, 1991.

3. Edward F. Murphy, *The Crown Treasury of Relevant Quotations* (New York: Crown, 1978), p. 73. Interest always attaches to those experiments in which a major-leaguer is asked to play a position other than his regular one. It is assumed that his skills will carry over and that he can perform at a high level elsewhere. This harkens back to an older rural America where a jack-of-all-trades would be expected to perform a wide variety of vital skills.

4. *Los Angeles Times,* July 1, 1988; *Sporting News,* July 30, 1990; *Newsday,* Aug. 15, 1989.

5. *Los Angeles Times,* April 4, 1988.

6. *Newsday,* Oct. 13, 1991; *Baseball Weekly,* May 13–19, 1992.

7. *New York Times Magazine,* January 14, 1990, p. 12.

8. *New York Times,* June 11, 1992; *Los Angeles Times,* Oct. 5, 1988; *Boston Globe,* Sept. 22, 1988.

Recently a popular poster of Nolan Ryan shows him wearing a baseball uniform and a cowboy hat, with a gun holster around his waist.

And in this imagined duel, should the pitched ball hit the batter or the batted ball crash into the pitcher, neither is expected to display any pain. Rather one expects them to be "manly," to "shake it off" and continue on as if nothing had happened.

4. A Regard For Order

1. Jerry Izenberg, *The Greatest Game Ever Played,* (New York: Henry Holt, 1987), p. 73; *New York Times Book Review,* May 31, 1992, p. 16.

2. Certain courtesies may also be observed. A batter will frequently retrieve a discarded mask and hand it to the opposing catcher. An infielder will usually signal a foul ball to an onrushing runner so that he need not slide into the base. When that runner must be tagged, the ball usually will be applied in delicate fashion so as to avoid giving offense. Indeed baseball, once a game featuring rough and tumble play, has shed a good portion of this abrasive aggressiveness, and unlike most other major sports, appears less combative than in the past.

3. While positions on the baseball field are largely fixed, when a ball is hit that is within reach of a number of players, one of them, to prevent confusion and possibly an awkward collision, must call out or signal that he intends to catch it, thereby averting confusion, disorder, and possibly injuries as well. It is often the aim of the offense to get defensive players on the move and out of position. A hit-and-run play, for example, will send infielders moving to assigned positions, thereby opening up "holes" in the infield.

4. Ironically, in this most orderly of sports, the "hit," the game's key offensive weapon, is almost always an altogether disorderly happening. That's because the batter ordinarily has little control over the ball, and consequently, it may head off in almost any direction. Hitters are urged simply to "put the ball in play," an acknowledgment that, for the most part, that's all they're capable of doing.

5. Just how rapidly and decisively order can be restored may be glimpsed in game one of the 1991 American League championship games. With the Twins ahead 5-1 in the sixth inning, the Blue Jays reached Jack Morris for five straight hits and three runs. At that point, Twin reliever Carl Willis entered the game with one out and two runners on base. He recorded two quick outs, then retired Toronto in order in the seventh, until relieved by Rick Aguilera, who completed the game. Thus, once the uprising in the sixth inning was quelled, Toronto never came close to threatening again.

6. *Baseball Weekly,* Apr. 5–11, 1991.

7. *New York Times,* Oct. 29, 1988.

8. *Los Angeles Times,* May 26, 1988.

5. Judgment Day

1. *Baseball America,* Sept. 25, 1988.

2. So precise is their authority that only they can give permission for pitchers

to moisten their fingers with fluid from their mouth on cold days. An umpire can listen in on pitcher-manager discussions if a pitcher is thought to be injured. If the conversation pertains *only* to the suspected injury the manager is not charged with a time at the mound. If other topics surface, the eavesdropping umpire can so rule. Umpires will also punish presumptuousness. A hitter with the count of three balls who presumes to judge the next pitch, however close, as a ball and instantly heads on down to first, will, in all likelihood, be called back by an umpire upset by this preemptive judgment.

3. The shame once associated with striking out has diminished considerably in recent years, perhaps an inevitable development given the rising level of strikeouts in the major leagues.

4. The search for a scapegoat here can prove elusive. In the past, it was the catcher who was most often held responsible for successful steals. More recently it has become fashionable to hold pitchers accountable, finding fault with their elaborate windups and predictable release points. First basemen who fail to keep runners close and second basemen who neglect to position themselves properly on the bag and apply tags promptly are, on occasion, also blamed. An interesting situation unfolds when the runner makes it to second after being virtually ignored and without drawing a throw. He is not credited with a steal, owing to the "indifference" of the defense.

5. Relievers, pitcher Sid Fernandez believes, are unduly burdened by the problems created for them by starting pitchers. "If you start," he remarks, "at least you're working on your own mistakes." *New York Times,* Sept. 22, 1988.

6. Related to the sacrifice is "taking one for the team"—allowing oneself to be hit by the pitched ball while up at the plate, and being awarded first base. (An equivalent play in basketball has a defender hold his position in front of an onrushing opponent, who's then penalized for a "charge.")

7. A somewhat misleading phrase since any position on the bases is in fact a scoring position—depending, of course, on the type of hit that follows; indeed, the batter himself is in a scoring position considering the fact that he can hit a home run, head round the bases, and score.

8. Occasionally they must be reminded of their obligations. Manny Mota recalls that Roberto Clemente for a time gained the reputation of being an excellent number-three hitter but not an especially productive run producer. "Well, in the spring training (1966) myself and a couple of his other friends on the team decided to get on him for not driving in runs." Clemente responded with 119 RBIs for the season which, according to Mota, "shows you that sometimes even the great hitters have to be reminded of their role for

the position they hit in." *Sporting News,* Aug. 12, 1991. Hitters are not held entirely responsible for their performances at the plate if they are not adequately "protected," that is, if the next batter in the lineup is not especially skilled. If such is the case the batter will likely see a succession of unhittable pitches frustrating his efforts to make solid contact. The pitcher is not overly concerned about walking him, so confident is he about retiring the next batter up. Thus an "unprotected" batter receives the benefit of the doubt, is assigned a diminished level of accountability.

9. Though a heavy burden is placed on players positioned in the heart of the order, it is certainly true in baseball that individuals on the offense cannot "take charge" of a game as readily or as consistently as in other team sports. In football, for example, the quarterback or other member of the backfield can be dominant, whereas in basketball, hockey, or soccer outstanding offensive players can control the game. In baseball, however, a hitter must await his turn at bat and may then come to the plate only four times in a given game. He is often simply not in a position to take charge. On the other hand, baseball presents us with the pitcher who, on given occasions, can be absolutely dominant, perhaps more so than any other defensive player in any other sport.

10. A similar situation pertains to the intentional walk where, instead of the batter heading immediately on down to first, a sequence of four "balls" must be thrown. (Notice, too, that the batter almost always plays out this charade by cocking the bat and preparing for each pitch. Baseball, as you see, takes its rituals most seriously; it tolerates no shortcuts.) Recall the player coming home, and remember that in baseball, it is people, not objects, who score; it is the players who are hailed for arriving home safely. In football, the ball must break the plane of the goal line. In hockey, the puck has to pass into the goal, and in basketball, a score depends on the ball passing through the basket. Then, too, in all these other games the score is simply numerical. In baseball, however, it's expressed as "runs" brought home by runners.

11. It is also almost obligatory in baseball that those hitting home runs excuse themselves and declare with due modesty that it was not their intention to do so. Home runs are supposed to be unexpected, inadvertent, simply the lucky consequences of solid contact. Indeed, there is a whole range of behavior that is monitored by the players themselves, committed as they are to enforcing acceptable conduct. Show-offs or "hot dogs" (for example, a pitcher who is too demonstrative after recording a strikeout) are not at all appreciated. Pitchers who throw too close to or hit batters may discover their own teammates have become the targets of opposing hurlers. Teams en route

to certain victory that nonetheless appear eager to "run up" the score will surely be held accountable for such improper behavior. Batters who peek at a catcher's glove position just before the pitch are also considered to be in violation of baseball's unwritten code of conduct.

12. *Baseball Weekly,* Apr. 22–27, 1992.

13. *Sporting News,* June 29, 1988.

14. He also serves as protector of his teammates. Those who have been hit by the opposing pitcher or brushed back under suspicious circumstances look to him to retaliate in similar fashion against the opposition, and thus, "even the score."

15. The entire field belongs to both teams, is morally neutral. There are no offensive and defensive zones, no places to make a goal-line stand or areas in which to ward off intrusions by aggressors (except home plate, which is shared). There's plenty of land in baseball, but no territorial imperative, no battle for turf. Instead the same field belongs to both teams. They alternate playing on it. They share it. "Baseball doesn't have sides because it isn't militaristic," A. Bartlett Giamatti once observed.

16. On certain plays, several fielders may be at fault, but always the error is assigned to an individual. There are no official team misplays. Individual responsibility, the American way, must of necessity prevail in the national pastime.

17. *New York Times,* Dec. 21, 1988.

18. Though no one seems to be keeping count, baseball fan mail may exceed in volume the flow of that in any other sport. In 1992 the Atlanta Braves reported that the mail was continuing to pile up despite efforts by the players to attend to it. Tom Glavine admitted he was "afraid to look at it all." Terry Pendleton asked fans not to be disappointed. "If they sent me something in August of last year, and they haven't received anything yet, they should just be patient because they will get it." *Sporting News,* May 11, 1992.

19. One can only speculate on the probable impact of the recent rapid increase in baseball salaries. More than in any other sport, fans constantly question whether players really "deserve" their pay, and wonder whether standards now are eroded and control relinquished. When now even mediocre performers will draw compensation in the high six figures, will not the whole structure of incentive rewards and punishments be compromised?

20. Baseball has faithful players as well, inasmuch as a commitment to evangelical Christianity may be seen among a significant number of major-league players.

6. Baseball Fundamentalism

1. Will, *Men at Work,* p. 7; Lee Eisenberg, "The Game without Violins or Apologies," *Esquire* 111 (Apr., 1989), p. 130; *Los Angeles Times,* Oct. 11, 1988; *New York Times,* Aug. 19, 1991.

2. *Los Angeles Times,* July 20, 1988.

3. Ibid., Aug. 1, 1988.

4. Ibid., July 15, 1991. *Sporting News,* May 11, 1992; *New York Times,* June 27, 1991.

5. Will, *Men at Work,* p. 55.

6. *USA Today,* June 26, 1991.

7. The current emphasis on exceptional leadoff men — Lenny Dykstra, Alex Cole, Luis Polonia, Brett Butler, Rickey Henderson, and Otis Nixon, suggests a revived appreciation of the fundamentals and the possibilities of manufacturing runs in creative fashion. Lead-off men are expected to be unusually versatile and imaginative hitters and runners, able to get on base and then advance in a variety of ways.

8. A lesson the Atlanta Braves will long remember when in the eighth inning of the seventh game Lonnie Smith, running from first on a hit, was thrown off stride by a common decoy play performed by Minnesota infielders Chuck Knoblauch and Greg Gagne. He went for the fake, slowed down, and failed to score what might have been the winning run.

7. A Surface Simplicity

1. Angell, *Late Innings,* p. 62.

2. Comment on WWOR Channel 9, New York, Aug. 1, 1992.

3. *Sporting News,* May 30, 1988; Edward F. Murphy, *The Crown Treasury of Relevant Quotations* (New York: Crown, 1978), p. 74; John Hough, Jr., *A Player for a Moment: Notes from Fenway Park* (New York: Ballantine, 1988), p. 335.

4. *Sporting News,* May 9, 1988; *The New York Times,* August 4, 1988.

5. Angell, *Late Innings,* p. 246; George Will interview on Larry King Show, April 19, 1990.

6. Comment on WWOR Channel 9, New York, July 14, 1992.

7. Major league officials, concerned about the growing size of gloves, called

upon umpires early in the 1990 season to enforce new size restrictions. Apparently they haven't. According to Steve Blass, that edict "died a quiet death like so many of the cows who made the gloves."

8. Catchers may be assaulted by incoming baserunners, but they are also vulnerable to another form of attack, generally overlooked—that on their eardrums. The sound of a bat making contact with a ball can at times prove most uncomfortable. Listen to Kansas City catcher Mike Macfarlane describing one such incident. "Rob Deer's homer was the loudest homer I've ever heard. It sounded like somebody had a 12-gauge shotgun right next to my head and pulled the trigger. *Sporting News,* June 8, 1992.

9. *Los Angeles Times,* May 12, 1988.

10. *Newsday,* July 29, 1988; *Washington Post,* Aug. 20, 1988; ibid., Sept. 1, 1988.

11. *Los Angeles Times,* Apr. 11, 1988.

12. *Newsday,* July 21, 1989.

13. *Los Angeles Times,* Oct. 7, 1988.

14. *New York Times,* Aug. 25, 1988; *Los Angeles Times,* Oct. 4, 1988; *Sporting News,* May 23, 1988; *Los Angeles Times,* Oct. 4, 1988.

15. Ibid., Oct. 3, 1988.

16. Hough, *A Player for a Moment,* p. 268.

17. Ibid., p. 270.

18. Warner Fusselle, *Baseball* (St. Louis: *Sporting News,* 1987), p. 67; *Los Angeles Times,* Oct. 3, 1988.

19. *Newsday,* Dec. 22, 1992.

20. *Los Angeles Times,* Oct. 12, 1988; *Washington Post,* June 24, 1988; Hough, *A Player for a Moment,* p. 224.

21. Roger Clemens, *The Rocket Man* (Boston: Stephen Green Press, 1987), p. 76.

22. *New York Times,* June 4, 1990.

23. *Newsday,* Mar. 8, 1991.

24. *Newsday,* June 21, 1990.

25. *New York Times,* Dec. 21, 1988.

26. *USA Today,* June 13, 1991.

27. *Newsday,* Mar. 23, 1993; Clemens, *The Rocket Man,* p. 82.

28. *Los Angeles Times,* Oct. 10, 1988.

29. Jinxes often arise in a manner most insidious from a source unknown to players. Broadcast announcers can in fact alter events on the fields by their

very comments. All they need do at times is to bring certain situations to light and then, most perversely, circumstances suddenly reverse themselves. Announcers are not unaware of their powers (indeed ordinarily will hesitate, for example, to discuss an ongoing no-hitter for fear of "ruining" it), but in the performance of their duties, they are often obliged to mention certain delicate matters. A batter described as a deft bunter will then promptly pop the ball into a double play. A pitcher praised for his exquisite control will suddenly lose sight of the strike zone and walk a couple of batters. In the Pittsburgh-Atlanta National League playoffs in 1991, for example, announcer Tim McCarver noted more than once that Pittsburgh's Gary Redus, about to bat, had not hit into a double play all season. Clearly the trap had been set, the jinx applied. Redus came to the plate and promptly grounded into a double play.

30. *Newsday,* Mar. 3, 1992. Though increasingly, players feel less of an obligation to talk to the reporters much, and that's not including players like Steve Carlton, George Hendricks, Dave Kingman, and others who never talked, and others who, angered by reporter comments, periodically clammed up for varying lengths of time. *New York Times* reporter George Vecsey believes that many players today don't feel they have to talk to the press. At one time, he notes, players who were friendly and open and provided "good copy" usually were rewarded by management with some extra dollars in their paychecks. Today, given the healthy salaries, there's less incentive to be cooperative. Still, Vecsey adds, players are probably more honest with the press than they once were, and the "smart" players "learn to give us something" rather than reject all overtures from reporters.

31. *Newsday,* June 2, 1990; Hough, A Player for a Moment, p. 199; Phil Niekro, *The Niekro Files,* Chicago: Contemporary Books, 1988), p. 59; *Baseball Weekly,* May 6–12, 1992.

32. *Los Angeles Times,* Oct. 4, 1988; *Newsday,* Oct. 5, 1988; *Baseball Weekly,* May 6–12, 1992.

33. Paul Dickson, *Baseball's Greatest Quotations* (New York: Harper Collins, 1991), p. 171; Sabo comment on WFAN radio in New York, July 12, 1988; *Washington Post,* May 27, 1988; Clemens, *The Rocket Man,* p. 43.

34. This posture by the press is a relatively new one. In the past the sports press, for the most part, played the role of booster, rooting for the home-town boys, covering up their misdeeds, cleaning up their language, and doing little to disturb the heroic mold in which they were cast. That such an approach has not yet disappeared can be seen in *Los Angeles Times* columnist Jim Murray's observations on the euphemisms still employed by some of today's base-

ball scribes. Here's a partial listing of recent terms and the realities behind them.

"Intense"—homicidal
"Scrappy"—talentless
"His Own Man"—selfish
"Team leader"—bully
"Good Power"—homer or nothing
"Fiery"—loud
"Patient Hitter"—Can't hit the curve and knows it
"Contact Hitter"—Makes sure he goes 2 for 4, the team is on its own.

Then, too, would the press today characterize Jose Canseco as "just a regular boring guy," which was how he chose to describe himself? No. By and large, the press tends to exaggerate talents, and create figures larger than life. Davey Johnson saw that happening all the time in New York. "Players playing in New York," he notes, "are perceived as better than they are. The good, solid player is perceived as great. The great ones become legends." Such perceptions, says Johnson, "are great in that they can make a lot of money for below-average players." *Los Angeles Times,* Oct. 14, 1988; *Washington Post,* Aug. 3, 1988.

35. *New York Times,* Mar. 21, 1993. To some observers, the most impressive part of baseball involves the throws—graceful, powerful, and accurate. (When Howard Johnson several seasons ago was experiencing trouble with his tosses to first base, he was blindfolded and proceeded to release seventeen successive accurate throws.) On display in a typical game is a wide variety of throws. Quite impressive is a series of quick pinpoint throws relayed from the outfield to the infield, then on to home, the ball arriving right on the mark to beat a sliding runner. Most majestic perhaps are the long distance "pegs" that originate in the outfield and arrive on a fly at home plate (usually eliciting "ohs" and "ahs" from a crowd impressed by the display of strength and precision). They'll take note, too, when a catcher unleashes a surprise, snap toss down to first in an effort to catch an unwary baserunner straying too far from the base. Third basemen enjoy putting their "cannons" on display demonstrating their ability to "gun" the ball over to first on a line in a flash. From shortstops we can on occasion witness acrobatic tosses launched from deep in the hole, arcing throws that nestle softly into the gloves of first basemen. Second basemen offer us the quick snap toss, often thrown sidearm, much like a slingshot. In baseball, good arms are good news.

36. A useful comparison may be highway driving. One can, when the distances

are great and the traffic light, cruise for mile after mile without having much to do other than stay awake. Then, all of a sudden, a crisis looms—it could be that the car ahead slams on the brakes, or another, without warning, cuts in front. To avoid disaster, one must shift instantly from virtual inattention to a heightened level of response that severely taxes an individual's abilities. That's what a typical baseball player must be able to do successfully each and every game.

37. *New York Times,* Apr. 28, 1992.

38. *USA Today,* Aug. 15, 1991.

39. *New York Times,* Oct. 1, 1991.

40. *Los Angeles Times,* Oct. 1, 1991.

41. *Sporting News,* May 11, 1992; Ibid., June 8, 1992; Angell, *Late Innings,* p. 283.

42. *Newsday,* Aug. 11, 1988.

43. *USA Today,* June 23, 1991.

44. *Los Angeles Times,* Oct. 4, 1988.

8. A Question of Balance

1. *Newsday,* Apr. 29, 1991.

2. *Sporting News,* May 30, 1988; *Washington Post,* May 13, 1988; Werner Fusselle, *Baseball* (St. Louis: The Sporting News, 1987), p. 10; *Los Angeles Times,* Aug. 1, 1988; Thomas Boswell, *Why Time Begins on Opening Day* (Garden City, N.Y.: Doubleday, 1984), p. 73; *Los Angeles Times,* May 23, 1988; *Los Angeles Times,* Aug. 1, 1988.

3. Los Angeles Times, Apr. 14, 1988; *Baseball Weekly,* May 27–June 2, 1992; *Sporting News,* Apr. 27, 1990; *Baseball Weekly,* Apr. 26–May 2, 1991; Fusselle, *Baseball,* p. 66; Murphy, *The Crown Treasury of Relevant Quotations,* p. 159; *Sporting News,* Apr. 23, 1990.

4. *The New York Times,* Apr. 11, 1990; *Newsday,* Aug. 5, 1988; *Washington Post,* Aug. 29, 1988.

5. Jacques Barzun saw baseball "as a kind of collective chess." Kenneth Duran accounted for its endurance "in part because it is a contemplative sport that delights in its nuances." To George Will the subtle maneuver, "the game within the game," was indisputably "elegant." So complicated can it become, according to Will, that "there is barely enough time between pitches for all the

thinking that is required." The appeal of baseball to men of letters and to intellectuals has been well-documented, although cautionary statements can be heard at times by those who remind us that it is just a game and that we may be straining a bit to read too much into it.

6. *Newsday,* Aug. 7, 1988; Angell, *Late Innings,* p. 189.

7. Angell, *Late Innings,* p. 357; *Los Angeles Times,* July 4, 1988; Nash and Zullo, *Baseball Confidential,* p. 57; *Los Angeles Times,* Aug. 8, 1988.

8. Angell, *Late Innings,* p. 356; *Sporting News,* Aug. 6, 1990.

9. *Newsday,* Sept. 5, 1988; Hough, Jr., *A Player for a Moment,* p. 121.

10. *New York Times Magazine,* Apr. 3, 1988, p. 23.

11. Mattingly, however, appears to be atypical. Hitters tend to be less prepared, less disciplined, and certainly more willing to take their chances than are pitchers. Tony LaRussa agrees. "I think there's a growing number of pitchers who want to have a plan going into a game about how they're going to go after that lineup . . . I know that 75 percent of hitters do not have that same type of plan against a pitcher [and] if you try to give them a scheme most hitters will rebel." *Sporting News,* May 11, 1992.

12. *Newsday,* Mar. 3, 1992.

13. Those, however, still blessed with blazing speed are less likely to consider the subtleties of pitching. Listen to Mark Wohlers, young fireballer for the Atlanta Braves. "I'm a fastball pitcher," he says. "I'm not looking to throw four pitches. I'm not going to trick anybody. You're not going to see 3-and-0 changeups." *Sporting News,* June 8, 1992.

14. Tim Leary, interview with author, Oct. 10, 1988.

15. Tom Boswell, *How Life Imitates the World Series* (Garden City, N.Y.: Doubleday, 1982), p. 37; *Sporting News,* May 9, 1988; *Los Angeles Times,* June 30, 1988.

16. Will, *Men at Work,* p. 146.

17. *Sporting News,* May 21, 1990; *Newsday,* July 18, 1988; *Sporting News,* June 29, 1992; *Newsday,* June 21, 1990.

18. *Los Angeles Times,* Apr. 24, 1988.

19. Boswell, *Why Time Begins on Opening Day,* p. 165; *Los Angeles Times,* Aug. 9, 1988.

20. A case, not quite as strong, could also be made for the shortstop. Listen to Barry Larkin explaining his responsibilities. "I like to think of the shortstop as a supervisor, that's the biggest part of the game . . . as a shortstop you're

always trying to anticipate. I have to take signs from the coaches on the bench and keep the other infielders up on what's going on all the time. When people talk about somebody taking charge they're talking about the short-stop." (Larkin's assertions apparently convinced the Cincinnati Reds, who early in 1992 awarded him a five-year contract for over $25 million, the highest amount ever paid a shortstop.) *Sporting News,* Apr. 1, 1991.

21. But not always. Today's batters will tend to watch their hits from the vicinity of home plate rather than start off immediately and energetically toward first. That's especially true of sluggers when convinced they've launched a home run. Observe Pedro Guerrero of the Cardinals on opening day of the 1989 season after he sends a long high fly to deep centerfield at Shea Stadium. He drops his bat deliberately, looks toward the outfield, fully expecting the ball to clear the fence. Accordingly, he begins a slow trot to first, then half-way down thinks better of it and suddenly accelerates. The ball has descended on a warning track, where it is misplayed by Mookie Wilson. Guerrero, by prematurely breaking into a triumphal trot, has lost the chance for a two-base hit and must settle for a four-hundred-foot single!

22. *Sporting News,* May 11, 1992; Christopher Lehmann-Haupt, *Me and Di-Maggio* (New York: Simon and Schuster, 1986), p. 53; Angell, *Late Innings,* p. 55.

23. *Newsday,* Oct. 11, 1988; *Sporting News,* May 11, 1992; *New York Times,* Oct. 16, 1988.

24. It was Green who, when managing the Yankees in 1989, criticized his players for their shortcomings in playing "game-situation baseball" and their inability to "think" baseball. *Washington Post,* July 4, 1988; *New York Times Magazine,* Mar. 26, 1989; p. 60.

25. There is also a sense that baseball should never become overly cerebral, mechanistic, and managed, but that optimum performance can only be expected when players are somehow "having fun." To "have fun" is a prescription central to baseball, especially applicable to players mired in slumps or otherwise underachieving (see pp. 89–91, 225).

26. Murphy, *Crown Treasury of Relevant Quotations,* p. 74; *Los Angeles Times,* Oct. 23, 1988; *Sporting News,* July 18, 1988.

27. *Washington Post,* May 23, 1990.

28. Murphy, *Crown Treasury of Relevant Quotations,* p. 72.

29. *Sporting News,* Apr. 1, 1991; *USA Today,* May 6, 1991.

30. Tony Gwynn, for example, maintains a home library of thousands of

videotapes recording his at bats, available for study. In no other sport do players give so much attention to correcting flaws, upgrading skills, and experimenting with new approaches at this, the highest level of the game.

9. Patience Rewarded

1. Boswell, *Why Time Begins on Opening Day,* p. 292.

2. After bemoaning his fate as a utility player in the final stages of 1989, Mark Carreon changed his attitude the following season. "I really learned a lesson from last year," he admitted. "I had a bad attitude just sitting on the bench and shaking hands. Now I'm happy to be in the big leagues. I had to get rid of that attitude real quick because it was interfering with my work habits." *Newsday,* Apr. 17, 1990.

3. Comment on ESPN telecast, May 20, 1990.

4. Nash and Zullo, *Baseball Confidential,* p. 78. You can keep your mouth shut or make your case discreetly, as Tom Seaver tells it. Once after giving up a home run, Seaver promptly hit the next batter, an act umpire Doug Harvey interpreted as deliberate. Heading out to the mound Harvey indicated that the pitch would cost Seaver. When Harvey arrived Seaver quietly explained that had he intended to hit the batter he would not have thrown a slider. "You're right," Harvey replied. "Forget about the fine." Comment on WPIX Channel 11, New York, Apr. 8, 1993.

5. Security is, of course, a relative matter ranging from the exceptional longevity of recent Dodger skippers Walter Alston and Tom Lasorda to the procession of sacrificial lambs who have managed the New York Yankees, in accordance with the whims and moods of owner George Steinbrenner. Sports columnists follow an annual rite of spring when they publish lists of all major-league managers and consider the likelihood of their completing the season. The dismissal of thirteen managers in 1991 suggests that more than idle speculation is involved.

6. Nash and Zullo, *Baseball Confidential,* p. 56.

7. After seeing his team throttled early in 1990 by both Oakland and California, Seattle manager Jim Lefebvre remained unfazed. "If this was a year ago [his first year as manager] I would have a real emptiness in my stomach right now. But there's too much talent here to be concerned. This club is going to score runs. All I'm concerned about as a manager is the quality of play and that has been good." *Newsday,* Apr. 17, 1990.

10. Foul Play

1. Compare this to amateur baseball where there is almost always a backstop built into the field. Were it not present, runaway balls would make the game decidedly unruly.

2. Foul territory, as befits its name, can also be untidy, populated with non-players and therefore troublesome. In addition to the tarpaulin, there are press sections jutting out, bullpen pitching mounds sticking up, benches strewn about, debris lying around, coaches wandering about, and ballgirls scampering here and there.

3. At Shea Stadium, New York, one avid fan, Anthony Manieri, sitting in his accustomed seat behind home plate, arrives at each game with a net. Early in 1990 he had, by his count, acquired ninety-nine foul-ball souvenirs!

4. Baseball, or at least the fans of baseball, seem strangely attracted to the subject of "might-have-beens," seeing these occurrences as melodramatic encounters between joyous possibility and abject disappointment, and representing the mysterious operations of unseen forces: the pitch, clearly a strike, but instead called a ball; the ball that lands just foul in the upper tier; the flyball caught over the fence by a leaping outfielder; the Texas leaguer caught in acrobatic fashion by a diving infielder. These and countless other "might-have-beens" serve continually as the grist for lively discussion, debate and dreams.

5. Ordinarily the powers that be recognize no such obligation. But on May 6th, 1990, Gregg Jefferies hit a foul "home run," then on the very next pitch clouted one fair. That was, and is, an occurrence most rare. Usually the resounding foul ball represents the batter's best shot and, in the overwhelming number of cases, he is subsequently retired (a development consistent with the belief that at each turn at bat the hitter can expect no more than one "fat" pitch, one golden opportunity).

11. Bending the Rules

1. They can be exquisitely specific. Recall our previous account of pitcher Zane Smith when he was obliged to remove his jacket after he reached base (see p. 41). How many times have umpires ordered pitchers to take off gold charms and medallions from their necks, concerned that they might in some fashion distract the batter? In 1990, umpire John McSherry ordered pitcher Ron Dibble to change his shirt after the pitcher had slit his sleeves, which then

flapped when he threw. This flapping, McSherry reasoned, might make it difficult for hitters to pick up the pitch. *Newsday,* Apr. 20, 1990. There will be no discussion here regarding doctored balls or corked bats, since these derelictions have been documented at length elsewhere. See, for example, Richard Skolnik, "In Baseball, It's Hit, Field, and Cheat," *TV Guide,* June 10, 1989.

2. The rules of baseball are many and precise, and the umpires all powerful; still, baseball tolerates more open and prolonged opposition to official decisions than any other sport. In football, basketball, hockey, and soccer protests are brief and not pursued with anything resembling the ardor and anger found in baseball. Managers have ready and easy access to the field of play in most instances (the major exception being the ban against protesting balls and strikes), and can remain out there for lengthy periods of time to press their case. Even when ejected from the game and expected to relinquish their authority, some, ever defiant, remain in the runway adjacent to the dugout issuing instructions, maintaining control of the team.

3. Jeff Reardon recalls Bob Gibson warning him not to socialize with opposing players on the field. Hard-nosed competitor that he was, Gibson would, Reardon remembers, get angry at young players who displayed any such inclination. *USA Today,* May 6, 1991.

4. Fielders were told in 1989 that they must discard their oversized gloves and stay within the prescribed dimensions. Some random enforcement followed but then the issue faded and glove sizes inched ahead once more. Some players wonder about these periodic crusades in one area or another by the leagues. "Who comes up with these things anyway?" Von Hayes remarked in 1990. "Last year it was balks. The year before that it was pine tar. It's crazy. Is somebody complaining? I haven't heard it." *Washington Post,* May 1, 1990.

5. Don Baylor notes how difficult this makes it for runners attempting to collide with the fielder in order to break up a double play. When the fielder "goes 'phantom' and moves off the bag to make his throw, I've got to get him. I can't slide to the base when he's over there somewhere trying to complete a double play." *Sporting News,* July 15, 1991.

6. Umpires, Ralph Kiner believes, often adjust to the norm. If players customarily do things in a particular way, umpires will tend not to "call it" even though, technically, it would be considered a violation. WPIX (Channel 9 New York) telecast, Feb. 9, 1991.

7. *Baseball Weekly,* May 13–19, 1992.

8. That's what occasioned an outburst from the Mets' Kevin Elster during a

game in 1991 when he thought umpire Harry Wendelstadt was being altogether too kind to St. Louis rookie pitcher Rheal Cormier. "Why don't you
give us that pitch?" Elster asked. "That kid [Cormier] has been in the league
for two weeks and you give it to him." *Newsday,* Sept. 16, 1991.

9. Manager Tom Trebelhorn thought that to be true but in reverse, for Rob Deer,
because of his consistently high strikeout totals. "I think there's a tendency
for guys [like Deer] not to get marginal pitches called balls whereas Dwight
Evans, Darrell Evans or a Rickey Henderson have a reputation for having
great eyes. I would say the same pitch these guys take, I would not want to
take 3-2 if I was Rob Deer." *Newsday,* July 4, 1989.

10. That umpires were partial to Rick Dempsey when he was behind the plate
was a claim made by Len Dykstra, which led to a fight between the two,
Dempsey claiming that "he said I was brownnosing to get strikes." *Sporting
News,* Sept. 3, 1990.

12. Fields of Fear

1. *Newsday,* Nov. 11, 1991; Nash and Zullo, *Baseball Confidential,* p. 68.

2. Ibid., p. 92.

3. Clemens, *Rocket Man,* p. 130; *Los Angeles Times,* Oct. 14, 1988; *Washington Post,* June 19, 1988.

4. *New York Times,* June 21, 1991. Early in spring training in 1993 John Franco,
after suffering an arm injury the previous year, awaited his first appearance.
"The whole day was kind of long for me, that's for sure. I didn't know how
I was going to feel and react out there. Sitting around from the early morning
stretch and waiting to get to pitch, I might have gone to the bathroom nine
or ten times. I felt like a rookie. But I just wanted to solve my own curiosity,
get out there and see how my arm would react." *Newsday,* Apr. 23, 1993.

5. Roger Angell, *Late Innings,* p. 357. This is true of most players, Coleman
believes, with some notable exceptions in his day including Pete Rose, Mickey
Mantle, Stan Musial, Enos Slaughter, and Frank Robinson. In recent years,
Ron Hunt and Don Baylor appeared to be uncommonly fearless, willing to
endanger life and limb rather than avoid close pitches. Once beaned, players
must learn to overcome the fear of again standing in close to the plate. Some
are never the same, while others like Dickie Thon have managed to take the
long road back. Interview on WFAN (AM), New York, May 5, 1991.

6. *Newsday,* Apr. 19, 1992.

7. James Simpson, *Contemporary Quotations* (New York: Crowell, 1964), p. 386; *Sporting News,* May 23, 1988; ibid., May 2, 1988; *Washington Post,* May 1, 1990.

8. Angell, *Late Innings,* p. 173.

9. Under the heading "hot dog" would come a player who takes too long to circle the bases after hitting a homerun. Minnesota pitcher Tim Drummond thought that was the case with Mel Hall of the Yankees in a 1990 game, and so the next time Hall came to bat, Drummond deliberately directed a pitch toward Hall's head, an action that Twins infielder Fred Manrique believed entirely justified. "Hall deserved to be thrown at for trying to show us up." Hall's teammates thought otherwise, and a bench-clearing brawl ensued.

10. He may also be scared away from the strike zone, and so alter his approach and begin to pitch defensively.

11. Nash and Zullo, *Baseball Confidential,* p. 70.

12. Ibid.

13. Ibid. To be a team's preeminent slugger puts a player at risk. Glenn Davis, when he was with Houston, understood this well. In one game against Cincinnati in 1990, he was hit three times by Reds' pitchers.

14. Interestingly, baseball permits "feared" hitters to be bypassed. When the likes of a Bobby Bonds, Frank Thomas, Jose Canseco, Joe Carter, or Wade Boggs are due to bat in a "dangerous" situation, they can be given an intentional pass by the pitcher so that they no longer pose a direct threat. In a 1990 game between Cincinnati and Chicago, Reds' manager Lou Piniella ordered Andre Dawson walked intentionally five times! Avoiding a feared hitter is also a factor in the general tendency to trade notable players across divisions or leagues, so that they will not return and take "revenge" while in the uniform of a rival team. Many players who are traded after failing to produce for a given team are eager to demonstrate that an error has been made. Listen to Rickey Henderson of the Athletics after he hit a home run against the Yankees, his former team. "I wanted to prove to the Yankees that I'm still a great player. I wanted to show them that they made a mistake trading me." *Washington Post,* May 1, 1990.

15. In the early spring of 1992, Mets' pitcher Wally Whitehurst was struck by a hard line drive off the bat of Deion Sanders, continuing a pattern from the previous season. In 1991, Kevin Mitchell smacked a ball off his thigh, Jerome Walton hit one off his shirt, Chris Sabo sent a shot bouncing off his other leg. The 1992 incident prompted Whitehurst to recall a time in col-

lege when he was wounded in the face by a batted ball, an injury that would require 110 stitches! *New York Times,* Mar. 10, 1992.

16. Ironically, it is baseball that has furnished one of the more lethal objects available to the public for use during heated disputes, fights, and general melees. Baseball bats have long been a weapon of choice among hooligans, gang members, mobs, and irate citizens.

13. As Time Goes By

1. Why are games getting longer? Sparky Anderson thinks he knows. "First, you've got two minutes between innings for TV. That adds 20 minutes right there. On a typical night, we'll make four pitching changes. Now that's 32 extra pitches per team, and the time it takes for the guy to walk in from the bullpen. And we throw over to first base more than ever." Former commissioner Fay Vincent believed umpires are not calling enough strikes, especially on pitches above the belt. Batters, he noted, are stepping out of the box continuously, further prolonging matters. *USA Today,* June 6, 1991.

2. Players sometimes do. An occasional game proceeds so slowly that they can get distracted, lose concentration, forget precisely what's happening. It's not at all uncommon to see runners, having lost track of the number of outs, dash away from a base, only to be doubled off because there was, in fact, only one out. Players sometimes appear bored, ambling about in slow motion, tobacco-filled jaws moving more rapidly than any other parts of their bodies. Major-league dugouts often reflect this sense of languor, players sitting around, chatting, staring off into space, some close to, or indeed, dozing off.

3. *New York Review of Books,* Nov. 5, 1991, p. 41.

4. No other sport features so many meetings or allows so much talk on the playing field. Admittedly, there is usually an umpire hovering in the wings to ensure that the game doesn't come to a complete halt or become little more than a series of gab fests punctuated by occasional action. Still, there's plenty of time-consuming talk (which offers little visual stimulation for fans, but encourages much analysis of the situation along with speculation as to just what is being discussed out on the field).

5. Nash and Zullo, *Baseball Confidential,* p. 65.

6. On the other hand, baseball is continuous in the sense that the game pro-

ceeds uninterruptedly to its conclusion without half-times as in football, or other stoppages of play between periods, as in basketball, hockey, and soccer. In some of these sports, commercial time-outs have drawn the ire of fans who view them as disturbing intrusions, impeding the natural flow of the game. Baseball's deliberate pace and overall length makes it unnecessary to call a halt in the game in order to insert commercial messages, though in recent years the introduction of commercials into the flow of the play-by-play commentary has upset many fans.

7. "In baseball there is always something to watch." That is the reasoned view of Merle Swenson, who should know, inasmuch as he has attended every Seattle Mariners home game since 1977 (a total of 1,149 through May, 1991). Indeed, even before a play is underway, a fan may be drawn in a number of different directions—to the updates of other games posted on the scoreboard, out to the bullpen to check on who is warming up, or into the dugout to learn who may appear as a pinch-hitter. Even as the pitch is about to be thrown other plays may already be underway—the second baseman sneaking in behind the runner, the first baseman charging in toward the plate, or the catcher stepping to the side for a pitchout. No other sport offers so many separate arenas of action operating simultaneously. *USA Today,* May 10–12, 1991.

8. Is there any hurrying in baseball? Are efforts ever made to accelerate the pace of a contest? When rain threatens to cancel a game, the home team, if it is leading, will endeavor to move things along in an attempt to complete the fifth inning when the game then becomes official, even if rain prevents further play. If weather conditions are adverse—cold, drizzle, or heat—and the game is one-sided, both teams are likely to proceed at a brisk pace. Both will be more eager to pack than to play, especially if the teams are scheduled to travel immediately after the game.

9. The game at such times of great tension and cautious deliberation, with the springs of action wound ever so tightly, may even come to a complete halt. In the fifth inning of a scoreless game seven of the 1991 World Series, the Braves had runners on first and third with Terry Pendleton facing Twins pitcher Jack Morris. The game and the season may well have been on the line. Morris, motionless, continues to peer in toward the plate. Pendleton, bat fixed, stares back. No one moved as the seconds ticked away. Pendleton finally broke the impasse by calling for a time-out.

10. Nash and Zullo, *Baseball Confidential,* p. 32.

11. Ibid., p. 65.

12. Ibid., p. 61.

13. On the other hand, a baseball game can seem to end prematurely, with time up before most imagined it would be. A case in point involved a game late in May of 1992 between the Cincinnati Reds and the New York Mets at Shea Stadium. Trailing 1-0 in the ninth, the Mets put a runner on first with one out. Dave Magadan stepped in to face Reds' pitcher Norm Charlton and the drama began to build. Then Magadan smashed a vicious liner toward first that seemed headed for a single or possibly a double and probably a tie game. But that proved to be wishful thinking on the part of Mets fans. The first baseman leaped and caught the ball high over his head and on the way down swiped at the runner attempting to return to the base. Double play. No more dramatics. In that electrifying instant time ran out, and the game ended abruptly.

14. Close Encounters

1. Nash and Zullo, *Baseball Confidential,* p. 54.

2. *New York Times,* July 22, 1991.

15. Talking a Good Game

1. Umpire Bruce Froeming notes that "Baseball is the only sport in which you have to learn to negotiate an argument. In football, an official can walk off a 15-yard unsportsmanlike conduct penalty against an abusive player; in baseball the only recourse is ejection. *Sporting News,* Apr. 13, 1992.

2. Abusive language may even be tolerated so long as it is not overheard by others. "You curse an umpire within earshot of another," says umpire Terry Tata, "and you can be out of there." Umpires will not accept being "shown up" in public, that is, being criticized or attacked in such a way that others on the field or in the stands become aware of the assault. A manager can hurl invectives at an umpire out of earshot of others and go unpunished, but if he kicks dirt at the ump in the course of the encounter, he's certain to be ejected for the blatant public act of defiance. Likewise, a catcher can complain heatedly about a call, but if he keeps looking ahead, it may be tolerated. Should he turn around, a clear signal of open disagreement, he will likely be forced to depart. "Private" abuse may be tolerated, but a public display will not be ignored or forgiven. *New York Times,* Sept. 7, 1992.

3. *New York Times,* June 19, 1989.

4. On occasion, players may just have emerged from a team meeting, periodic get-togethers convened by management or sometimes by the players themselves to clear the air or restore morale when the team's fortunes have sagged. Players differ over the value of these gatherings. To some, such "pep rallies" have little impact on professionals fully capable of providing their own incentives. Others support such practices, and agree that they can galvanize a team that is adrift. Sound the right notes, celebrate team unity, and you can expect, they say, positive dividends.

5. *Sporting News,* June 17, 1991. In baseball, each year produces a list of players who attract notice precisely because they have decided to stop "talking" to the press. In 1990 for example, Cincinnati pitcher Jose Rijo joined the ranks, breaking off communications. "I'm giving 100% to pitching," he explained, "100% to my wife and 100% to my family and 0% to you guys. I'm gonna be like Steve Carlton" [former star pitcher who rarely, if ever, talked with reporters].

6. Ibid., June 17, 1991. There is talk even as the game is about to start, when the managers (or their designates) meet with the umpires to exchange lineup cards and review the ground rules. Sprinkled amidst these business matters is some informal gab and friendly exchanges.

7. In other sports, such as basketball and football, there is some talk, but it's often provocative, intended to goad or incite opponents (commonly referred to as "talking trash").

8. *Sporting News,* May 11, 1992.

9. It's not uncommon, however, to see a baserunner on first chatting amiably with the first baseman, and a moment later diving headlong back to the base to avoid a slap tag forcefully applied. To some fans, this abrupt change in relationships appears jarring.

10. *Los Angeles Times,* July 1, 1988; Nash and Zullo, *Baseball Confidential,* p. 12.

11. Ibid., p. 13.

12. Ibid., p. 14.

13. Indeed, it may even be a violation of the rules if umpire Dave Phillips has his way. In a June, 1992, game against Minnesota, Chicago catcher Carleton Fisk was ejected by Phillips after turning around to question a call. Phillips indicated there was a rule against turning around, one Fisk insisted did not exist. Fisk "knows the rules," Phillips retorted. "If he wants to be treated as a professional, he needs to act like one." *Baseball Weekly,* June 24–30, 1992.

14. Nash and Zullo, *Baseball Confidential,* p. 19.

15. This is usually preceded by a strategy session in the dugout, where the manager and his coaches can be seen discussing the situation, talking about what moves should be made.

16. In the first inning of game six of the 1988 National League Championship Series, Mets pitcher David Cone was staggering, having walked Steve Sax on four straight pitches and gone 3 and 0 on Mickey Hatcher. The Dodger crowd was screaming for blood. New York pitching coach Mel Stottlemyre hastened to the mound to try and settle him down. "He was nervous. I could see it in his face. I could also see he was tense and over keyed up. He didn't say anything. I said, 'I know you're nervous. Try to relax. Step off and throw to first, twice, three times if necessary, to get loose.'" That wasn't the only advice Cone received. Here's how some other Met players responded to the situation. "Hey, settle down!" Gary Carter implored. "You don't need to be as pumped up as you are. Have some fun! I was assertive . . . because he wasn't 'OK.'" Keith Hernandez tried a different approach. "I was trying to pump him up. He was tight, nervous. I was trying to bring out the competitor in him. I was screaming, trying to pump him up." Then Wally Backman made his contribution. "I just told him to concentrate a little more, to get 'em. I was trying to build the guy up in a calming way." It's a wonder Cone ever survived the inning. Reporter Scott Ostler took note of the conflicting voices. "So his pals were trying to pump Cone up and calm him down, soothe him and ruffle him, pat him on the back and yell in his face, and kick him in the butt in a nice and hostile way." *Los Angeles Times,* Oct. 12, 1988.

17. It may be that these disputes are becoming more heated because a traditional form of verbal discharge has diminished. Many observers see "bench jockeying," the use of verbal barbs directed at opposing players on the field by those positioned in the dugout, as a lost art with but few really skilled practitioners remaining.

18. In 1991, major-league baseball produced a promotional commercial that featured not action from the ballpark, but scenes of fans listening to the game mostly on their radios, clear confirmation of the fact that even in this quintessentially visual age, millions of fans continue to enjoy listening to others describe the action and talking about the game.

19. Some of them take time in the telling, a fact that prompted announcer Gary Thorne to caution those in the ESPN broadcasting booth with him "never to start a story with 2 outs."

16. A Taste for Drama

1. Not to the initiated, however. As Harold Baines reminds us, there's something always happening. "There's nothing boring about baseball," he insists. "There's always something going on. The manager is giving signals to the coach, the coach is giving signals to the batter, the catcher is giving signals to the pitcher and infielders, and the infielders are giving little signs to the outfielders as to what pitch is coming." *Sporting News,* Apr. 15, 1991.

17. Mysteries of the Game

1. *Los Angeles Times,* Oct. 13, 1988; Ibid., May 16, 1988.
2. *Newsday,* Oct. 9, 1988.
3. Murphy, *The Crown Treasury of Relevant Quotations,* p. 73.
4. *Baseball Weekly,* May 13–19, 1992. Pitcher Hoyt Wilhelm probably never worried about it but still must have found it strange that having hit a home run in his very first major league at bat, he never hit another one, despite playing twenty-one years in the majors.

18. Statistically Significant

1. The level of numerical literacy in baseball is exceptionally high. Most every fan will with ease be able to explain the significance of the following numbers:

A) 60'6"   I) 40/40   Q) 410'

B) 90'   J) 56   R) 4 8 1
                          3 6 0

C) .300   K) 714

D) .400   L) 1951   S) .982

E) 20   M) 3000   T) 25

F) 60   N) 300   U) 90 mph

G) 61   O) 3   V) 3 and 2

H) 30/30   P) 9   W) magic number

X) mathematically eliminated

In 1992, *The New York Times* ran a television advertisement for its sports section featuring a veteran writer grilling a would-be baseball reporter by asking him every manner of statistical trivia question. When at last the job seeker flubs a particularly obscure statistical question he is promptly dismissed as unsuited to work for the *Times*.

2. *New York Times*, June 13, 1976; George Will interviewed on the Larry King Show, Apr. 19, 1990.

3. Here's how *Sporting News* explained the addition of new statistical information into its pages. "We began a research project more than a year ago, interviewing current and former subscribers. One of the things that came through quite clearly was your intense desire for statistics that help you analyze the game. You already know the results; you asked us, simply, to explain how and why things happen." *Sporting News*, July 7, 1991.

Suggesting that a "New Age of Baseball Statistics has arrived," the publishers of *The Tenth Man*, by Bill Welch, hailed the value of its new Baseball Analysis and Reporting System (The BARS System) "which uses a powerful computer to show batting averages for nine locations in the strike zone for every player in the major leagues." The enthusiasm of those who offer us the numbers game is boundless.

4. *Sporting News*, May 21, 1990. So eager are baseball's statisticians to call attention to potentially record-breaking streaks that they are announced and given substance early on in the process, when little more than a promise may exist. Don Mattingly had this in mind when during the 1991 season his fifteen-game hitting streak drew attention. "I have no streak," he declared somewhat petulantly. "Fifteen games is no streak. Thirty games is a streak, maybe." *New York Times*, July 4, 1991.

5. *New York Times*, June 21, 1991; *Newsday*, Feb. 28, 1991.

6. Seymour Siwoff, et al., *The 1991 Elias Baseball Analyst*, (New York: Simon and Schuster, 1991), pp. 47–51.

7. Ibid., pp. 71, 286.

8. Will, *Men at Work*, p. 230; Siwoff, *Elias Baseball*, p. 133; *New York Times*, July 15, 1991.

9. Siwoff, *Elias Baseball*, pp. 145, 111; *USA Today*, May 1, 1991.

10. Siwoff, *Elias Baseball*, p. 54.

11. *USA Today*, May 6, 1991.

12. Angell, "Homeric Tales," *The New Yorker* 67 (May 27, 1991), p. 72.

13. Some examples. Honus Wagner at age forty-two years and four months was

the oldest player ever to hit an inside-the-park home run. Consider those statistics that provide the batting averages of players for every day of the week. What of the fact that Ozzie Guillen of Chicago, a free-swinger, saw the fewest pitches of any major-leaguer during the 1990 season?

14. *Baseball Weekly,* Apr. 26–May 2, 1991; here is a not atypical account of a game in 1991 appearing in *New York Times.* Note the frequency of statistical information (italics mine) and the emphasis on streaks and numbers in general.

Sanderson and Yanks
Seem Downright Cozy
By Michael Martinez
Special to *The New York Times*

BOSTON, June 26—Their road record has been their big weakness, but the Yankees are playing at Fenway Park as if it's in the heart of the Bronx.

One night after they beat Roger Clemens, the Yankees beat the Boston Red Sox again, this time by 5-1, assuring themselves of a series victory. Before the Yanks began their six-game trip, they had an *11-21 road record,* but they have recovered here.

The Yankees haven't *won a series at Fenway since October 1986,* but Scott Sanderson pitched seven strong innings and was supported by a three-run third and a two-run sixth. Sanderson now has a *4-0 career record* against the Red Sox, including two victories this season in which he had given up just *one run in 13 innings.*

Burks Gets Homer

Sanderson *(8-3)* took a shutout into the sixth before giving up a home run to Ellis Burks. The shot ended his *scoreless string of 21 innings* against the Red Sox and marked the *first time this season* he has given up a homer in a game and still won.

Steve Howe pitched the final three innings for his second save.

Despite his record, Sanderson has struggled lately, going more than *three weeks without a victory* and losing last Friday night to the Minnesota Twins when he gave up five runs in five innings. He was bothered, in part, by a stiff neck that persisted for several days.

But he said then—and continued to maintain—that the injury would not prevent him making his next start. It didn't, of course, and after a slow beginning tonight, he seemed to find the sort of groove that had eluded him.

The Red Sox, in fact, had two base runners in the first inning before Sanderson retired a batter. Shortstop Alvaro Espinoza mishandled a grounder by Ellis Burks, then threw wide for an *error, his league-leading 14th* of the season. But Ellis was thrown out attempting to steal second.

Jody Reed followed with a single, but Sanderson got Wade Boggs and Jack Clark to bounce into force-outs.

Mike Greenwell opened the second with a double to extend his *hitting streak to 17 games,* longest in the American League this season, but he failed to advance. Sanderson struck out Tom Brunansky, then retired Carlos Quintana and Tony Peña on infield grounders.

He was rewarded in the third when the Yanks scored four times off Red Sox rookie Mike Gardiner, who had three victories but had also been supported by an *average of 7.2 runs a start.*

Statistical excess is not limited to newspaper accounts. When Eddie Murray hit a homerun early in 1993, announcer Fran Healy called it a home run followed by the words, "as he adds to his numbers," hardly an example of rhetorical grace.

15. *Sporting News,* May 11, 1992, p. 15.

16. *Washington Post,* May 12, 1990.

17. Comment on ESPN, June 26, 1991. So there is, in the end, no reason to worry. While the high priests of statistics acknowledge that their intention has been "to cut through the sport's aphorisms and sacred truths" they are willing to declare that "chance is several hundred times more powerful than anyone thinks it is." "It is," John Thorne tells us, like the "elephant in the middle of the room that nobody is willing to acknowledge. We crave certainty [but] we are always dealing with chance in baseball."—an admission that will never appear on a blurb for a new volume of baseball statistics. *New York Times,* June 26, 1989.

19. Fans: A Special Connection

1. *Sporting News,* May 13, 1991.

2. In the 1991 movie *City Slickers,* one of the principal characters recalls that the only subject he could even discuss with his father was baseball. So it was for newspaper columnist Lawrence Levy, who admitted that baseball "was the most dependable, enduring tie between my father and me; it gave us a way to reach each other when all other channels failed, a place for a troubled teenager to meet a strong-willed man."

3. Edwin Pope, sports editor of the *Miami Herald* since 1956, surely is typical.

he remembers well how as a youngster he burrowed "into the sports section of the *Atlanta Constitution* every morning; he memorized every batting average of every player at every position." *Sporting News,* May 20, 1991.

4. *New York Times,* Apr. 22, 1990.

5. When teams act without sufficient prior public debate, fans feel a sense of betrayal. This was expressed most poignantly during a 1991 episode of the television series "Brooklyn Bridge." When news spread that the Dodgers had traded Jackie Robinson, one of the young fans on the show in utter disbelief expressed his sense of loss and disappointment. "I don't understand; if Jackie plays for Brooklyn and we're Brooklyn, how can they trade him without asking us?" *Newsday,* Dec. 10, 1991.

6. There is, nevertheless, a growing dissatisfaction with player salaries. In a 1991 *USA Today* fan poll, 84 percent of the respondents agreed that the ballplayers were overpaid. Whether this will in some way diminish fan support for the game is uncertain. Nevertheless, a *Sports Illustrated* poll released in June of 1991 showed baseball to be trailing football in overall popularity. Furthermore, fan attachment to baseball had slipped 7 percent in the last five years. Still, baseball attendance in 1993 showed a substantial increase, even when one discounts the addition of two new franchises in Denver and Florida. Also note the recent popularity of baseball caps, representing 70 percent of all hats sold in the United States. According to one analyst, the hats "embody a vision of manhood that is really about boyishness and the exuberance of youth." *Newsday,* June 17, 1991; *New York Times,* Aug. 10, 1991.

7. Kevin Maas' prolonged batting slump in 1991 caused him to take his telephone off the hook because so many fans were calling to offer advice. *Los Angeles Times,* June 3, 1988; ibid., Apr. 7, 1988; *Sporting News,* July 4, 1988; *Newsday,* Aug. 20, 1991.

8. Some are reputedly buried under Chicago's Comiskey Park, now defunct itself. When some of the older ones are torn down, fans flock to collect stadium memorabilia—seats, signs, soil—anything that will help recall its past glories.

9. In 1991, a Montana prison escapee fled to Seattle, whereupon he decided to attend a ballgame at the King Dome. To his great surprise and misfortune, there he encountered the warden of the Montana State Prison. "I guess I'll see you back there," the prisoner was reported to have said. *Newsday,* Aug. 4, 1991.

10. In recent years, the play *Bleacher Bums* has been performed in various Ameri-

can cities. It focuses, during a single game, on those by now legendary Chicago Cubs fans who occupy the right-field bleachers year after disappointing year. The common man need not even be present in the ballpark to witness the game. In the old Polo Grounds (New York) and today at Wrigley Field fans are able to look in on the game from the rooftops of adjoining buildings, a most unusual connection between baseball and its followers. Fans wait outside of Fenway Park in the event a ball is hit out of the stadium and into the adjacent street. Indeed, in 1991 a ball, propelled out of Fenway, smacked into a vehicle passing by. For years Rick Kecher positioned himself outside of Wrigley Field to retrieve balls hit out of the stadium. At one point he had collected over four hundred baseballs. *Newsday,* June 12, 1992; ibid., May 30, 1991.

11. *USA Today,* May 15, 1991.

12. *Newsday,* Aug. 7, 1991; *The Sporting News,* Apr. 1, 1991; *Newsday,* Aug. 15, 1989; Hough, *A Player for a Moment,* p. 208; *Sporting News,* Sept. 17, 1990; Clemens, *Rocket Man,* p. 76; *Sporting News,* May 2, 1988; *Newsday,* June 8, 1988. The volatility of fans disturbs some players. Several years back Ron Kittle refused to come out of the dugout after hitting a homerun. "I ain't into it," he exclaimed. "The same guys who cheer me are the ones who boo you the next day. So the hell with it." Most players, however, tend to be more receptive when it comes to cheers. Indeed, baseball is one of the few sports whose players openly acknowledge the applause of spectators. *Newsday,* June 18, 1988.

13. *Los Angeles Times,* Aug. 14, 1988; *Sporting News,* Mar. 8, 1993. After the Twins were battered by the Braves 14-5 in Game five of the 1991 World Series in Minnesota, manager Tom Kelly commented on the players' postgame reactions: "Five or seven minutes after the game the players forget about it. . . . That's just the way it is today. That's what players are like today." *New York Times,* Oct. 27, 1991.

14. *Sporting News,* Sept. 17, 1990; ibid., June 10, 1991; ibid., May 11, 1992.

15. The 1991 season saw incidents involving Jose Canseco and Albert Belle in which both players responded quite directly to taunting by fans. Sociologist Jerry Lewis speculates as to the reasons behind a decline in player passivity. The players, he says, are now "millionaires, they're executives. If you've been around upper class powerful men, they just don't take a lot. It's power." *New York Times,* June 30, 1991.

16. One mode of revenge available to umpires is the rule that prevents the showing of replays involving umpires on the stadium screen. When, for example,

in 1991, scoreboard operators at Shea Stadium showed an obviously safe Gregg Jefferies sliding home (he had been called out), Paul Runge, the chief umpire at the game, ordered the replay screen to be turned off. Scoreboard operators, Runge explained, "are not supposed to show any play involving umpires whether they're right or wrong, close or not." *Newsday,* Aug. 23, 1991.

17. *Newsday,* Aug. 18, 1988; *New York Times,* Oct. 9, 1988; *Newsday,* Apr. 22, 1988; *New York Times,* July 31, 1992.

18. In most instances they do; quite a few of them, in fact, keep score as the game proceeds. In no other sport do spectators generally engage in keeping an ongoing record of developments out on the field. Crowds can play a part in the game in other ways as well. Doc Gooden admitted that early in his career when he was an outstanding strikeout pitcher the posting of "K" signs by spectators after each of his strikeouts had the effect of pumping him up and getting him to try for additional strikeouts. Crowd noise can help runners for the home team in a very specific way. On a hit-and-run, the baserunner—having taken off for second on a ball hit to the right side—need not look back but can head on to third because the roar of the crowd "tells" him the ball is a base hit. Interview on SportsChannel, Apr. 28, 1993.

19. More ominously, fans for one reason or another will toss objects of all sorts out onto the field, usually aimed at the opposition. Several years ago, for example, Lenny Dykstra charged into the ivy at Wrigley Field in pursuit of a flyball, which he never caught, largely because Cub fans in the vicinity poured beer all over him. (Had Dykstra "had his mouth open," teammate Kevin Mc-Reynolds remarked, "he'd have registered as driving while intoxicated.") Not long afterwards, Dodger manager Tommy Lasorda was hit in the eye by a quarter tossed out of the stands at Shea Stadium. ("I wanted to sign that SOB. He had such great control," Lasorda quipped.) It could be worse. In the nineteenth century, fans used to flash mirrors into the eyes of batters. John McNamara recalls that while managing winter ball in the Dominican Republic "people [would] light newspapers and throw 'em down on the field." *Newsday,* Aug. 8, 1988; *ibid.,* Oct. 5, 1988; Hough, *A Player for a Moment,* p. 283.

20. Baseball has nearly institutionalized the kissing fan, inevitably a young woman of generous dimensions who is bent on leaving the stands and embracing one of the players. For years it was Morganna (called by sports writer Mike Lupica "an American icon") who performed this curious ritual. In 1991, the cast was enlarged to include the stripper, Topsy Curvy. Then too, there are the stadium mascots such as the Philadelphia Phanatic or the San Diego Chicken,

whose antics entertain both the crowd and TV audiences. Of interest is the fact that these mascots perform both on the field and in the stands, and in that sense symbolically unite the two, bringing fans and players together. *Newsday,* Oct. 14, 1991; *Baseball Weekly,* Apr. 22–28, 1992.

21. Players, demonstrating their connection with fans, will often toss foul balls into the stands for the spectators rather than put them back into play. Occasionally, bats or portions thereof fly into the stands as well. Fans are inclined to claim these and usually do. In a game at Shea Stadium, Lenny Dykstra, swinging at a pitch, had his bat go flying amidst the spectators. It was retrieved by a security guard. But the fans began chanting, "We want the bat," whereupon it was brought to the fan who had caught it. *Newsday,* Apr. 16, 1991.

22. Baseball may be the only sport (excepting car racing or the running of the bulls at Pamplona) where spectators are at physical risk when attending a game. A ball sent crashing into the stands is a dangerous object likely to injure anyone in the way. Bats sent flying into the stands also cannot be taken lightly. Though injuries to spectators are not frequent, they are also not uncommon. During the 1991 season, Andy Van Slyke casually tossed a ball to the fans behind home plate. One fan, in his eagerness to catch the souvenir, toppled over the railing, fell six feet, and dislocated his shoulder. Pitcher Ron Dibble, on the other hand, hurled one into the centerfield stands, plunking a first-grade teacher on the elbow. *Sporting News,* May 13, 1991. In some instances, notably at Wrigley Field, fans will throw homerun balls hit by the opposition back onto the field, in an example of sacrifice and contempt.

23. At Dodger Stadium in August of 1991, Cal Daniels of Los Angeles never caught up to a ball he was chasing in the outfield. Instead, a fan did, having jumped onto the field and scooped up the baseball. Fans will also badger ball girls (positioned on the sidelines to retrieve ground balls hit foul) to turn over some of these balls to them. From time to time their pleas meet with success. We should not ignore these ball girls or the bat boys (employed by all teams) in the dugout as an additional element in humanizing the game—part of the larger process of connecting field and stands, the game and its followers.

24. Jesse Barfield in 1991 hit a fair ball into the seats where a fan lunged for it but then dropped it onto the field. It was declared a ground-rule double instead of a home run, prompting Barfield to recommend that more fans "bring gloves to the park, because if they catch it, it's a home run." *Sporting News,* June 10, 1991.

20. Anticipation

1. Fielders will shift to the left for a right-handed pull-hitter. A fastball hitter will receive a steady diet of off-speed pitches. A catcher will check the feet of a batter to anticipate where he's likely to hit, and a pitcher will vary his deliveries to deceive a baserunner attempting to study his "moves." We will, in this discussion of edges and opportunities, focus on the general ebb and flow of a game, not on the above-mentioned play-by-play tactics that players employ to gain an advantage, however slight. *New York Times,* May 15, 1990; Will, *Men at Work,* p. 250; Boswell, *Why Time Begins on Opening Day,* p. 296; comment on ESPN, Apr. 12, 1990; *Sporting News,* Aug. 27, 1990.

2. A statistical study of the outcomes of all World-Series games since the beginning of the century revealed that "even a mediocre team . . . has about one chance in three of defeating a dominant team . . . in the Series." *Sporting News,* Oct. 29, 1990.

3. Andre Dawson, on the other hand, says he tends to get hot on the road but "can't explain it. Maybe I just get more rest when I'm out of town." *Washington Post,* May 21, 1990.

4. Do visiting teams have any advantages? The subject has unfortunately not received much attention. It might be fruitful to consider the possibility of heightened awareness and aggressiveness within that "alien" environment. It has been suggested, moreover, that playing amidst "hostile" surroundings and unsympathetic fans does activate the competitive instincts of players, and stirs within them a desire to show up the hometown fans. On the other hand, home-cooked meals and family life may promote undue complacency and comfort, elements not ordinarily associated with winning teams.

5. Many sports pages, it should be noted, daily list "streaks" and the "home" and "away" records of each team. On the other hand, those who have studied streaks reject the idea that they do, in fact, provide any momentum, any level of predictability at any one particular point. The statistical chance of having a streak extended is no better than seeing it conclude.

6. One must also factor in playing conditions at game time. Cold weather tends to favor the pitchers (always in motion, it is easier for them to stay warm and loose). Furthermore, cold air will reduce the distance balls hit to the outfield will travel.

7. Going into the 1991 season opposing batters hit a healthy .289 against Cone in the first inning. Thereafter, the collective batting average for all other innings was an anemic .215.

8. Predictably, there are those pitchers who, uncommonly sharp in the first inning, consistently contain the opposition early in the game. Doug Drabek, Scott Sanderson, Tim Belcher, Rick Mahler, and Dennis Cook are among those with whom one must be patient and hopeful that they will falter in the later innings.

9. In 1988, the following results were achieved with first pitches: 43 percent were balls and 25 percent called strikes. There were an additional swinging strikes (6 percent), foul balls (12 percent), and balls put in play (14 percent). So, remarkably enough, 43 percent were balls and 43 percent were strikes.

10. Will, *Men at Work*, p. 23.

11. The count is virtually absent at such times when hitters swing and make contact on the first pitch, or early on in the count. Some do so because they are impatient and prefer to swing away at the outset. Others reason that the best pitch they'll see in the sequence is the first one, so concerned is the pitcher with getting ahead in the count. Others fear that the pitcher, ahead in the count, will resort to pitches that are especially "nasty" and decidedly unhittable.

12. A hitter, given the natural advantages of the pitcher, is never really in "command," certainly not to the extent of a pitcher with a favorable count. In such instances, the encounter may be effectively over, the pitcher most assuredly prevailing, barring some lucky hit or foolish "mistake" on his part.

13. What team is not delighted to see the opposing pitcher leading off? Most always he will make out and put a damper on the prospect of his team scoring that inning. Should he get on base, the situation changes dramatically, especially as the top of the order follows. Having your pitcher lead off and get on base is not, however, an unalloyed good. He is liable to remain on the base paths for some time, obliged to run hard, and concentrate on something other than his pitching and the batters he will face the next inning. As a result he may, after running the bases, be "roughed up" when he returns to the mound.

14. Amidst this talk of edges and opportunities it's important to note how quickly and dramatically it can all disappear. A leadoff runner picked off first or thrown out stealing, a bunt that fails to move the runner to second, a runner out stretching a single into a double, a double play—these are but a few of the many negative outcomes that can snuff out a potential rally, and turn raised expectations into shattered hopes. Fans often excited are nonetheless rewarded on far fewer occasions.

15. For a contrary view, some might contend that ordinarily a pitcher will face

just so many threats in a game. If he is equal to the task early on, or if the opposition is turned away, they simply may not get another chance to mount another challenge.

16. A more exaggerated instance occurs during a rain delay when a pitcher must cool his heels in the dugout or clubhouse. More often than not, he is replaced when the game resumes.

17. Fouling off a lot of pitches may not seem to be accomplishing much, yet in a sense, it may be preparing the way for the pitcher's ultimate downfall. A parallel situation prevails in boxing, where early blows taken to the body, seemingly uneventful, will later on prove to be a fighter's undoing.

18. Middle relievers, or "setup men," generally lack the stature of starting pitchers and "closers." Though differences may be slight, these relievers are the weakest members of most pitching staffs.

21. Looking Ahead

1. Similar experiences can be encountered with the lob in tennis and the high jump and pole vault. In each instance, there is that suspenseful moment when the end is in doubt, and all strain to "predict" the outcome.

2. Jack Buck, an announcer during the 1991 playoffs and World Series, was criticized for his tendency to predict the conclusion and results of plays even while they were underway. Buck admitted being somewhat overzealous on a number of occasions. He was, however, penalized for this bit of presumptuousness, losing his position as World Series announcer in 1992. On the other hand, many announcers customarily declare, after a ground ball is hit with runners on, that it "should be a double play" even before the ball reaches an infielder.

3. *New York Times,* Oct. 16, 1992.

4. Pitchers, on the other hand, do their own projecting about whether the ball is headed for home-run territory. Is there a more forlorn figure than that of a pitcher on the mound staring helplessly toward the outfield, considering whether the ball has the home run distance? Tim McCarver has remarked that if a pitcher, after making his delivery, swirls his head quickly after the ball's been hit, it is because he suspects it may be a home run. On the other hand, pitchers know immediately if the fly ball just launched will fall short. In the seventh game of the National League Championship Series in 1991, Atlanta's John Smoltz pitched to Pittsburgh's Barry Bonds in the eighth in-

ning with two runners on. The instant Bonds swung, Smoltz pounded his fist into his glove in triumph. Sure enough, it was a harmless outfield flyball.

5. One final thought on visualization in baseball: no other report offers so wide an array of visual snapshots that when viewed in a newspaper, magazine, book, or poster instantly conjures up the action sequence in all its richness and drama.

22. Argument as Art Form

1. This would have made perfect sense to sports writer Arthur Daly, who once wrote that the typical baseball fan possesses "the digestive apparatus of a billy goat. He can and does devour any set of diamond statistics with insatiable appetite and then nuzzles hungrily for more." Would such an individual shy away from any worthy opponent? Murphy, *Crown Treasury of Relevant Quotations,* p. 74.

2. More than any other sport, the language of baseball has entered into common parlance. The following words and phrases are likely to appear in most everyday conversations.

"Strikeout"	"Three strikes"
"Out of left field"	"Grand slam"
"Can't get to first base"	"Squeeze play"
"Off base"	"Home run"
"Heavy hitter"	"Thrown a curve"
"Pinch hitting"	"Here's the pitch"
"Touch base"	"It's a hit"
"Raincheck"	"Playing the field"
"Hardball"	"Step up to the plate"
"Touch all the bases"	"Ballpark figure"
"Bush League"	"Screwball"
"Batting average"	"Play ball with"
"Field" (a question)	"Lowballing"
Make his "pitch"	"Go to bat for"
"Bat this around"	"Softball" question
"Keep your eye on the ball"	"Switch hitter"
"Right off the bat"	"On deck"

"Dugout chatter" (name given to daily Senate leadership briefing for reporters).

3. Murphy, *Crown Treasury of Relevant Quotations,* pp. 74–75; Eugene Brussell,

Webster's New World Dictionary of Quotable Definitions (New York: Prentice-Hall, 1988), p. 41.

4. Defenders of the game today are not much interested in viewing baseball as a barometer of society, of burdening it with moral baggage best deposited elsewhere. They will, if pressed on the point, remind listeners that the "glory days" of yesteryear featured unbridled racism, petty dictators in the front office, and crude, often inebriated, and loutish players out on the field. Today's ballplayers are far better conditioned—which is probably why so many more of them play into their later years—endure longer schedules, perform by day and by night, and crisscross the country by airplane, month after month, over a lengthy season. Relief pitching is better than ever, the split-fingered fastball is often unhittable, acrobatic fielding plays are considerably more prevalent, outfielders are faster, base-stealing techniques are far in advance of earlier levels, and baserunners are more adventurous with far more attempting head-first slides than ever before.

5. Statistics can be deceptive in yet another way, they will insist. Had this or that ballplayer played elsewhere, in a place or on a team where his strength might have been maximized, his output and recognition would have been enhanced most measurably. In no other sport are such hypothetical scenarios indulged in with such regularity or zest. How many deep flies to left center-field at Yankee Stadium by Joe DiMaggio would have been home runs elsewhere? Consider what Ted Williams could have accomplished had he been able to target the short right-field porch at Yankee Stadium. For reasons not entirely clear, baseball fans indulge their imaginations more in such musings than fans in any other sport.

6. The above discussion, meant to be suggestive, hardly exhausts the possibilities. Nothing has been said about the ongoing debate over the designated hitter. Scorn and contempt can be expected from baseball's traditionalists, while defenders insist it has remedied a grievous flaw in the game. Differences of opinion are sharp on the matter of expansion. Will it spark additional interest in the game, or will a dilution of talent seriously weaken its appeal? Players will join fans in debating the quality of baseball in the National, as opposed to the American League. The ballparks are sized differently, the pitchers throw differently, and the umpires call them differently, it is asserted. Actually, there will be many who question whether there is much substance to such claims. A "sacrosanct community of monks"—that is how general counsel to the baseball players' union, Gene Orza, chose to comment on the behavior of umpires. Are they becoming too sensitive, too assertive, projecting themselves into the game as a disruptive element? Some would agree;

others would insist umpires are doing what needs to be done to maintain control of the game. Is baseball's All-Star Game best served when the votes of fans determine the teams or are the press corps and the players better positioned to make the selections? Such a debate surfaces each year as the All-Star Game approaches.

23. Innocence as Salvation

1. *Newsday,* Feb. 20, 1993; ibid., Mar. 1, 1993; *New York Times,* Mar. 8, 1993.

2. *Sporting News,* Apr. 5, 1993.

3. *Newsday,* Sept. 20, 1992.

4. Feinstein, John, *Play Ball: The Life and Hard Times of Major League Baseball* (New York: Villard, 1993); Jack Sands and Peter Gammons, *Coming apart at the Seams* (New York: Macmillan, 1993).

5. Richard Ford, "Stop Blaming Baseball," *New York Times Magazine,* Apr. 1, 1993, p. 40.

6. *Sporting News,* Mar. 22, 1993; ibid., Apr. 12, 1993.

7. *USA Today,* Apr. 16, 1993; ibid., Newsday, Apr. 4, 1993.

Index

Baseball and the Pursuit of Innocence was composed into type on a
Compugraphic digital phototypesetter in ten and one half point Sabon
with two and one half points of spacing between the lines. Sabon was
also selected for display. The book was designed by Cameron Poulter,
typeset by Metricomp, Inc., printed offset by Thomson Shore, Inc.,
and bound by John H. Dekker & Sons, Inc. The paper on which this
book is printed carries acid-free characteristics for an effective life of
at least three hundred years.

TEXAS A&M UNIVERSITY PRESS : COLLEGE STATION